LAUGHTER IN HELL

LAUGHTER IN HELL

The Use of Humor during the Holocaust

Steve Lipman

JASON ARONSON INC.
Northvale, New Jersey
London

Production Editors: *Bernard F. Horan and Leslie Block*
Editorial Director: *Muriel Jorgensen*

This book was set in 12 point Garamond by BOOKS INTERNATIONAL, INC. of Deatsville, Alabama, and printed and bound by Haddon Craftsmen of Scranton, Pennsylvania.

First softcover edition—1993

Library of Congress Cataloging-in-Publication Data

Lipman, Steve.
   Laughter in hell : the use of humor during the Holocaust / by
Steve Lipman.
     p. cm.
   Includes bibliographical references and index.
   ISBN 0-87668-585-8 (hardcover)
   ISBN 1-56821-029-9 (softcover)
   1. Jewish wit and humor. 2. Germany—Politics and
government—1933-1945—Humor. 3. Political satire, German.
4. Holocaust, Jewish (1933-1945)—Humor.   I. Title.
PN6231.J5L54 1991
808.88′2′089924—dc 20   90-28101

Manufactured in the United States of America. Jason Aronson Inc. offers books and cassettes. For information and catalog write to Jason Aronson Inc., 230 Livingston Street, Northvale, New Jersey 07647.

To
Peter and Helene Lipman,
who taught me the value of a sense of humor,
and
Dr. Milton Plesur, *z"l,* and Elenore Lester, *z"l,*
whose lives were an inspiration to me

Contents

Acknowledgment   ix

1

Humor, Faith, and the Holocaust
1

2

Laughter under Oppression
23

3

The Humor of Optimism
61

4

Werner Finck and the Cabaret World
111

5

Jewish Humor
131

6

The Flavor of Humor: Anti-Nazi, Pro-Victim
189

7

Outside the Walls, after the War
213

Notes   249

Index   269

Acknowledgment

I owe thanks, in the most heart-wrenching way, to Saddam Hussein.

A child of the post-Holocaust generation, I have pursued my interest in the topic of this book for more than 20 years. But documenting the humor that grew out of the Holocaust, the capacity of Adolf Hitler's victims to employ their sense of irony as a spiritual weapon, could not help but be a historical exercise for me. No amount of library research or interviews with survivors and experts could hope to convey the terror under which parts of Europe lived—and coped—from 1933 to 1945.

Until 1991.

I had the fortune then to be in Israel during the most unfortunate of times—the first two weeks of the Persian Gulf war. Like millions of Israelis, I learned how to use a gas mask, how to prepare a sealed room, and, God forbid, how to administer any number of medical treatments should this decade's Semitic Hitler unleash his arsenal of chemical weapons.

I also learned how the citizens of Israel, including countless descendants of World War II European Jewry, turned to humor to dispel their fear and apprehension. In sealed rooms, during alerts, they made jokes—in many cases, reworked versions of those that

circled in Nazi Germany—about Hussein. In the morning, following the nocturnal missile attacks, they were quick to share the latest
humorous tale. "Saddam buster" T-shirts became bestsellers, and
several books of jokes about the war found a ready market.

True, there is no comparison between Europe under the
shadow of Nazism and Israel under attack by Scud missiles. There
is even less cause to find any commonality with the United States
during the early days of the Persian Gulf war; Americans, while not
under direct fire or threat thereof, were gripped by the military
buildup that sent hundreds of thousands of its soldiers to the Gulf
sands. Americans also relieved the pressure with humor—with
popular jokes and editorial cartoons and routines by standup
comedians.

Because of Iraqi censorship, there were no press reports from
occupied Kuwait on how Kuwaitis—who undoubtedly gained the
closest empathy in today's Arab world for Jewish life in Nazi-
occupied Europe—used humor to keep their spirits from sagging.
But in the days after the cease-fire, there was an account of one
Kuwaiti who affixed a picture of Hussein to the posterior of a
donkey during a liberation celebration. I suspect that citizen's
humor was not an isolated case.

The conditions of Nazi Europe clearly defy comparison to any
time or place. But the Israelis I observed, and with whom I found
shelter, were again under attack by a deranged man who sought
their annihilation. The people, unwilling residents of sealed rooms,
the Holocaust survivors among them again facing the specter of
poison gas; the leadership, its hands tied by the coalition forces'
insistence that Israel refrain from retaliating—all this evoked old
feelings of helplessness and uncertainty.

In a small way, for a short time, I saw how a population
overcame the fear that failed to paralyze the generation of the Final
Solution. I am more sure than ever that humor is one of the greatest
gifts God gave mankind to pull itself out of despair. It wasn't just

the persecuted of Nazi Europe—Jew or Gentile—who found that value, and will continue to do so, of this gift.

Without a doubt, I would have preferred that the hypotheses I propose in these pages about the efficacy of humor remain in the historical realm. Like any weapon, humor's power to fight oppression is best kept unsheathed, as a deterrent. Better, that there was never the need to document the humor produced in Europe in the 1930s and 1940s or in Israel in early 1991. Or anytime, under any dictator.

Jewish tradition teaches a dual, and seemingly contradictory, approach to evil. We are enjoined, when mentioning the name of an evil man such as Hitler or Hussein, to adjoin the Hebrew phrase, *umach b'shmo*, may his name be blotted out. We want to forget the memory of such people. Yet God instructs the Jewish people in the Sinai desert, as they are about to enter the Promised Land, to eternally recall the deeds of Amalek, the prototypical enemy of the Jews who sought to prevent the Hebrews' exodus. "Remember what Amalek did to you. . . . You must not forget."

One explanation for this apparent dichotomy. God is preaching moderation: keep your guard up. Don't forget the evildoers; be prepared for the next battle. But don't dwell on the subject; recognize the evil in the world, fight the good fight, then put it behind you.

Humor, as the battles against Hitler and Hussein show, is a ready weapon.

Many people, from close friends to strangers I know only through correspondence, have a role in the development of this book. If I forget to thank anyone, it is an oversight and I apologize.

Above all, I owe thanks to Linda and Heshy Friedman, who convinced me that my collection of fragmentary notes could comprise a full book, and to Anthony Cardinale, who did not spare my manuscript his criticism.

For help in translating texts from foreign languages, I thank Toby Axelrod, Michael Brenner, Chavi Friedlander, Judith Friedlander, Karin Nerenberg, and Rabbi Harvey Falk. Source material is available in a host of languages; because of my linguistic limitations, I was forced, in general, to use excerpts from German and Hebrew. I recognize the drawbacks in this, but consider the importance of documenting the topic in the available tongues to outweigh waiting for extensive translations. In most cases, I've cited only the English translation of sources that came from other languages; the original version is included when available and appropriate.

The staffs of several research institutions have gone out of their way to further my research. These are the Library of Congress; the New York Public Library; the Leo Baeck Institute; the Goethe Institute; the YIVO Institute for Jewish Research; Yad Vashem; the Wiener Library at Tel Aviv University; the National Yiddish Book Center; the House of Humour and Satire in Gabrovo, Bulgaria; the Center for Holocaust Studies in Brooklyn, New York; the libraries of Yeshiva University, Hebrew Union College–Jewish Institute of Religion, and the Jewish Theological Seminary of America. The Institut fur Zeitgeschichte in Munich provided invaluable background on political humor in Nazi Germany, as did regional archives in Koblenz, Augsburg, Bamberg, Coburg, Amberg, Landshut, Nurnberg, and Munich.

I am indebted to several people who have lent their support to my work: Dr. William Sheridan Allen, Tibor Baranski, Dr. Judith Tydor Baumel, Steven Bloom, Frederick Brainin, Dr. Diane Cypkin, Dr. Yael Danieli, Elisabeth Degasperi, Arnold Doowes, Dr. Joseph Dorinson, A. Dzialoszynski, Arnd Lothar Falk, Michael Feuer, Dr. Itzhak Galnoor, Rabbi Yaacov Haber, Steve Hanson, David Harris, Dr. Rudi Hartmann, Eric Hauser, Maria Jaworski, Dr. Edward Johnson, Pedro Kanof, Eliahu Khazoum, Daniel Kij, Dennis Klein, Dr. Jack Kugelmass, Dr. Lawrence Langer, Robert

Lasson, Gabriel Laury, Leon Lewis, Steven Lukes, Hans Joachim Margulis, Sybil Milton, Manny Mittelman, Manfried Mauskopf, Ilse Mollenhauer, Miriam Nick, Dr. Israel Oppenheim, Edith Raim, Dr. Joachim Rasch, Helena Salomon, Myra Shays, Dr. E. A. M. Speijer, Dr. Norman Solkoff, Frank Stiffel, Elaine Taibi, Judith Turnbull, Dr. Ralph Wiener, Dorothee Wittekind, and Dr. Avner Ziv.

I have tried to combine the experiences and insight of all who showed interest in my project. Keeping in mind how unusual my topic is, and how sensitive are the feelings of persons who went through the Holocaust, any errors in fact, interpretation, or awareness are, of course, entirely mine.

Humor, Faith, and the Holocaust

The secret source of humor itself is not joy but sorrow. There is no humor in heaven.

—Mark Twain

There is no laughter in the holy of holies. There laughter is swallowed up in prayer and humor is fulfilled by faith.

—Reinhold Niebuhr

October 3, 1940. More than a year after Nazi Germany launched its invasion of Poland, starting World War II, Rosh Hashanah has come to the Warsaw Ghetto, the walled-in area that is the prison of the Polish capital's Jewish population. The Jewish New Year brings another day of beatings, typhus, starvation, and deportations. Even so, some pious residents of the ghetto hurry to daybreak services in the three out-of-repair synagogues that remain open with the permission of the occupying Germans. They wear the Nazi-imposed identification: a blue Star of David on a white armband.

"A Jew prayed badly on Rosh Hashanah, the Jewish New Year,"[1] notes Emmanuel Ringelblum in his journal entry on that date. The archivist of Jewish life and resistance in the ghetto does not record the name of this particular Jew, or the specific reasons why the traditional petitions for judgment and deliverance faltered on the man's tongue. But Ringelblum does preserve the man's explanation: "Asked why, the Jew replied, 'The prayer fits the year.'"[2]

A cynical answer. Yet fitting, in a cynical age.

The dozen years of the German National Socialist Workers' Party's "Thousand-Year Reich," 1933–1945, was a time for scoffers. Nazi Germany nearly reached its goal of conquering Europe. And it added a new word to the world's lexicon, the Holocaust—the murder of 6 million European Jews and a nearly equal number of Gentiles. Hitler's unprecedented campaign against civilian targets strained the limits of credulity, requiring any number of symbolic images to convey the tragedy in terms that can be grasped—Anne Frank as the Jew in hiding, the voyage of the *Exodus* as the band of resilient survivors.

The Warsaw Ghetto, and its ultimate destruction, has joined this metaphorical group. Just as the spring 1943 Ghetto Uprising—a band of outgunned, outnumbered Jewish fighters held out for six weeks against German troops—has become the war's preeminent illustration of resistance, the words of Ringelblum's anonymous supplicant may symbolize an outlook that permeated a persecuted generation.

Neither his faith nor his humor shaken, the Warsaw Jew prayed, albeit poorly, and joked, although sarcastically, in a time that tried men's ability to do either. While the crucible of Nazi Europe forged souls that turned to heaven and to humor—as they do in all times of crisis—his spirit was a synthesis of the two "illegal" actions. Only a man at peace with his creator could reverse the tradition of Judaism's holiest season—during which the Lord weighs the deeds of mankind—by judging the work of a God whom he seemingly found lacking.

The man's answer survives as his testament; his own fate is not recorded. Did he merit another year of life? Or did the Heavenly Court spare him further torment? If he was typical of the 400,000

4

Jews packed into the ghetto at one point, he perished, either within its walls, or in one of the death camps to which the inhabitants were shipped.

But his answer invites another question. How could man pray or laugh in Europe in World War II? Religious belief, even when tempered with a mocking spirit of disbelief, seems foreign to many who view the Nazi crimes against humanity at a distance of miles or decades. Humor seems equally inappropriate. Both responses to reality appear illogical at best, madness at worst. God, if not dead, was silent or impotent.

How could man pray or laugh?

He saw no other choice.

And those very acts made him stronger.

"There were those who thought that we could laugh Mussolini and Hitler out of court,"[3] Christian theologian Reinhold Niebuhr wrote of prewar naiveté. Many mistakenly held that view in the early 1930s. The Nazis in turn feared actions that accentuated their spiritual mortality. Their supremacy threatened by religion and humor, they tried to eliminate or co-opt both. Synagogues were burned and desecrated; church bells were stilled, confiscated for bullet casings; priests and pastors were silenced or turned into shills for the Nazi creed of secular *Volkism*.

At least one Nazi general, according to a possibly apocryphal story, understood religion's influence on the population. This unnamed military leader was once heard railing against the state's war on the churches. "But I did not know you were such a religious man," observed a foreigner who was present.

"I'm not," said the general. "I look at it from the technical point of view, and I know that no army which goes into battle without some hope of an afterlife will fight well. Hitler and his Nazis are ruining our raw material."[4]

The Nazi effort boomeranged. The "frontal attack" on religion was an open failure that "only intensified"[5] religious commitment.

5

"By possessing some religious belief," one World War II historian observed, "the person was able to remove himself from the [concentration] camp world to another world of different values and meanings."[6]

A Jewish inmate in one concentration camp would repeat the *Shema,* the Hebrew declaration of faith in the unity of one God, "and it would give me extra strength. To say the *Shema* was to say that somewhere, even in this period of great loneliness and antihumanity, there is someone to whom you can address yourself."[7]

Although the lure of temporal honors for supporters of the Nazi state and the horrors of unspoken torture for its opponents immeasurably decreased the size of God's flock, it is a matter of record that countless Jews and Christians remained steadfast in their piety, defying the bounds of common sense and the laws of an outlaw state. Righteous Gentiles sheltered Jews under the noses of occupying German soldiers. Both Jew and Gentile gathered for surreptitious prayer services in concentration camps. Starving Jews bartered a piece of bread, a days' sustenance, for a prayer book, fasted when the Hebrew calendar so dictated, and risked their already imperiled lives to observe any number of biblical commandments.

Similar examples of faith in action emerged from nearly every ghetto and concentration camp, every major city and isolated village under Nazi rule. Even the nonbeliever may recognize the need for and the role of religious expression in the foxhole of Hitler's Europe.

But humor? Its pervasiveness during the Nazi period—from the cabarets in Germany's major cities to the sanctioned inmate theater in Czechoslovakia's Theresienstadt camp and the jokes that spread in hushed tones in the Polish death camps—is common knowledge among survivors of Hitler's genocide. Scores of books in German and the other languages of the liberated countries, many published soon after the war, document aspects of humor's omni-presence. Fictional accounts of the period also contain a share of humor. The pages of *King of the Jews*, Leslie Epstein's novel about the Warsaw Ghetto and its Judenrat (Nazi-appointed Jewish council), are full of the jokes and witticisms found in ghetto diaries.

But the phenomenon is little known and less accepted among the general public. Jokes about Nazi Germany are part of an unwritten list of topics—including sex, private love affairs, and bodily defects—that are taboo among members of the Israeli Knesset.

According to Terrence Des Pres, author of *The Survivor—An Anatomy of Life in the Death Camp*, a landmark study of the subject, literary accounts of the Holocaust have come to require three elements: insistence on the tragedy's uniqueness, minimal deviation from the historical facts, and a *humorless presentation* (author's emphasis). "The Holocaust shall be approached as a solemn event, with a seriousness admitting no response that might obscure its enormity or dishonor its dead."

Des Pres questions the third assumption. "Is laughter possible in literary treatment of the Holocaust?" he asked. "If possible, is it permitted? Is the general absence of humor a function of the event in itself, or the result of Holocaust etiquette—or both?"

His answer: Yes, laughter is permitted. Yes, it is possible. Its absence is a result of the tragedy itself and a sensitivity dis-played by the post-Holocaust generation. "Since the time of Hippocrates . . . laughter's medicinal power has been recog-nized, and most of us would agree that humor heals," he wrote. "Even so, can laughter be restorative in a case as extreme as the Holocaust? That something so slight should alleviate the burden of something so gigantic might, on the face of it, be a joke in itself. But then, humor counts most in precisely those situations where more decisive remedies fail."[8]

Understandably, it seems disrespectful, sacrilegious, to pollute the contemplation of mass murder with such profane matters as comic rhymes and punch lines—the very thought cheapens the victims' lives. "Silence would be the highest form of our respect for the writings of the resistance and the martyrs condemned to death by the German occupier,"[9] Nobel Peace Prize Laureate René Cassin wrote in the introduction to a French book on writings of the condemned.

When Hitler's victims themselves laugh at their plight—as many did, to preserve their own sanity—the door is left open for others. Does that explain the questionable contributions of recent mass entertainment: "Hogan's Heroes" on television, Mel Brooks' "Springtime for Hitler" parody in *The Producers* on the screen, *The Last of Hitler* on the New York stage? Has the post-Holocaust generation usurped the survivors' prerogative to laugh at the Hitler years? Were jokes about an eminently unfunny time really funny? Are these efforts ultimate proof of the dictum that humor equals tragedy plus time?

That the period of the *Shoah*—Hebrew for destruction—could not be a "time to laugh"[10] of Ecclesiastes is a common view even among academic authorities. A psychoanalytic authority on humor: "I do not see how the Holocaust can be comical."[11] An anthropology expert: "It is hard to imagine that any humor could possibly arise from the mass gassing of thousands of individuals."[12] An expert on films about the Holocaust whose mother survived it: "Black humor . . . was infinitely more possible in ghettos and in hiding than in concentration camps. I don't mean to suggest that my mother told jokes in Auschwitz, so she survived."[13]

Such opinions miss the point. Wit produced on the precipice of hell was not frivolity, but psychological necessity. "We kept our morale through humor,"[14] says philosopher Emil Fachenheim, an Auschwitz survivor.

Nothing about the Holocaust was funny. By appreciating the humor from the period we are not laughing at the victims or their suffering; we are simply recognizing that laughter was a part of their lives, a part nurtured by their suffering. They found humor, sometimes sardonic humor, in all aspects of their disrupted existence. "People who live in absolute uncertainty as to their lives and property find a refuge in inventing, repeating, and spreading through the channels of whispering counterpropaganda, anecdotes and jokes about their oppressors," wrote sociologist Antonin Obrdlik, who studied the role of humor in occupied Czechoslovakia. "Some of them even dare to collect the jokes as philatelists collect stamps. One young man whom I knew was very proud of having a collection of more than two hundred pieces which he kept safe in a jar interred in the corner of his father's garden."[15]

Whether we, who did not share the victims' pain, can fully share their laughter is another question.

Marcel Ophuls, producer of the documentary film *Hotel Terminus: The Life and Times of Klaus Barbie,* tells the story of a middle-aged woman he met in London several years ago. A survivor of German and Soviet prison camps, she was doing the voiceover for an Ophuls film on the Nuremberg trials. Between takes, she told of her own own camp experiences. "Most of her tales turned out to be uproariously funny, I'm sorry to say,"[16] Ophuls recalled.

"I used to be indignant at the jokes which took as their butt the most tragic events in ghetto life, including the Gestapo, Nazi decrees and typhus," Mary Berg wrote in her Warsaw diary. "But I have gradually come to realize that there is no other remedy for our ills."[17]

"Now and then that bright and bubbling good humour of mine rises to the surface again," Etty Hillesum, a Dutch Jew, wrote in her journal in occupied Amsterdam in 1942. "It never really leaves me, and it isn't gallows humor either, I'm quite sure."[18] She died in Auschwitz a year later. Another Dutch Jew, Rachella Velt Meekcoms, would stage vaudeville shows in Auschwitz with other teenage inmates.

9

"In spite of all our agony and pain we never lost our ability to laugh at ourselves and our miserable situation. We had to make jokes to survive and save ourselves from deep depression. We mimicked top overseers and I did impersonations about camp life and somebody did a little tapdance, different funny, crazy things," she recounted. "The overseers slipped into the barracks while we weren't looking, and instead of giving us a punishment they were laughing their heads off. I couldn't believe it: one day they were hitting us black and blue, and then they were laughing while we made fun of them."[19] She survived the death camp.

Humor, the currency of hope, certainly did not flourish in the Holocaust for its own sake, but for a deeper reason. Like the outline of a fish that early Christians would sketch in the dirt to identify fellow-believers—other followers of Jesus, spiritual heirs of Galilean fishermen, who considered themselves fishers for lost souls—humor was both a psychological weapon and a defense mechanism. It was a social bond among trusted friends. It was a diversion, a shield, a morale booster, an equalizer, a drop of truth in a world founded on lies. In short, a cryptic redefining of the victims' world.

"Anti-Nazi humour was both a low-key expression of resistance (or at least disapproval) and a form of therapy," according to British social historian Richard Grunberger. Telling a joke fulfilled "the raconteur's perennial craving for an audience." For many Germans, Grunberger wrote, "the circulation of political jokes represented a comfortable (or even socially admired) substitute for thinking—let alone acting—about evils which existed on a plane extraneous to word-play and punch-lines."[20]

In the death camps and ghettoes, one's style of humor was a mark of culture, along with songs and stories, that marked the individuality of each group. This truism crossed national boundaries.

There is a "fellowship of those who bear the mark of pain,"[21] wrote humanitarian Albert Schweitzer, whose serious illness in

10

middle age, from which he recovered, sensitized him to the suffering of others.

Philip Mechanicus, a reporter interned at the Westerbork transit camp in Holland, kept a diary during 1943 and parts of 1944. "Captivity means the barbed wire fence and the discipline of hut life," he wrote, "but with a little imagination and a sense of humor and a love of nature you can create a world of your own in which it is possible to forget the captivity of the material body."[22]

Psychiatrist Victor Frankl observed that in Auschwitz an operative sense of humor both afforded detachment from one's predicament and forced one to recognize it. He relates the prisoners' reactions upon being shaved of every bodily hair and then being herded into showers. "The illusions some of us still held were destroyed one by one, and then, quite unexpectedly, most of us were overcome by a grim sense of humor. We knew that we had nothing to lose except our so ridiculously naked lives. When the showers started to run, we all tried very hard to make fun, both about ourselves and about each other. After all, real water did flow from the sprays!"[23]

Humor, like religious profession, was a form of spiritual resistance among the oppressed. Where it ranked in the hierarchy of more substantive acts of opposition to the Nazis, and how it was related to them, is admittedly open to debate. Did humor make a more steadfast fighter? Or did it make an individual docile, less likely to retaliate? Is laughter ultimately "a safe and civilized alternative to violence?"[24] Both sides can be argued, as in the case of the black church in the antebellum American South that bound the slaves together yet directed their angry murmuring to promises of redemption in another world.

During the Holocaust, religion and humor served a like—though not identical—purpose: the former oriented one's thoughts to a better existence in the next world, the latter pointed to

11

emotional salvation in this one. Both gave succor and provided an intellectual respite beyond the immediate physical surroundings.

"Humor," wrote Reinhold Niebuhr, "is, in fact, a prelude to faith; and laughter is the beginning of prayer. Laughter must be heard in the outer courts of religion; and the echoes of it should resound in the sanctuary. Humor is concerned with the immediate incongruities of life and faith the ultimate ones."[25]

The claim that religion and humor ranked among the most common forms of nonmilitary resistance to the Nazi occupation in no way belittles the physical acts of resistance committed by hundreds of thousands of individuals. But how many had the physical means of resistance—grenades, a paintbrush, a printing press—or the ability to use them? Even the unimaginative could laugh.

The man of faith or humor needed only an open heart.

For those who found no solace in the Creator, a few moments of shared laughter—man's modest creation—kept countless persons from taking their own lives or slipping into the zombie-like state of the "Muselmänner." The so-called Muslims, concentration camp inmates who became soulless shells, spent their days in an emotionless stupor, too detached to smile at any joke or strike at any provocation.

To psychoanalyst Theodor Reik, a contemporary of Sigmund Freud, the ability to appreciate humor is no less than a divine endowment. Reik fled his native Austria in 1938. "By conferring upon him the gift of wit, his God has given him the power to speak of what he suffers," Reik wrote. "Life is often tragic, but its pathos reflects itself most distinctly in jokes. There is behind the comic façade not only something serious . . . but sheer horror."[26]

According to Jewish tradition, while Moses was on Mount Sinai receiving the Torah from the Lord, he asked to see the face of God. "No man can look at Me and live," God replied. Instead God allowed Moses a fleeting glance at the back of the Eternal One's

12

head, which bore an anthropomorphic form of the black leather *tefillin* straps worn by Orthodox men in prayer.

Likewise, could any man directly face the evil that Satan unleashed in 1933 and live? Is the death by suicide of such writers as Primo Levi, André Schwarz-Bart, Tadeusz Borowski, and Jean Amery—survivors whose works rank among the most vivid of Holocaust literature—an answer? An element of humor turns up in all these men's writings.[27]

In Auschwitz, the prisoners' motto of resistance was "Let's not give in," according to Anna Pawelczynska, a Polish-born sociologist and survivor of the camp. A sense of humor was "one important weapon of inner resistance that could not be taken away."

"The first indications that the odds for survival were unequal among the prisoners showed up in their first reactions to the camp," Pawelczynska wrote. "There could be a complete breakdown; there could also be strained efforts at humor—symptoms of a vitality and a greater capacity to adapt. The prisoner who managed (with humor and calmness, or relative calmness) to accept the reduction of his material needs in the first days was capable, later on, of adding to his arsenal [of survival skills]. Sometimes a whispered quip could bring release from the paralysis of fear. We could laugh at our own appearance and the fact of still being alive; we could caricature the agents of camp authority. Everyone who refused to 'give in' had his own defense mechanisms. The sight of a raging SS officer became less menacing as soon as one imagined him with his pants down or lying drunk in the mud."

She cited the value of "games [that] had to be naive and primitive. Those who hauled sewage could pretend to be horses. The crew's horsy sounds and behavior would draw the overseer, a German prostitute, into the game, which suited her level, and she would change from a dangerous official into a harmless wagon-driver."[28]

"The prisoners who had not yet adapted themselves and still

13

found themselves in the struggle for daily existence," one Dutch-born survivor observed, "had little sense of humor."[29]

George Eisen, a California college professor who spent his youth in hiding from the Nazis, has documented grisly games Jewish children played in concentration camps and ghettoes. Among them were "Gas Chamber," "Gestapo Agent," and other games that mirrored the horror of their surroundings. In "Burial," mimicking the mass burials, children would lie down and play dead while others would roll them into shallow graves.[30]

Alfred Kantor, a young Czech artist who survived Auschwitz and Schwarzheide, a slave-labor compound in Germany, found that "a youth spent in detention camps does not rule out a sense of humor or an appreciation of the ridiculous." In a two-month frenzy in a displaced persons' camp following liberation, he painted 127 watercolors of scenes from his captivity, and his brush fairly dripped with sarcasm.[31]

Another Auschwitz survivor, a professional humorist and film gagman before the war, returned to Budapest afterward to write a funny novel about the death camp. It was an attempt, a friend speculated, "to persuade himself that Auschwitz was quite an amusing place and he only went there to collect material for a funny book." The survivor was "no less terrified, of course," than the other prisoners when an S.S. officer, a central character in the novel, was making up his mind who to kick down a precipice "to certain death." The survivor "had to convince himself that all the horrors were just a joke—not to be taken seriously. The thought that ordinary human beings intentionally organized Auschwitz—that they really *meant* it—was unendurable to him. Perhaps this was madness but if it was, it was a mad reaction destined to preserve—or restore—his sanity."[32]

Victor Frankl, the Austrian psychiatrist who observed various forms of humor among inmates during his three years in Auschwitz and other camps, "practically trained a friend" who worked next to

14

him as a laborer on an Auschwitz building site to "develop a sense of humor."

Frankl proposed that he and his comrade invent at least "one amusing story" a day about an incident that could happen some time after their liberation. His friend, a surgeon, had been an assistant on the staff of a large hospital. "So I once tried to get him to smile by describing to him how he would be unable to lose the habits of camp life when he returned to his former work," Frankl wrote in *Man's Search for Meaning,* his autobiographical volume on logotherapy, the branch of psychotherapy that grew out of his death camp experiences. On the building site where Frankl worked, "the foremen encouraged us to work faster by shouting: 'Action! Action!' I told my friend, 'One day you will be back in the operating room, performing a big abdominal operation. Suddenly an orderly will rush in announcing the arrival of the senior surgeon by shouting, "Action! Action!"'"

Frankl's scenario presupposed an end to the war—the defeat of the Germans and the victims' triumphant return to better lives. Other Auschwitz inmates would invent "amusing dreams about the future, such as forecasting that during a future dinner engagement they might forget themselves when the soup was served and beg the hostess to ladle it 'from the bottom.'"[33] This was because priceless but scarce pieces of solid food sank to the bottom of the pot in the concentration camp's gruel.

Alfred Kantor, as an eighteen-year-old aspiring artist in Theresienstadt, was smuggled pencils, paper, and other drawing supplies by other prisoners. They beseiged him with requests "for a sketch of their bunk, or some other scene" of the camp. "'Just for a souvenir,' they would say, since they expected to return to their previous lives some day and wanted something to show their families and friends."[34]

This optimistic spirit, to be sure, was not shared by every victim. Human character varies too much, and the suffering was too intense. But many of the oppressed found a lasting niche for humor; many survivors delight in sharing a treasured story or wisecrack that brought a smile fifty years ago.

Humor in this context means more than jokes or funny dialogue. The term is employed in its broadest sense, as a liberating sense of perspective, and in its classical meaning—irony, parody, sardonic exaggeration, situation reversals, morbid twists on reality. "Do you believe in life after wagon?"[35] Jews being carted away to the concentration camps would ask each other.

One classic World War II joke illustrates how humor turned reality upside-down:

> Two Jews had a plan to assassinate Hitler. They learned that he drove by a certain corner at noon each day, and they waited for him there with their guns well hidden.
>
> At exactly noon they were ready to shoot, but there was no sign of Hitler. Five minutes later, nothing. Another five minutes went by, but no sign of Hitler. By 12:15 they had started to give up hope.
>
> "My goodness," said one of the men. "I hope nothing's happened to him."

Such humor vicariously reverses the roles of oppressor and oppressed, in the view of Harvey Mindess, a psychoanalytic authority on the topic. "The very act of making fun of our inferior position raises us above it,"[36] he writes. In other words, the pain can't be that bad if we can laugh at it.

"How is it possible not to laugh?" one survivor mused. "I find it more surprising that people could remain serious. Because the only thing that keeps them alive is a sense of humor."[37]

The humor was "more likely to make you cry than to make you laugh, or to laugh through tears," says Judy Baumel, a Holocaust researcher who lives in Israel. "It was a hollow, mocking laugh."[38]

16

Laughter *through* the tears or laughter *because* of tears?

In a time of deportations, Zyklon-B gas, and *Einsatzgruppen* mobile killing squads, what was there to laugh about? And where? The political cabarets, whose barbs mocked the Fatherland's leaders in the early days of the Reich, were closed with dispatch. Criticism of the government in the press or radio broadcasts of the occupied lands, even in jocular terms, was forbidden. Banter among trusted friends in an Orwellian police state was also suspect.

Nevertheless, humor cropped up in many guises, on many subjects, during the Nazi era. It was conveyed in many forms—situational quips, art, poetry, classical music, and work songs—but jokes were the most common medium. They numbered in the hundreds, if not thousands. They were the easiest to create—"Their very brevity is a God-sent gift,"[39] said one observer—and share. They translated easily. They were the most universal means of expressing humor.

"Hitler's Germany," it was reported, "became history's most productive source of political jokes."[40] Frederick Goetz, a Munich student and discharged German soldier (he had served reluctantly during World War II) took out a classified ad in an October 1945 issue of the *Süddeutschen Zeitung*, two months after the Nazi surrender, asking readers to send him examples of anti-Nazi humor. He wanted to "round off the picture of the German people in the Nazi time." The response was "gigantic"; readers sent Goetz more than 500 letters, with "some 350 political jokes and anecdotes."

In Goetz's view, this "needleprick politics" became a virtual obsession of the German population as the war wore on. "At the beginning," he wrote, "it was just a few uncomprising opponents and fighters of the Brown Terror who made use of such political jokes. But it became more and more, till finally it enveloped the vast majority of the people. Political jokes circulated everywhere, in plants, in offices, in inns, even in [Nazi] party agencies and organizations, in the city and in the country."[41]

17

The literature that emerged from occupied Europe—journals written during the period, and reflective pieces written after the war—bears testimony to the valued place of humor. Funny tales turn up throughout the memoirs from the ghettoes and death camps. They were such an uncontested part of daily life that the authors did not deem it necessary to preface their reports of popular jokes with explanations of the jokes' propriety. "Even the ghetto has its wags who can sum up an entire situation with a well-aimed joke,"[42] wrote a resident of the Lodz Ghetto.

These witticisms—*Flüsterwitze*, German for whispered jokes—spread steadily across the continent through the underground papers published in ghettoes and partisan units, and via the inmates shipped from site to site. Ringelblum's Warsaw journal reported: "The German Jews, deported here from Hanover, Berlin, etc. have brought a number of jokes with them."[43]

The language of the persecuted "was the whispering tone, but sometimes it sounded like a cry," wrote Ralph Wiener, a native of Vienna who joined a resistance group during the war. He wrote *Als das Lachen Tödlich war* [When Laughter Was Fatal], a study of anti-Nazi humor. "The victims belonged to different people, different races, different classes, different religions, different outlooks," he wrote. "What unified them was the common fate."[44]

More than jokes, humor during the Holocaust was sometimes simply the facade of irreverence. This spirit led one inmate to paint the words "Road to Heaven"[45] on a sign marking a road in the Sobibor death camp. The same spirit inspired a resident of the hunger-ravaged Warsaw Ghetto, upon being wished a "calm Passover"—the previous year's greeting before the normally festive holiday of liberation—to respond: "Rather wish me an easy fast."[46] It allowed one Westerbork survivor, after liberation, to create a mock travel album with humorous drawings and assorted "souvenirs"[47] from his stay. It led one multilingual refugee, upon being asked who had taught him an impressive array of European and

Asian languages, to reply: "Hitler." It inspired ghetto wits to brand Hitler's polemic as *Mein Krampf* [My Cramp] and to confer stereotypically Jewish code names on the Axis dictators. Hitler was known as Horowitz; Mussolini, as Moshe Ber.

> "Twin babies were born in Germany, one called Horowitz, the other Moshe Ber," went one tale. "They were bathed, and then got mixed up; no one knew which was Horowitz, which Moshe Ber. They asked a Jewish passer-by to tell. He answered, 'The one who makes in his pants first is Moshe Ber' . . ."[48]

Jokes were made about every facet of life and death in the Nazi era. No target, including God himself and His prophets—the Jewish parentage of Jesus was often cited as endangering Christ's life—was out of bounds. Starvation, disease, beatings, murder, and every form of persecution were grist for the victim's joke mill. Nazi pomposity, the spotless uniforms, the exaggerated reports of military triumphs, and the hyperbolic use of language similarly lent themselves to mockery. Both the foibles of prominent German leaders and the behavior of "average" Nazis—civilians and soldiers—became topics of underground wit. "The Nazis were easy to caricature,"[49] says Wolfgang Roth, a set designer who worked in Berlin's cabaret world in the early days of the Third Reich.

And there were a host of jokes about jokes, including the story of a comic who was locked in solitary confinement until he recited every anti-Nazi joke he knew. His internment, of course, lasted several years.

If humor is a sugar coating that hides the bitter taste of its message, when was such a palliative more needed? The times, and the victims of the times, demanded it. Following the farewell performance of Max Ehrlich, a popular cabaret comic, in Berlin in 1939, the Nazi-supervised *Jüdisches Nachrichtenblatt* newspaper wrote: "In troubled times, you have taught us that we must not

19

forget the ability to laugh."[50] Psychologists who work with survivors speculate that a functioning sense of humor has helped many overcome the plague of nightmares and guilt about outliving the Nazis' other victims—common symptoms of the so-called survivor's syndrome.

In recent years, the powerful effects of humor and laughter have come under closer scrutiny. The most celebrated case is Norman Cousins, former editor of the *Saturday Review*, who virtually laughed his way out of a crippling illness that doctors believed to be irreversible. He described his novel treatment in *Anatomy of an Illness.*[51]

Other studies of humor's therapeutic value have found similar results. Avner Ziv, an Israeli educator, interviewed groups of children who had spent lengthy periods of time in underground fallout shelters in Israel's border settlements. He found fewer lingering psychological problems, such as nightmares, among those who were billeted with a peer who demonstrated a viable sense of humor.[52] According to humor researcher Paul McGhee, laughter has been noted among individuals about to be shot or burned, "apparently in a desperate attempt to master the fear of death. In ritual burnings in India in the past, individuals were expected to laugh as they approached their fiery deaths."[53]

Hospitals have established "humor rooms"[54] where patients can get a videotaped shot in the arm of W. C. Fields or Groucho Marx. "Future doctors, instead of saying 'Take two aspirin and call me in the morning,' will say 'Watch a Lily Tomlin special and call me in the morning,'"[55] predicts Joel Goodman, director of a humor resource center in Saratoga Springs, New York.

One practitioner of this so-called humor therapy, Susan Ziemer-Brender, a Viennese-born, California-based nurse, spent half her teenage years in a series of concentration camps. She lost her "raucous" laughter in Auschwitz, she says, and regained it, with the help of her surrogate family, in Gross Rosen, her final camp.

Working on the kitchen crew, she mastered the ability to hide food in her prisoner's dress. "Now my laughter was not really raucous, but I laughed," she says. "And I could dream and I could pray for freedom." Her message: "Laughter and spirituality compose the celebration of aliveness. Combined, they seem like a delicate blanket."[56]

Ziemer-Brender's career and life after the Holocaust were undoubtedly influenced by one overriding fact—she survived.

What of the millions who didn't? Like the man in the Warsaw Ghetto whose Rosh Hashanah prayer faltered, their humor outlived them.

Is that enough of a legacy? Did their jokes and quips have any ultimate meaning? Did their possibly Pyrrhic victories change history?

Judy Baumel offers one answer: Wit does not stop Nazi bullets, but the victims' abandonment of humor would be a concession of moral defeat. "The Nazis got the last shot in," she says, but the victims did what was within their power—"They had the last word."[57]

The clearest moral victory won by a victim in the face of physical defeat was claimed by a nameless young Jewish woman in Maidanek, a death camp near Lublin, Poland. She was about 26. She was taken one day to be hanged in front of other inmates.

"Together with her sister she ran away from the airport at Lublin, where they were put to work," philosopher Eliezer Berkowitz recounts. "The sister managed to escape, but she was caught. It was a beautiful day in May. The gallows were set up at the center of the commando square, the victim and the hangman standing beside it.

"The hangman started to question her: 'Who helped you to get away?' Her answer was: 'A Jewess does not betray those who tried to help her.'

"'Don't you see how everybody laughs at you!' said the

21

German. 'You are beautiful. One word could save you. And the world is delightful.'"

The woman's final words were: "Today you laugh, tomorrow you will be laughed at!"[58]

2

Laughter under Oppression

Even he who fears nothing, fears laughter.

—Nikolay Gogol

Freedom begets wit, and wit begets freedom.

—Jean Paul

The perfectly happy man in a perfect world does not laugh, for he has no need of laughter. But he may smile.

—William McDougall

In Nazi Germany, as in all totalitarian societies, humor was no laughing matter. Dictators are by nature a humorless lot, and Adolf Hitler was no exception. Through legislation and intimidation, he spared no effort to prevent political jokes against him; he was as unsuccessful in that attempt as he ultimately was in military battle. Immediately after he became chancellor in 1933—two years after the label "the Austrian comedian"[1] was pinned on him by German wags—anti-Reich jokes became a criminal offense. Satirical books were burned and censored under the Nazis, authors forced into exile. Political jokes, which George Orwell called "tiny revolutions," were considered a direct attack on the government, and violators were subject to harassment, arrest, imprisonment, or death.

25

As the German occupation of Europe spread, so did the illegality of anti-German humor—in one instance, two citizens in occupied Holland were sentenced to four months in prison, the *New York Times* reported in 1941, "for singing songs in a drunken condition, the contents of which were insulting to the Fuhrer and Germany."[2] Oswald Mosley, the pro-German leader of the British Union of Fascists who negotiated with the Nazis to establish an English-language commercial radio station on German soil before England's entry into World War II, was duly instructed that political humor was not on the list of approved topics. Programs would be monitored by Nazi officials. "They [would post] their man in the studio to censor everything put out. We understood they did not want any jokes by comedians about the Nazi regime."[3]

Nazi Germany was not alone in its attempts to suppress critical humor. Any number of other oppressive regimes, also taken with their precarious importance, have made similar efforts. In Russia under the czar and Stalin, telling or listening to an improper political joke could spell "10 years forced labor, which in those days often meant death."[4] No less important when used, no less dangerous when detected, antitotalitarian humor—"the *vox populi*"[5] in one observer's words—could imperil the teller in Mussolini's Italy, in the Soviet Union under Stalin's successors, in Eastern bloc lands, and in any number of extant dictatorships around the world. As recently as 1987, Krishna Prasad Bhattarai, a political dissident in Nepal, was arrested and briefly jailed for telling a "slightly risqué joke"[6] in a clandestine political meeting about presidents Reagan and Gorbachev. Bhattarai became prime minister of the Himalayan kingdom three years later, obtaining the ultimate last laugh the political world offers.

"Jokes may not be able to topple a dictatorial regime," wrote Egon Larsen, a self-exiled German refugee who was active in London's cabaret world during World War II, "but there is one important point which adds to the effectiveness of political humor:

the oppressors have no defense against it. If they try to fight back they appear only more ridiculous."[7]

Humor has "of course, quite a different role in a democracy to that in a totalitarian state," according to Oxford University political scientist Steven Lukes, co-author of *No Laughing Matter: A Collection of Political Jokes.* In his Great Britain, he wrote, "a political joke is a joke the subject of which happens to be politics. It needs no greater courage to tell a joke against [Prime Minister Margaret] Thatcher . . . than to tell one about the English weather. In a tyranny political jokes are acts of defiance and of great courage."[8]

That was the message of a tale set in Germany thirty years after the end of World War II. Walter Ulbricht and Willy Brandt, the leaders of East and West Germany, respectively, are conversing. "Have you a hobby, Herr Brandt?"

"Yes, I collect jokes that people tell about me," Brandt says. "And you?"

"Oh, I collect people who tell jokes about me,"[9] answers Ulbricht.

"Underground political humor is a natural vent for collective frustrations built up as a result of the hardships of daily life and is a self-satisfying retort to the incessant propaganda,"[10] according to Algis Ruksenas, who has studied political humor in the Soviet Union.

Citizens of the West can only vicariously appreciate the role, and the risk, of telling a joke in totalitarian states. "A joke told in a totalitarian dictatorship is an act of resistance and is most certainly regarded as such by the political police," wrote George Mikes, a Hungarian-born author and humorist who immigrated to England to escape the Nazis. "Many people spent years in prison for telling and indeed for listening to jokes and a few even died for the sake of a good story."

"In a free society the joke is like a pleasant spice—just an after-dinner anecdote which goes down well with coffee and brandy," Mikes observed. "In the West it is indeed a luxury. Jokes are not necessities. They are only one out of many possible ways of criticism. In totalitarian countries jokes are the *only* way. The next step after the joke is the political assassination. There is nothing in between."

"In lands more familiar with oppression," he asserted, "a joke is necessary for one's self-esteem. Laughter is the only weapon the oppressed can use against the oppressor. It is an aggressive weapon and a safety valve at one and the same time. The joke is an art of rebellion at its best. . . ."[11]

To Mikes, political jokes, like those about death, are a coward's cloak of cynicism, an attempt to "show that . . . he can take it . . . that he is not afraid of things that worry the rest of us. The cynic tries to get on familiar terms with Death, or God, or cancer, tries to make Death his chum; just a chap standing around the bar . . . an amiable fellow. This is one way of taming Death, of making it look less frightful."

"But, of course," Mikes wrote, "he is even more afraid; he is permanently preoccupied with the fear that he is joking about . . . it is always the man who is afraid of, or preoccupied with, death who jokes about it." In Mikes's *Weltanschauung* it is neither the man of faith nor "the convinced atheist," but the agnostic who makes jokes about the Diety. The man unsure of his convictions, or lack thereof, "is afraid lest God may, after all, exist and punish him."[12]

According to Mikes, antigovernment jokes when cleverly channeled could be used to strengthen a regime. "The tyrants know the value and power of jokes only too well," he wrote. "That is why tyrants and their henchmen cannot possibly have a sense of humor, any more than an archbishop can be an atheist. Some of the more intelligent ones realize that jokes are also safety valves. A country where people may joke about their rulers seems to be a free country. In some of the East European countries the Secret Police try to control even the joke output of the population: they invent and spread censored and licensed anti-regime jokes."[13]

Nazi Germany, of course, was not among the governments that countenanced humor at their expense. Humor there, particularly the crude anti-Semitic brand, was one of the tools at the disposal of the Reich. *Der Stürmer*, Julius Streicher's rabidly anti-Semitic publication, regularly carried cartoons that featured stereotypes of Jewish society. Anti-Jewish jokes found a willing audience among German citizens with Nazi leanings; such humor continues to enjoy a limited popularity in parts of Germany today, and in other European countries. Ironically, a tinge of sympathy for Europe's endangered Jews, or at least a recognition of their condition, could be found in the anti-Allied humor favored by the Germans and their World War II accomplices in some occupied lands. "The safest way to get vital military transports to the fronts," collaborators in Hungary and Czechoslovakia would say, "was to put some Jews in them and write on cars in large letters: 'This is a Jew transport to an extermination camp.' Thus it was sure not to be molested by the Allies," who declined to bomb the death camps and railway lines for "military reasons."[14]

Repression, of course, merely whets the public's appetite for satire. Mikes, who lived through the 1956 Hungarian revolution, remembers that "jokes died out . . . during the victorious days . . . of 1956. As soon as the Russian tanks started roaring back into the country, causing devastation and death everywhere—while declaring that 'We are coming as friends'—the wits of Budapest retorted: 'A good thing. Imagine how they'd behave if they came as enemies.'"[15] Antigovernment jokes "dried up"[16] in Poland during the heady days of the Solidarity movement in the early 1980s, but reappeared after the government cracked down on dissidents.

In Nazi Germany, the very suppression of humor generated one more topic upon which to comment. Outlawed in public meetings and in the government-controlled press, satirical attacks on the German leadership multiplied, "either pushed underground, or abroad."[17] As early as 1933, British newspapers which printed the anti-Nazi editorial cartoons by the *Evening Standard*'s David Low were banned in Germany, after one drawing angered Hitler. The particular drawing—"It Worked at the Reichstag, Why Not Here?"—implied that Hitler could destroy the League of Nations as he had destroyed the Reichstag. (The Nazis usurped the power of the German parliament and burned the legislative building in 1933, blaming the fire on Communists.)

The ban on Low's work represented an about-face; three years earlier the Führer, himself a former postcard illustrator, had requested from the British cartoonist, "as one artist to another,"[18] a few of Low's original drawings pillorying democratic politicians.

The first concerted comic attack on the young Nazi government was staged across the border, in Prague, in the form of a 1934 exhibition of anti-Nazi cartoons. The display included the work of Czech cartoonists and German artists, many of whom had been "silenced, exiled or imprisoned"[19] in their homeland. The exhibit "showed a comprehensive, and basically accurate, picture of the Nazi phenomenon. It stressed the inherent inhumanity and cruelty of Hitler's movement."[20] And it drew the ire of Hitler, who put pressure on the Czech government to ban such displays. The Czechs slowly acceded to the wishes of their powerful neighbor; by the end of 1938 the Czech press instituted preventive censorship.[21] Some writers and artists left for the freer shores of Great Britain and the United States.

Later, in occupied Czechoslovakia, the frequency and stridency of anti-Nazi jokes were found to increase in direct proportion to the harshness of the occupation and the grimness of the news reports from other parts of Europe.[22] The barbs usually stung local targets: Czech traitors were more often the subjects of such jokes than the Nazis themselves.[23]

Inside Germany anti-Nazi humor, which became more sarcastic as the war continued, was lamely blamed by the Party on the efforts of foreign propagandists. A campaign to raise public morale—and eliminate derisive humor through public appeals, Party rap sessions, and word-of-mouth propaganda—failed. One German writer went so far as to issue a defense against attacks on the Reich's putative supporters, the Scots. Will Vesper, poet and author, said that many Scots "love and esteem Germany," and called for a ban on anti-Scotch humor. "The Scots are the healthiest, most respectable and also most Germanic people of the British Isles," he wrote in a German magazine. "That is reason enough for the Jews and Jew-ridden in England to hate them and to attempt to make fools of them. That is reason enough for us and our press no longer to provide foolish jokes to the advantage of these Jewish proselytes."[24]

From the earliest days of the Nazi regime, laws were enacted that made jokes prosecutable as treacherous attacks on the state and Party. Political jokes became the subject of secret Gestapo reports, which "reported in detail on criticism and discontent."[25] A newspaper editor in Germany who had angered the Nazis in 1938 for publishing some political jokes was reportedly taken to local Gestapo headquarters, where he was shown a bulging file of jokes collected by the secret police.[26] The file, as far as is known, was destroyed by the Nazis.

A 1941 security memo by the secret police in Berlin, titled "Rumors, political jokes and people's humor," voiced concern over jokes: "Jokes, favorable as well as such detrimental to the nation and especially those of a spiteful nature (so-called concentration camp jokes), jokes about events in the war, for example about the flak, Italy, England and so forth, knockdowns of the people's humor in poems, anecdotes and so forth, for example air raid shelter humor. Every single one is to be brought to a halt." The memo sought to establish where the jokes originated, where they were still "in

31

circulation,"[27] and whether they were being spread in select circles or among the general population. A security memo two months later reported that "besides rumors and jokes of a harmless and entirely favorable nature, numerous political jokes and rumors especially detrimental to the state and of a spiteful nature, for example spiteful jokes about the Führer, leading personalities, the party, army and so on, were being spread everywhere."[28] A later secret police report, in 1943, lamented that "The telling of detrimental and vile jokes even about the character of the Führer [has] increased dramatically since Stalingrad."[29] The German people were apparently emboldened by their army's defeat in the Russian campaign that year.

Government agents monitored the performers in political cabarets, whose shows were especially popular among the liberal, independent-minded class—Goebbels' "parlor intellectuals"[30]—in Germany's major cities. Every facet of the Reich was lampooned in the shows. Popular cabaret lines, "lyrics, dialogues and jokes, satirical and hardhitting, often made their way . . . to the general public,"[31] while the reverse path was also traveled.

One special target was Kurt Tucholsky, a Jewish-turned-Protestant satirist whose essays and cabaret songs established him among the most popular social critics during the Weimer Republic. He was an antimilitarist, non-Communist member of Germany's "homeless left" who spent most of the 1920s in self-imposed exile in a series of European capitals. He took his own life with poison in Sweden in 1935. Tucholsky's pre-1933 descriptions of life under a Nazi reign were prescient: a 1930 sketch, *Herr Wendriner steht unter der Diktatur* [Mr. Wendriner under the Dictatorship], centering around a fictional middle-class Jewish businessman, foretold the imposition of the yellow armband on Jews and other aspects of daily life under National Socialism; in *Zwischen zwei Kriegen* [Between Two Wars], a 1925 essay, he outlined the annexation of Austria, the invasion of Poland, and other features of German foreign policy.

32

Tucholsky's clearest contempt for the Nazis was reflected in the songs he wrote for Berlin cabarets. He mocked the Nazis' racist posturing and dismissed Hitler as a "Mussolini with beer."[32]

"Satire has a boundary from above," he wrote in 1932. "Satire also has a boundary down here. In Germany, for example, [the boundary includes] the powerful, fascist rulers. It is its own reward—that's how deep you can shoot."[33] Believing the Nazis "too vulgar and irrational to be worthy of serious analysis . . . he therefore believed the only recourse was to make them look ridiculous." [34]

By 1933, safe in Sweden, Tucholsky was declared persona non grata in Germany. His books were banned by the Reich, and he was stripped of German citizenship. His works were among those burned by a rally of Nazi youth in Berlin in May 1933, in one of the first major book burnings under Hitler. He was part of a group of 34 German writers—some others were Sigmund Freud and Bertolt Brecht—who were so honored. The loudspeaker at the square on Berlin's Unter den Linden blared: "Because of insolence and arrogance! With honor and respect for the immortal German folk spirit! Consume also, flames, the writings of Tucholsky."

At the same time, Goebbels mounted a "systematic defamation of Tucholsky's character and writings."[35] (Tucholsky, in turn, found in the propaganda minister "Nothing, no humor, no warmth, no fire, nothing.")[36] The satirist's name was attacked in nearly every anti-Semitic pamphlet. He was vilified as a "stateless"[37] Jew. The Nazi Institute for the Study of the Jewish Question devoted 23 pages in its pseudoscientific study, *Die Juden in Deutschland* [The Jews in Germany], to Tucholsky.

On a wider level, the Nazis tried to quash political humor in Germany. An undetermined number of court cases were brought against citizens for such "popular opposition" and "malicious offenses."[38] In legislation promulgated as early as 1933, the "Law against treacherous attacks on the state and party and for the protection of the party uniform," jokes told about the Reich and its leading personalities were lumped with other acts defined as treason. Both teller and listener were subject to sentences ranging from imprisonment to capital punishment at the hands of the Volksgerichtshof, or People's Court. The threat of punishment apparently caused widespread concern, but it did not eliminate the jokes.

The court, based in Berlin, was established to set quick verdicts against accused traitors. The panel of two professional judges and five other members—from the ranks of the army, the SS, and Party officials—met in closed session in the chambers of Berlin's law courts, in a room decorated with three large swastikas and busts of Hitler and Frederick the Great. There was no appeal from its verdicts.

The tribunal handed down 5,286 death sentences, about one-third of the death verdicts handed down by all German courts between 1933 and 1945, and the tellers of political jokes comprised a considerable part of the total. After the war, West German prosecutors attempted to bring the wartime "hanging judges" to trial. As late as 1967, a West Berlin court established that a People's Court judge in 1944 had collaborated in passing a death sentence on one Josef Müller, a Catholic priest in Grossdungen who had told an anti-Nazi joke. According to the indictment, Müller had related to two congregants an incident involving a fatally wounded German soldier who called on his unit's chaplain to grant a final wish. "Place a picture of Hitler on one side of me," the soldier reportedly asked the chaplain, "and a picture of Goering on the other side. That way I can die like Jesus between two thieves."[39]

"By this and by other undermining remarks he has gnawed at our strength to bring about a total victory," stated the indictment, which called Müller's act "one of the most vile and most dangerous attacks directed on our confidence in our Führer. Such behavior is not only an irresponsible misuse of the priestly authority, but is more: it is a betrayal of the people, the Führer and the Reich."

"In doing so he has become dishonorable forever," the indictment concluded. "Because Müller is condemned, he must bear the consequences. He is punished with death."[40]

Telling jokes about the regime in public became "an increasingly dangerous occupation in Nazi Germany."[41] The act of looking over one's shoulder to make sure no one was within earshot was called the "German look."[42]

> "Well, what's new today?" Simon asks his friend Nathan in a joke from Germany, circa early 1930s.
>
> "At last," replies Nathan, "I do have something new. I have just heard a brand new Nazi joke. What do I get to tell it?"
>
> "Don't you know by this time?" answers Simon. "Six months in a concentration camp."

During the war's first few years, German poet Karl Schnog wrote *Witze machen verboten* [Making Jokes Is Forbidden], which warned:

Dachau ist im Volk beliebt.
Wenn du Witze machst, dann weiche.
Weil's im schönen Dritten Reiche
Einfach nichts zu lachen gibt![43]

The people love Dachau, no doubt.
You'll go there if you make jokes.
Because the beautiful Third Reich evokes
Simply nothing to laugh about.

The only safe way to share the latest quip was in private, under one's breath. Understandably, few written records show exactly how and where these examples originated; the source of any particular

joke—when and where it was born, who fathered it, who preserved
it, who brought it to the outside world—is nearly impossible to
trace. Most instances of humor that survived—and there is no way
of knowing how much was lost—came to us through the refugees
and survivors themselves and through Western journalists who
brought the jokes out of Europe. Some of the best humor was
beamed back to the occupied lands on Allied shortwave broadcasts.

The danger of expressing an unfavorable opinion became itself
the subject of many jokes. In a famous early 1930s cabaret sketch by
Werner Finck, a popular satirist and proprietor of a Berlin
nightclub, he is asked by the dentist to open his mouth:

"Why just me, of all people?" asks Finck, sitting in the
dentist's chair.

"Now, now," the dentist reassures him, "don't be afraid, and
open your mouth."

"Either one or the other," Finck answers.[44]

Weiss Ferdl, a Munich comedian, gave a cabaret crowd his
observations about Dachau, the concentration camp near the
Bavarian capital: "Most impressive and well protected, I must say.
The walls are ten meters high, with barbed wire along the top,
electrically charged, and machine gun towers at every corner—still,
I only have to say a word or two, and I'll be inside in a jiffy."[45]

That line "spread like wildfire through the entire country."[46]

At times the cabaret criticism was nonverbal. There is a story
attributed to several German cabaret comedians: The comedian
walked onto a cabaret stage with a muzzle over his mouth one
night, sat down on a chair and remained silent for several minutes.
Finally he stood up and walked off the stage, still silent. Whereupon the master of ceremonies announced: "Ladies and gentlemen,
now that the political part of our program is over, we come to the
entertainment."[47]

A popular joke of the time described a scene in a streetcar. Two
men are making strange gestures to each other, then they suddenly

36

break out in laughter. "What on earth are they doing?" one passenger asks another. "They are deaf-and-dumb," is the answer. "They are telling each other political jokes."[48]

Graphic artists also joined the battle against the Nazis. Caricatures of the Nazi hierarchy, in periodicals and pamphlets, "helped to shape attitudes to Hitler and his henchmen inside and outside Germany."[49] The drawings' simplicity, understandable without translation of the accompanying text, contributed to their "long-term effect on the historiography of the period. There is no doubt that they helped . . . to mount a broadly based campaign, both in Europe and especially in America, against Hitler's creations."[50] Viktor Weisz, a Berlin-born cartoonist known professionally as Vicky, immigrated to London in 1935. There his anti-Nazi sketches launched a successful career on the *Evening Standard*. He took his own life in 1966. George Grosz, another noted Berlin cartoonist, turned his pen against German militarism and the nascent Nazi Party during the Weimar years. He moved to the United States in 1932, on the eve of Hitler's ascent to power, and the fire left his political drawings.

Graffiti too carried anti-Nazi messages. Antonin Obrdlik, who had the "luck" to spend nine months in his native Czechoslovakia after its invasion by the German Army, recalled "with what haste and anger the Germans . . . washed inscriptions insulting or making fun of their Führer and their regime from the walls of houses and wooden fences where they appeared overnight."[51]

According to a tale reported by Obrdlik, the Germans searched for a Czech loyal to the Reich. Finally, the Gestapo found one likely candidate. "He was an old man walking up and down the street and speaking seriously to himself aloud: 'Adolf Hitler is the greatest leader. The Germans are a noble nation. I would rather work for ten Germans than for one Czech.' When the Gestapo agent asked him what was his occupation, this Czech admirer of Nazism confessed that he was a gravedigger."[52]

37

The world created by Hitler's propaganda machine—bogus mandates at the polls, newsreels filled with frenzied crowds of intimidated "supporters"—inevitably conflicted with popular opinion. Hitler's actual ranking among a substantial part of the masses was best expressed in the tales that Goebbels dismissed as discontented "grumbling."[53] Humor, and its illegitimate-in-the-eyes-of-the-Reich brother, rumor, were devoured by a public satiated with the government's hyperbolic "news," both in Germany and in the occupied countries. SSJF (Radio Station Jewish Fantasy) was a steady source of information in the Warsaw Ghetto, where the question "Anything new?" was answered with, "What's the matter—are you too lazy to think up your own news?"[54]

Several jokes had Hitler donning a disguise to walk anonymously in public for an accurate glimpse at public opinion, his concern for the masses itself being a laughable proposition. According to one story, he shaved off his moustache, put on a hat and long coat, and went to a movie theater. Every movie had to flash Hitler's photo on the screen and everyone would rise and proclaim "Heil, Hitler." When his likeness appeared on the screen this day and the crowd saluted, Hitler remained in his seat. The man next to the Führer prodded Hitler and said, "Look friend, we all feel the way you do, but you're taking a chance by not standing up."

In another story a disguised Hitler asks the first person he meets: "What is your opinion of the Führer?"

"The man whispers 'I can't tell you that in the street,' and leads Hitler to a side road, goes into a hotel, takes him up to his room, checks under the bed, locks the door, checks the drawers, and places a cushion on top of the telephone. Then he goes toward Hitler and whispers in his ear: 'I sympathize with the Führer.'"

Aware of his true unpopularity among a substantial part of the German population, driven by megalomaniac insecurity, Hitler would brook no criticism of him or his policies. He took himself seriously and would "flare up in a temperamental rage at the least impingement by act or attitude on the dignity and holiness of state and Führer."[55] He had, according to one biographer, "a horror of being laughed at."[56]

Hitler's sense of humor, invariably manifested through some form of teasing, taunting, or mimicry, "was strongly tinged with a malicious pleasure in other people s misfortunes or stupidities. He would laugh delightedly at the description by Goebbels of the indignities the Jews had suffered at the hands of the Berlin S.A."[57] Architect Albert Speer, who had many occasions to observe Hitler, stated that the Führer "had no humor; he liked laughing, but it was always at the expense of others."[58] As chancellor, Hitler delighted in repeating decades-old stories of pranks he had pulled on others.

In his early years he would act the part of the class clown and bait "any teacher who showed signs of weakness."[59] A childhood friend remembered Hitler as possessing no spirit of self-irony.[60] A soldier who later served with Hitler in the German Army during World War I described the young corporal as "always deadly serious—he never laughed or joked."[61] When his comrades mocked his rantings about the Jewish threat to the Motherland, "Hitler furiously promised that one day he would show them. He would rule over them all and get rid of the Jews."[62]

The Führer's disinterest in humor and aversion to mockery were common to other Nazi leaders. Among his inner circle only Joseph Goebbels, the Reich's propaganda minister whose "malicious wit"[63] was known to offend Hitler, and Reich Marshal Hermann Goering, head of the Gestapo, the secret police, were known to have a shred of a sense of humor.

Among the top Nazi leaders, Hitler, Goering, and Goebbels were the butt of countless jokes; the trio figured in several jokes as a unit. Hitler was der Mächtige [the powerful one], Goering, der Prächtige [the splendid one, for his narcissistic leanings], and Goebbels, der Schmächtige [the scrawny one, for his slight build]. Goering was simply "Hermann" in most jokes. It was said

39

he circulated jokes against himself, "about his love of medals and uniforms and exhibitionism. The purpose . . . was to create an image of himself as a jolly, good-natured fellow with a few human weaknesses, to correct his reputation as a Nazi bully. . . ."[64] The Brandenburg Gate in Berlin was known as "Goering's clothes closet,"[65] for his love of flashy threads. A "Goer" was the maximum amount of tin a man could carry on his chest without falling flat on his face. According to a popular rumor, Goering was supposed to have promised a glass of beer to his chauffeurs for every joke about him they passed on, "with the result that they got drunk every day."[66] Goering's role in the 1933 burning of the Reichstag brought the story of a subordinate who reported the conflagration. "No, not until tomorrow!" Goering replied. And this:

> "I saw Goering on Leipziger Street yesterday," one Berliner told a friend.
> "So?" said the other. "What did he burn there?"

Goebbels became the butt of popular jokes for his diminutive size (he was known as "Wotan's Mickey Mouse"), his affected speaking style ("Mahatma Propagandhi"), and his clubfoot ("Humpelstilzchen"). Though he reputedly had the ability to poke fun at himself, Goebbels "certainly had no intention of granting others this right."[67] Goebbels condoned jokes against the Jews and the Communists, but labeled anti-Nazi political jokes "faeces of the soul."[68] As the designated protector of the Reich's image, he jealously guarded it against any affronts. "He understands no jest," a German correspondent for a British newsmagazine reported. "Where Mr. Goebbels is, there is no laughter. Mr. Goebbels has forbidden wit."[69]

As part of his internal and external propaganda campaign, Goebbels turned all the government's weapons against critics of the Reich. First to feel his wrath were two Berlin cabarets, Werner

Fincks's Die Katakombe and the Tingeltangel, which Goebbels called "breeding places of subversion."[70] The clubs were closed; the performers were charged with degrading the Nazi uniform, ridiculing the party organization, and even depicting "a prostitute in connection with the pick-up service of the Winter Relief Work."[71]

In November 1938, about the time that the anti-Jewish *Kristallnacht* riots in Germany and Austria showed the outside world's indifference toward the Reich's infringement of human rights, Goebbels suggested a change of theme to the entertainers still at work: "How come these frivolous satirists don't attack the Jews, the philistines, the mischief makers, the indolent social drones, the vain and the irresponsible rumormongers?"[72]

Despairing at first of overtly silencing the cabaret comics, the propaganda minister sought to dampen their ever-more-accurate ardor through veiled threats and the presence of uniformed soldiers in cabaret crowds. Goebbels eventually realized the futility of this course, and in 1939 political jokes were outlawed outright. In January 1941 cabaret masters of ceremonies were banned, and in 1943 cabaret entertainment was ordered off the radio.

Following one rash of cabaret closings in early 1939, before the invasion of Poland and the start of World War II, Goebbels grew concerned about Germany's public image. "In no country of Europe today is there so much joy as in Germany," he said at the time. Apparently fearful that his actions against entertainers who dealt flippantly with the Nazi system "might give the impression that there is no humor in Germany,"[73] his *Angriff* newspaper announced a joke contest. The paper invited Germans to submit any kind of "genuine humor"—verses, jokes, or funny experiences—"to give proof that 'we really still have humor.'"[74] First prize was 100 marks, about $40.

The month long competition drew more than a thousand entries, proving to Goebbels that "joy in robust fun seems widespread." The winner was Kurt Naumann, a "humble construc-

41

tion worker" from Grossenhain. Naumann's winning entry was a cartoon showing a row of scantily clad women. "I won't perform in this costume," says one figure attired only in a helmet and saber. "Why not?" asks a male onlooker. "Does one see too much?" "Rubbish," replies the woman. "Too little." The *Angriff* printed two similar racy Naumann cartoons, which some readers of the paper branded "healthy eroticism."[75]

In another attempt to develop a Teutonic sense of humor, "free from all corrupting influences, especially Jewish," the town council of Hamburg established a thousand-mark prize for the best satirical story reflecting "the wit and wisdom of the north German region."[76] The winning entry was submitted by Hanns ut Haum; his story, "Das Magdalenennaus," a home for wayward girls; its plot, a visit to a house for fallen girls by a solemn philanthropic society; its fate, mockery. The story had been plagiarized from Egon Erwin Kisch, a well-known Prague Jewish journalist, who proceeded to lambaste the town council.

Concerned by Germany's continuing image as a land devoid of wit, Goebbels at one point felt compelled to answer a question posed by cabaret owner Werner Finck in a Berlin newspaper column: "Do we have a sense of humor any more?" "Yes," the propaganda minister replied in the Nazi *Völkischer Beobachter*, adding that the traditional German folk humor did not countenance the ridiculing of sacred values fostered by "effete intellectuals and the amusement-greedy mob." After all, he said, there was no variety show in Vatican City where "the sacraments or the articles of faith of the Catholic Church are made the butt of cabaret ridicule."[77]

Anti-Nazi humor from occupied Europe, particularly the period's Jewish humor, bears similarities to two other prominent forms of antiestablishment humor—among African-Americans in the United States, and among dissidents in the Soviet Union.

With black American humor, which grew out of the whispered

protests against conditions of slavery in the South, it shares a tenor of "retaliation and mockery, of control and defensiveness,"[78] according to Boston University social historian Joseph Boskin. "What's the matter with you?" the captain of one of the first ships of enchained Africans is supposed to have barked to a muttering slave. "You've been in this country for five minutes and already you're complaining!"[79] Slave laughter was at first a ruse—smiling workers suggested contented workers—and a way to deflect slave-owners' wrath. "You scoundrel, you ate my turkey," a master scolds a young slave. "Yes, suh, Massa, you got less turkey but you sho got more nigger,"[80] the slave replies. Once the slave population mastered "this protective mimicry of laughter,"[81] it developed its own style of humor, "something worthy of laughter." This indigenous black humor combined with "dance, songs, and vocal inflections"[82] as tacit means to preserve the slaves' unity, their longings for freedom, and the vestiges of their African heritage. Though based on the slaves' African tradition of oral folk tales, black humor in America was unmistakably shaped by the slavery experience. "There is a feeling among most Americans," civil rights leader W. E. B. DuBois wrote, "that the Negro is quite naturally and incurably humorous. One has only to see Africa to be cured of this."[83]

Early slave humor, often self-critical, centered around the master's power of life and death, and his frequent impotence in the face of lying, sabotage, malingering, and pretended witlessness, Boskin wrote. Just as Jews used intellect to score psychic points against the Nazis, American blacks "have savored language as a means of conflict and control"[84] against what they perceive as the white power structure. The black pose was called "puttin' on ole massa [the old master]," an antebellum forerunner of the practice labeled psychological resistance in the Holocaust.

Boskin's description of slave humor suggests further similarities with anti-Nazi wit: "The object was to create humor in order to

43

laugh at the oppressor. The outstanding characteristics of black humor . . . are its play qualities, which ward off punishment, a style that permits quick retaliation, a deep scrutiny, which enables an important time lapse for assessment purposes, and a type of control humor vital for the maintenance, especially among the young, of a highly attuned and carefully sensitized community."[85]

He draws parallels between black and Jewish "techniques of disguise for addressing their adversaries. . . . Each has utilized accents of body or voice to deflect suspicion of improper thought or action."[86] Compare the Jewish male's supposed desire for Aryan women and the black man's avowed lust for Caucasian conquests. "In Jewish folklore," Boskin says, the response is "the ironic curse, an intent disguised by a statement meaning the opposite, and in the black community it has been the double entendre."[87]

During the civil rights movement, American blacks continued to use humor to ridicule the white establishment and to "lessen the tension which accompanied the non-violent demonstrations."[88] Jokes from the period made light of segregation, political leaders, and political inequities:

> A Mississippi law provided that a prospective voter be required to give a reasonable interpretation of any clause in the state or federal constitution. It left to the local registrar the decision as to whether the answer was correct.
>
> One day Rastus walked into the local registrar's office. "Well, Rastus," said the registrar, "tell me what is meant when it says that no state shall grant letter of marque and reprisal?"
>
> "Why, suh," replied Rastus, "that means this ol'niggah ain't goin' to vote in Sunflower County."[89]

Sharing a clear geographic and political genesis, jokes against the czar and a succession of Russian Communist leaders are closer in tone and text to those that came out of World War II Europe.

However, unlike the pre-Glasnost political jokes in the Soviet Union, whose usual targets were individual leaders and temporary deprivations, much anti-Nazi humor was aimed at the legitimacy of the Reich itself. Undoubtedly, many of Hitler's victims drew on their neighbors' tradition of anti-authority humor for their own verbal snipes.

Up to a decade ago in the Soviet Union, a government minister ruled on the propriety of jokes told by sanctioned comedians,[90] and underground jokes were said to spread by the OBS—*Odna Baba Skazala* [an old lady said]—network. "Jokes, or *anecdoty*, are the homemade glue that binds together all Soviet citizens in their dislike for the empty falsehoods of the government's longplaying propaganda machine,"[91] a collector of political jokes from Leningrad wrote. Glasnost has opened the gates for freer criticism of the Kremlin and apparently eliminated the danger associated with telling a critical joke in the USSR; but the television screens and newspaper columns in the Communist world are not yet entirely open to such humor.

"At first, I thought [President Mikhail] Gorbachev was bad for business," says David Harris, a student of humor behind the Iron Curtain. But Gorbachev's attempts to open up the Soviet Union's political and economic structure created havoc in the Soviet economy as well as a new generation of political jokes. "There are still a lot of jokes."[92] Harris, who gathered jokes from Soviet Jewish emigrés in the 1970s, found several common elements among the examples coming from the USSR and its Eastern European satellites. Tales about secret police, food shortages, and discredited doctrines were recycled from place to place; the names were changed to condemn the guilty. Jews often played a prominent role as the carriers and foils of wit. "Soviet Jews, finding themselves unable to live as Jews or to leave the country in substantial numbers, long ago turned to humor to deflate the extraordinary pressure and tensions in their daily lives,"[93] Harris says.

45

Unlike the political humor of Soviet Jews, which featured such trickster figures as Hershel Ostropoler and Abram Rabinovich, anti-Nazi humor had no such central character. The languages of Europe were too diverse, the physical distances too great, the cultural backgrounds too varied to allow one common figure to represent the common suffering. Instead, any number of archetypal figures, named and unnamed, appeared in countless anti-Nazi jokes. Like their Soviet counterparts, however, the protagonists always had the last laugh on their oppressors.

Some Jokes and Poetry under the Nazi Occupation

The poem "Der Flüsterwitz" [The Whispered Joke] was written in Germany in 1941:

> The Flüsterwitz is a fly,
> that is hatched on manure,
> from the germs: malice, a lie.
> No one knows who is the father.
>
> The Flüsterwitz thinks itself forbidden,
> Twofold is its life's purpose:
> Slander or obscenities,
> in every case just swinish.
>
> At the tavern table or other corners
> his face bears a secret grin,
> with a blunt twinkle in his eyes.
> He lives, no doubt—though not out in the open.
>
> The Flüsterwitz tiptoes around in circles
> for the creation, hunched over.
> It is like indigestion,
> that one gulps from his dear neighbor.[94]

There was a saying in Nazi Germany:

All roads lead to Rome—but all of Hitler's streets lead to "Irrland."

Irrland, comparable to the English "Errland," means land of insanity and is a play on Irland, the German spelling of Ireland.

The reputed lack of a German sense of humor was clearly conveyed in this tale, based on an old joke:

Hitler was at his wit's end, enraged at having heard it repeated everywhere that Germans did not have a sense of humor. He revealed this to his counselors, who, after thinking it over, decided to send one of their ranks—an eminent Herr Professor—to search the world for the secret of *witz.*

The Herr Professor took to the road, and visited the five continents without finding a single person who was in a position to light his lamp. Finally, for the sake of peace and quiet, he headed back home. Before returning to Germany, he discovered on his route an inn. The proprietor was called, so the sign announced, Moche Kretchmer.

The man gave a warm reception to his visitor, who decided to stay the night. The sociable innkeeper, being the amiable sort, permitted himself to ask his business. And the Herr Professor confided in him his torment. Having heard the story, Moche Kretchmer let out a good laugh and told him:

"Stop worrying, Herr Professor, I'm going to explain to you what 'witz' is. Not being very wise, I'm going to give you an example. Listen well to this question:

"Who is the son of my father and yet isn't my brother?"

47

Herr Professor thought this over, looking at the question from all angles, but couldn't find a satisfactory answer. Finally Moche Kretchmer, with a broad grin, told him the answer:

"The son of my father who isn't my brother, that's me. Moche Kretchmer!"

This was a revelation for Herr Professor, who could barely express his gratitude to his astute host.

He spent the night imagining the triumphant reception awaiting him in Berlin. At dawn, he returned to the road, in a hurry to reach his destination.

In Berlin, the authorities gave an enthusiastic reception for this extraordinary emissary of the Führer. The Führer gathered together his counselors, before whom Herr Professor would give an account of his discoveries.

At the appointed hour, he, in a state of high emotion, took the floor. After a long dissertation, full of citations, he came to the crucial point of the program. And there, repeating the words of the innkeeper, he posed the trick question:

"Who is the son of my father, yet isn't my brother?"

The Nazi dignitaries, stunned, sat mute. For long minutes, silence reigned; it felt as if everyone was making an effort to find a logical explanation for this question. But nothing came. Finally, Herr Professor, throwing a condescending look toward his audience, announced:

"Let us see . . . think a little, meine Herren: The son of my father who isn't my brother, why, that's Moche Kretchmer."

Hitler dies and goes to Heaven. "Heil Hitler! dear God," he says. "God's greeting [*gruss Gott*], dear Hitler!" comes the greeting in return.

48

It was said that Goebbels, in order to refute the "lies" of immigrants in the foreign press, wanted to arrange an essay contest for the best political jokes about the Third Reich.

The prizes:

First prize—Three years of hard labor.

Second prize—Two years in a concentration camp.

Third prize—A tour of the Gestapo cellar on Prince Albrecht Street with padlocked interrogation.

Before 1939, Goebbels greeted some foreign journalists, to whom he said, "Gentlemen, people often state in your countries that we want war. That is total slander. If you look around in Germany, you will have to ascertain this: the people are ruled with an iron fist; they are wearing clothing out of artificial fabrics; we can't even provide butter substitutes, coffee substitutes, or tea substitutes. We have artificial rubber and substitutes for many raw materials. Hard labor has already been introduced, terror reigns, and we even commit murder since taking power. Then, gentlemen, if we have all of this in freedom, why do we still need war?"

Goebbels, suffering from chronic self-consciousness, goes to a psychoanalyst. "You are suffering from a pronounced inferiority complex," the psychoanalyst advises. "The antidote is auto-suggestion. Stand in front of a mirror for 15 minutes each day and repeat, I am important . . . I am significant . . . I am indispensable. This will cure your self-consciousness."

"Your remedy is useless," says Goebbels. "I never believe a word I say."

Goebbels is rejected from Heaven and banished to Hell. To ease his way, St. Peter allows him a glance at Hell through a telescope. He sees a high-class bar, well stocked with expensive drinks and scantily dressed waitresses. When he arrives in Hell, he finds it entirely different: a place of terror and agony. To his exasperated question—What was everything that he had seen?—the Devil shrugs his shoulders and answers, "Propaganda."

Goebbels was speaking to an American journalist at a reception for the press. "If your President Roosevelt had an SS like our Führer's, then there wouldn't be any more gangsters," he said.

"Certainly not," answered the American, "then they all would be officers."

Hitler, Goering, and Goebbels were once discussing what they would do if Germany lost the war.

"I would flee to Japan," Hitler declared.

"I would go back to Sweden," said Goering.

Goebbels laughed and said," "I would put my nightgown on, sit on the chamberpot, and if someone came, I'd say, 'Father isn't home.'"

At a private conference, Goering, Goebbels, and Hitler are discussing what they will do should the Communists get the upper hand and revolt against the Nazis.

"As soon as I hear of a revolution in Berlin," says Goering, "I shall make for my private plane and dash off to Italy."

"I, too, would make for a plane," says Goebbels, "and go to Warsaw. I could easily pass for a Polish Jew."

"Unlike you fellows," says Hitler, "I would stay right here and claim immunity as a foreigner."

Goering was an accomplished pilot, Goebbels was rumored to have Jewish ancestry, and Hitler, of course, was born in Austria.

Goering asks Goebbels, "What are you going to do after the war?"

"I am going to take several years off to visit every part of the empire."

"I didn't know you had bought a bicycle."

Goering arrived in Heaven and the archangel in charge, acquainted with the newcomer's special weakness, decorated him with a huge star. Goering was delighted, but later returned from a walk on the Milky Way, indignantly declaring that he had seen a bigger star than his own.

"Do be reasonable, Goering," replied the archangel. "That star belongs to Nero. He set fire to the whole of Rome, you only set fire to the Reichstag."

Goering's act of promoting an Air Force officer to general, and of exacting a million-mark "atonement contribution" from the German Jewish community for Herschel Grynszpan's shooting of a German diplomat in November 1938 prompted the following joke:

"Who is the greatest alchemist?"

"Goering! He made an Air Force Marshal out of milk [Milch,

the officer's name] and a million from verdigris [the bluish patina that forms on the surface of copper and other metals].''

On Christmas 1939 Goering and Goebbels stand under a crucifix.

"They will nail us on the cross if things go badly," Goebbels declares.

"Have no fear," says Goering. "I'll see to it that there isn't any more wood or nails."

Goering and Goebbels die and go to Hell. Their punishment: for Goering, 1,000 new uniforms and no mirrors; for Goebbels, 1,000 radios and no microphone.

What is the difference between Japan and Goering?
Japan is the land of laughs and Goering is the laugh of the land.

What is fratricide?
If Hermann Goering slaughters a pig.
What is suicide?
If someone tells this joke in public.

"Goering tried to commit suicide."
"Why?"
"He was so pleased by the festivities at President Hindenburg's funeral that he wanted the same for himself."

Goering was asked out to dinner, but to his intense annoyance, only 10 of the 12 medals he was to wear could be found. His servants searched frantically through the 12 uniforms he had worn during the day, but without avail.

At last, in came Goering's valet, triumphantly carrying the missing medals. "You left them on your pajamas, Your Excellency," he said.

Hitler decided to make peace with the Vatican. He sent his Minister of the Interior, Dr. Wilhelm Frick, to Rome. But Frick found the job a rather awkward one and returned to Berlin for further instructions. Goebbels, next selected as negotiator, also returned, the mission unfulfilled. At least Hitler sent for Goering, who was ordered to settle the matter at once. A few days later the following telegram came from Goering in Rome:

"Everything settled. Vatican burning. Pope in flight. Papal ornaments suit me admirably."

Recently the four main pillars of the Nazi Party visited a Berlin café. No one recognized them: Goering wore a business suit, Goebbels did not open his mouth, Schacht paid the bill, and Hitler had with him a Jewish girl.

While out walking one morning, Hitler, Goering, and Goebbels get lost. Finally they meet a farmer driving down the road in a cart. The farmer gives them a lift.

As they get in and drive off, Hitler can not resist a little bragging.

53

"My man," he says, "imagine the great honor that has come to you. In your humble cart sits Adolf Hitler."

"You are Adolf Hitler?" asks the farmer doubtfully.

"Der Führer!" cries Hitler impatiently. "Don't you know me?"

The farmer glances at the man with the little moustache, shakes his head, and coldly replies, "I never saw you before."

Then Goering speaks up. "Then, farmer, look at me closely and tell me who am I?"

The farmer glances around again, shakes his head, and says in an unfriendly tone, "No, I don't know you either."

"I am Marshal Goering."

Now the farmer feels sure he is being made a fool of. He says angrily, "Goering? You? Next thing you'll be telling me is that the Jew back there with you is Goebbels."

"Considering our station, it would befit us to act according to etiquette," Goering says. Goebbels concurs. "In the Middle Ages, people latinized their first names; I choose for myself the name Josephus."

"And I will call myself Hermannus," Goering says.

Hitler shakes his head vigorously: "Impossible. I can't call myself A-Dollfuss."

George Herbert Dolfuss was the dictatorial Austrian chancellor assassinated in 1934.

Hitler wants to know what kind of weather there is in Heaven, and he sends Goering to St. Peter. When Hermann does not return, Hitler sends Goebbels up too. Josef does not come back either. Now Hitler goes himself and asks what happened to Goering and Goebbels.

"I sent them to Hell," St. Peter declares.

"But why?"

"Goering stole one of my stars immediately and Goebbels seduced one of my angels."

Goebbels was renowned for harboring an active libido.

Hitler and Goering make an inspection flight. Over a lighted-up Vienna they drop a bomb—the city is plunged immediately into darkness. Then on to Prague, which they find in total darkness.

Says Hitler: "I don't trust these Czechs." With those words he drops a bomb on the city. Instantly, everything lights up and a great illuminated sign shines from below. The sign states: "WELCOME R.A.F."

Here is a similar version:

Early 1941. The bombing attacks of the British Air Force are becoming more frequent. Hitler and Goering undertake an inspection flight over the occupied European lands, to see whether the prescribed protection measures against the air attacks are being observed.

They fly over Brussels and see that lights are burning in many houses, despite the blackout orders. Goering orders two bombs dropped, and all the lights go out immediately. They come over Amsterdam and again see many well-lit houses. The Führer complains, and Goering orders three bombs dropped this time. The city becomes dark in an instant. Now they come to Poland, flying over Warsaw. It is dark; not a light is to be seen. Goering remarks:

"Well here, with the Poles, the blackout is being observed."

55

"Yes," says the Führer, "the Poles have finally become submissive and obedient."

Goering laughs: "But nonetheless, my Führer, let's still drop a bomb on the Pollacks."

Hitler agrees. As the bomb explodes, the whole city lights up, the people hurry on the streets and shout in joy, "Finally, finally, the British are here."

Air Force Commander Goering, a successful pilot in World War I, wanted to resume his old avocation after 1933. However, Hitler was not ready to allow him to keep flying—the Führer has ascertained that a couple of stars were already missing from the sky.

Pictures of Hitler and Goering hung side by side in a Catholic school. Hindenburg was still alive then, and the teacher therefore asked the class which picture belonged between these two figures. He had in mind, of course, a picture of the former president.

Little Franz held up his hand and said: "A picture of Christ."

"Why?" asked the teacher.

"Because Christ already was hanged once between two criminals."

Goering says to Goebbels, "I've noticed that the people don't greet each other with 'Heil Hitler' any more. How would it be if we encourage the use of 'Good day' for a change?"

Answers Goebbels, "Out of the question. As long as our beloved Führer lives there will be no more good days."

"Who are the three greatest inventors?"
"Hitler, Goering, and Goebbels."
"Why?"
"Hitler invented voluntary coercion, Goering invented plain pomp, and Goebbels invented subjective truth."

"Who are the three best photographers?"
"Mussolini, Hitler, and Goebbels."
"Why?"
"Mussolini develops, Hitler copies, and Goebbels enlarges."

After Austria's annexation in 1938, a German gets into a conversation with an Austrian.

"Hitler is Heaven's gift to the German people," says the German.

The Austrian answers, "Hitler? We Austrians set him upon you as revenge for 1866."

Prussia had defeated Austria in war in 1866.

An Air Force orchestra serenades Goering in a small town on his birthday. Hermann rushes to the balcony, just after donning a uniform laden with all sorts of medals and decorations.

Suddenly a tree falls near the band with a loud bang. Goerings's wife, Emmy, still in the bedroom at the vanity mirror, calls out: "Hermann, are you hurt?"

"Did you know the Green Forest is going to be cleared?"
"Why?"
"Goering needs a new pair of pants."

Because of a domestic shortage of cloth fabrics during World War II, German clothing contained a large amount of wooden fibers.

During a stroll through Berlin, Goering meets a group of children at play, making figures out of mud and horse manure.
"What are you making there?" asks Goering.
"We're making figures of Dr. Goebbels and Dr. Ley," one child answers.
"Have you also made one of Hermann Goering?" the corpulent Air Force Marshal asks.
"No," says the child. "We still haven't found a big enough pile of manure."

As a great Allied victory parade rolled through Berlin in the summer of 1945, a sewer lid opened suddenly. Goebbels' ghost stuck his head out of the manhole cover and bellowed, "We did win!"

Several years after the end of the Second World War an elegantly clothed man enters a cigarette shop in Berlin. He is dressed in English fashion and carefully selects his cigarettes. With an English accent he inquires about events in Germany.
"You once had a leader named Adolf Hitler—where did he end up?"
"Oh, you mean Adolf—we deported him to Argentina. He's become a cowboy."

"And Hermann Goering, the beloved Reich Marshal—what's he up to?"

"Hermann? See that crane by the new building over there? He's sitting there winding the reel."

"And Dr. Goebbels, the imaginative propaganda minister?"

"Josef is standing at the corner of Kranzler Street with a vendor's tray selling shoestrings and suspenders. He's doing good business, because he can outshout all the other salesmen. But you are so well-informed about all our bigshots. May I ask who you are?"

"Lord Hess."

This tale made the rounds after Rudolf Hess, Hitler's secretary, made his "peace flight" to England.

3

The Humor of Optimism

Nothing is so properly applied to the false Grandeur, either of Good or Evil, as Ridicule.

—Francis Hutcheson

Whoever wants to survive, must be able to put on an act. Whoever wants to resist, must slyly renounce his identity and be able to play his roles better than the Fascists.

—Uwe Naumann

Gallows humor. The term—*Galgenhumor* in its original German— can be traced back to 1848. It describes the fatalistic wit of the condemned, the last quip before the inevitable meeting with the hangman, the guillotine, or the barrel of a rifle. The archetypal gallows joke tells of a man, about to face a firing squad, who refuses a last cigarette because he's trying to give up smoking.

The expression is commonly—and incorrectly—thought to apply to the humor that came out of occupied Europe. The assumption is that a population vying daily with the hangman must have been capable of only the most bitter humor. On the contrary, the period's humor, from the German cabaret routines in the early 1930s to the anti-Nazi jests in a series of conquered lands and the jokes shared in secret among the ghetto and death camp prisoners,

63

was defiant, confident, even smug. There was little sign of a defeatist attitude. There was, to be sure, a small amount of bitter, biting wit—but "black humor," macabre humor, was scarce. The tacit message: The Nazis are intellectually and morally inferior, sure to suffer ultimate loss and disgrace. Hitler's designs on Europe quickly became the object of continent-wide derision.

Czech sociologist Antonin Obrdlik reported that ascerbic attacks on Nazi Germany began in his homeland "long before the actual invasion took place" in 1939. "Especially after the annexation of Austria [in 1938], there was a whole crop of jokes and anecdotes. People tried not to see the bad omens, and many of them found in anecdotes an intellectual and emotional escape from the disturbing realities."[1] After the German invasion, a story circulated in Slovakia that Sano Mach, an unpopular Czech official, declined to let a public square bear his name. The proposed name, Sano Mach Platz, would translate into German as "Sano, make room."[2] That is, disappear. The Gestapo found a hanged hen in one Czech village with this inscription fastened to her neck: "I'd rather commit suicide than lay eggs for Hitler."[3] A sign appeared on the walls of a cemetery in another town: "Hey, you Czechs, get out of here! Don't you know that this is the German *Lebensraum* [living space]?"[4]

Obrdlik called this brand of humor "an unmistakable index of good morale and of the spirit of resistance of the oppressed peoples." One good anecdote, he said, "changed completely the mood of persons who have heard it—pessimists changed into optimists. Its decline or disappearance reveals either indifference or a breakdown of the will to resist evil."[5] Czechs who accepted the "New Order" in Europe would refuse to listen to political jokes, stating that "This is no time to live on jokes."[6]

Across occupied Europe, a sense of humor was evident in the work of resistance forces. Arrows at highway crossings were turned around and street signs switched, "creating utter confusion among the supermen of the German armies."[7] Cooks stirred laxatives into food for German troops. The "Only for Germans" signs were removed from places of entertainment and hung from lampposts. German films in Danish theaters were surreptitiously replaced by such offerings as *In Which We Serve*, a British war film.[8] *"Le nazisme, c'est la victoire des boches sur les allemands"* [Nazism is the victory of krauts over the Germans] was a popular saying in France.[9]

In Belgium, the Nazi occupiers were subjected to a barrage of disrespectful stories and practical jokes. Bookstores ostentatiously, and courageously, displayed publications with such titles as *Swimming in 10 Lessons* and *Learn to Swim,* at a time when Germany was contemplating a waterborne invasion of Great Britain. *L'Espoir* [Hope], an underground organization, sold a pamphlet with cartoons by anonymous Belgian artists. The drawings lampooned the occupation, the Nazi regulations, food shortages, and inflation. One piece, entitled "Bread Lines," showed two preoccupied sparrows standing in line for sustenance at the back of a horse. Another cartoon showed two women talking. "Got any provisions?" asks one. "Yes, of patience," says the other. In another, an applicant for a coal ration card is advised by a clerk: "Take good care of it. You can use it for a fan when you get too warm." These cartoons were smuggled out of Belgium and reprinted abroad.[10]

Resistance members in occupied Norway would sing this folk tune:

This is a story of passive resistance,
Of a man who refused to give Nazis assistance.

A farmer there lived once in occupied Norway
who found this grim warning tacked on to his doorway:
It said: "You have failed to come up to your quota,
Next week if you fail by a single iota,
Your farm will be taken and you will be killed.
This is the law, and it must be fulfilled."

The farmer replied, "Sirs, the undersigned begs
To inform you concerning my quota of eggs,
I posted your notice just where the hens live,
But the stubborn old bi-peds refused to give,
So I wrung all their necks, the foul saboteurs,
Delighted to serve you. Sincerely yours."[11]

In Poland, a year after the 1939 German invasion, this advertisement for a tanning firm appeared in a Krakow newspaper: "We are tanning the skins of Überalleses and other wild animals."[12] Überalleses, ostensibly a beast with hide sought by the tanner, was a bald reference to the German occupiers; the German national anthem is "Deutschland über alles."

In Germany itself, citizens flaunted their contempt for the regime with greetings of *Morjen* and *Wiedasehn*, Berlin dialect for *Guten Morgen* and *Auf Wiedersehen*, instead of the *de rigueur* "Heil Hitler." When the salute was unavoidable, it "resembled the gesture with which one brushes a fly off his forehead, and the words became indistinct in a sudden fit of coughing."[13]

One story told in Germany had two friends meeting in Cologne's famed cathedral. One was carrying a radio. Why? asked the other. "The radio has to go to confession, it has lied too much in recent weeks."[14]

As the war turned against Germany, jokes became more defiant. One, from Hamburg, featured Fietje and Tetje, characters in several tales from the port city:

> Fietje and Tetje are standing on the street, holding out their collection cups. Fietje keeps coming back with a full cup, in order to get a new, empty cup. Tetje gets almost no coins. "What's your secret, that you're collecting so much?" Tetje asks. "That's simple," Fietje grins, "I always whisper: 'This is a collection for the new government.'"

The Reich's efforts to dissuade Germans from tuning into Allied shortwave broadcasts were mocked. Weiss Ferdl appeared at his Munich cabaret one night with a brand new radio set. He turned the knob and announced:

> I have Berlin here, if I turn a little further I get Munich, then Salzburg and Vienna, and if you keep on turning, you get to Dachau.[15]

One tale in Germany pointed up the popularity of the foreign broadcasts:

> A young boy is picked up on the street. He knows neither his family name nor his address—only that his first name is Hansel. Finally, a policeman tells him, "We'll simply make a report about you on the radio—that there is a child here, and his name is Hansel."
> Young Hansel answered brightly, "Please make the report over English radio. My father doesn't listen to any other."[16]

The Propaganda Ministry's documentary films about the German war successes were dismissed as "Goebbels' fairy tales."[17] Following Allied bombing attacks in 1940, stories about the erection of gallows with effigies of Hitler hanging from them circulated throughout the Reich. This joke was reportedly passed on in many regions:

> A Berliner and an Essener were discussing the extent of their damages.
> The Berliner exclaimed the bombardment had been so bad in Berlin that windowpanes were still shattering five hours after the attack.
> The Essener replied, "That's nothing; in Essen, Führer-pictures were still flying out of windows 14 days after the last attack."[18]

Hitler's pledges to exact revenge on the Allies for damaging Germany were greeted with skepticism:

> "Retribution," it was said, "will come when homes for the aged post signs, 'closed due to induction.'"[19]

Jokes about the increasingly advanced age of Germans pressed into the national service during the war were common. According to another joke:

> During the last attack on Berlin, the English dropped hay for the jackasses who still believe in revenge.[20]

Another example:

> 1950. Conference in the Führer's headquarters about the date for retaliation. It is adjourned for lack of agreement on the question of whether the two planes should fly beside or behind each other.[21]

While the victims of Nazi Europe produced a substantial amount of original humor, quite a few jokes were reworked versions of earlier ones against the Russian czar and other despised regimes. The tale of the youth who pulls a drowning Hitler out of a lake, and when asked what reward he desires, simply replies, "For God's sake, don't tell my father," has turned up in a score of settings. Old jokes, it seems, may find new targets, but they never die.

Humor expressed itself during World War II in many forms, including art, poetry, and theater.

Political cartoonists, particularly in the Allied lands, found Hitler an irresistible target. Avas, a Pole working in Great Britain, showed the Führer brandishing an "olive branch"—a knife entwined with a few leaves.[22] Stanislaw Dobrzynski, another Pole, published a book of sketches in Jerusalem in 1944. In one, a bloated Hitler floats above Berlin, made airborne by absorbing his own hot air.

Another drawing, entitled "Sein Kampf" [His Battle], showed wolves and vultures and other scavangers prowling a field of skeletons.[23] The Russian artist Boris Efimov had Hitler declaring, "Each one of you, my faithful SS men, will receive 'lebensräume,'" in front of a row of graves. In another Efimov work, "Goebbels' Anti-aircraft Battery," the propaganda minister's weapon was rifle-sized fountain pens that issued spurious battle reports.[24] Boris Angeloushev, a Bulgarian cartoonist who trained in Germany and fled after the Nazi takeover, produced a series of satirical anti-Nazi sketches during and immediately after the war. In one, a portrait of Napoleon scowls at a tattered Hitler. "Didn't I tell you to keep your hands off Russia?" asks the French conquerer, who, like the German dictator, was conquered by the Russian winter. In a 1939 drawing, a faceless Nazi soldier stands atop a pile of bodies. The title of that sketch: "Neutralizing the Neutrals." Another Angeloushev work shows a ragged Hitler at the door of Heaven. St. Peter declares: "As long as I don't have a report from the Soviet Information Bureau, I can't handle your case."[25] Another Bulgarian artist, Iliya Beshkov, also caricatured Hitler. "The End of a Philosophy," done in 1944, as the war was turning against Germany, shows a skeleton-like Hitler, his pants legs eaten away, one hand holding a cocked revolver, the other resting on a volume of Nietzsche, the nineteenth-century philosopher credited with inspiring the Nazi creed.[26]

Rhymes, from simple couplets to multiverse creations, were a barometer of the public mood in Germany throughout the war. Schoolchildren, who heard the latest takeoffs in the secrecy of their homes, openly shared them in class. The quixotic 1941 flight of Hitler's personal secretary, Rudolf Hess, to England on a "peace mission" inspired this verse, which became popular in Germany:

Es geht ein Lied im ganzen Land
Wir fahren gegen Engelland

Doch wenn dann wirklich einer fährt
So wird er fur verrückt erklärt[27.]

There is a song across the land
That we are going to England,
But if one person makes the trip,
It's said that he has flipped his lid.

After Goebbels made his impassioned plea, "Do you want total war?"—a call for victory on all military and nationalistic fronts—at a Berlin Sports Palace rally in 1943, drawing enthusiastic shouts of "Yes," this rhyme addressed to the English bomber pilots (the so-called Tommies) made the rounds in the Ruhr region:

Lieber Tommy, fliege weiter,
wir sind alle Bergarbeiter,
fliege weiter nach Berlin,
die haben alle "Ja" geschrien.[28]

Tommy, please stop flying here,
We're just simple mountaineers,
Berlin's really your address,
They're the ones who shouted "Yes."

Incidentally, the word "total" soon turned up in several jokes, mocking Goebbels' usage.

Ruth Andreas-Friedrich, a Berliner who was active in the "Uncle Emil" resistance group during the war, was in an apartment building bombed by the Allies in the fighting's final month. On the way down to an air raid shelter, at a time when the war was nearly lost, a friend entertained her by singing:

The Chancellery is a glorious sight:
Bigwigs are hanging from every street light.

70

They've got the Führer up there too
What a clever thing to do!
But doesn't he look an awful sight.[29]

During the German occupation, an illegal puppet show operated in Amsterdam. Marionettes of Hitler and his consorts were depicted in Hell. For a brief time in 1943, a cabaret existed openly in Westerbork, a Dutch transit camp where such events as track and field, soccer, boxing, and classical music performances were also allowed while they pleased the commandant. The performances featured "no politics"—just pure escapism. "Two comedians, one fat and one skinny; about five pounds of sex appeal, a couple of catchy tunes; some old jokes and a lot of new ones."[30]

"Of all the diversions . . . none pleased the inmates more than the cabarets," remembers Jacob Boas, a survivor of the camp. "Westerbork's cabaret bred the illusion that things were not as hopeless as they seemed. For weeks on end, the hit songs and jokes of the latest revue would be on everybody's lips."

Why did Commandant Albert Gemmecker sanction the cabaret? "Probably he was bored and craved diversion," Boas guesses. "He would have his own theater company. The fantasy of power would be augmented, the legend of his munificence broadened."

The performers gained self-confidence and prestige from the prisoners; their craft earned extensions at Westerbork, delays on the trains to the extermination camps. But only temporarily. "For much as the Commandant might have liked to save his court jesters," Boas writes, "he could not."[31]

Similarly, a prisoners' theater performed "under the eyes of the SS,"[32] in Dachau, with transparent allusions to the Nazis, in the summer of 1943. Prisoners of the first Nazi concentration camp, which was located in a Munich suburb, performed in the open, between rows of barracks. The "world premiere" of *Die Blutnacht auf dem Schreckenstein oder Ritter Adolars Brautfahrt und ihr grausiges Ende*

oder Die wahre Liebe ist das nicht [The Night of Blood on the Rock of
Horrors or Knight Adolar's Maiden Voyage and Its Gruesome End
or That Is Not the True Love], a play written clandestinely in the
camp on discarded scraps of paper by Viennese journalist Rudolf
Kalmar, took place there. The plot: Count Adolar is visited at his
castle by three knights. Adolar, a thinly disguised Hitler figure,
ends up killing the three visitors after he rapes Anneliese, the
heroine. The role of Adolar was played by Erwin Geschonneck, a
prisoner who survived Dachau and became a popular actor in East
Germany after the war. By the time Geschonneck portrayed Adolar,
he had perfected his impersonation of Hitler's speech and gestures
by putting on brief skits to amuse fellow prisoners.

Kalmar, who also survived his incarceration, called his play "a
parable of the small spirit of the great Reich."[33] It closed with these
words:

> *Es ist das alte Lied,*
> *Was man im Stück hier sieht.*
> *Doch bleib für immer Euch ein Wort im Ohr:*
> *Ist alles auch ganz schlecht,*
> *Es wird schon wieder recht*
> *Durch dieses Zauberwort: Humor, Humor!*[34]

> It is the old song,
> That you see here in this play.
> But always keep a word in mind:
> Everything is hell,
> Soon it will get well
> Through this magic word: humor, humor!

The ground between the barracks was packed for each show;
prisoners brought their own stools. Members of the SS sat as
"honored guests" in the front row at each show, apparently taking

no offense at the anti-Nazi jibes. Kalmar supposed that the double meaning of his lines escaped some of the Nazi guards, whose "benevolence" was confined to the actual hours of the performance. True to their usual sadistic style, they forced the prisoners to hastily erect and tear down the makeshift stage. "The platform could not be built until an hour before the performance," a survivor recalled. Shows were on Saturday and Sunday afternoons. Immediately after every Sunday's performance, "the stage had to be cleared away as if it had never stood there."

Kalmar recalled that "The prisoners . . . the Czechs, Poles, Russians, Slavs, the Serbs and Croatians, shook with pleasure" during the performances. "I know with certainty," said Karl Roder, a participant in the production, "that the few hours of laughter, not just during the play, inhibited every thought of suicide."[35] Another survivor praised the play for raising the inmates' spirits: "Many of them, who sat behind the rows of the SS each night and laughed with a full heart, didn't experience the day of freedom. But most among them took from this demonstration strength to endure their situation. How many of them, who performed the play on powdery barrels, survived the Fascism? Only a few. They had the certainty, as they lay at night on their wooden bunks: We have done something that gives strength to our comrades. We have made the Nazis look ridiculous."[36]

The prisoners' artistic breath of freedom at Dachau was eventually suffocated: Six weeks after the first performance of *The Night of Blood,* a prohibition from Berlin closed it down.

During a beer hall rally in the early 1930s, a Nazi speaker declared from the platform, "The expression 'fear' has been deleted from our dictionaries."

A small voice at the rear of the room piped up, "Please look under 'Moire.'"

"Moire" is a Hebrew form of the verb "to fear."

Three Swiss citizens were talking in July 1939 about their vacation plans. They wanted to get to know all of Germany—the first Swiss wanted to see Munich, the second, Berlin. The third said, "I'm going to Warsaw."

"But Warsaw is, of course, not in Germany," the others replied.

Said their friend, "I'm not going till October."

Germany invaded Poland in September 1939.

Hitler is standing with his aides in front of two aquariums. On one is stuck a swastika, but it is empty. The other tank has no swastika, but in its place a beautiful fish is splashing in the water. Hitler glances around, perplexed. He would love to have the fish in his tank. But how should he start? He doesn't want to steal it; that would cast a bad light on him. Finally he decides on an idea. He pulls the plug from the aquarium that holds the fish. "The poor fish," Hitler murmurs, while the water is flowing out. "Look at it. If only he could be helped." The water goes lower and lower.

"Oh, the poor fish," he cries out. "Isn't it terrible what's happening to him? Someone must rescue it! He would have it so good in my aquarium!" Finally all the water drains out, and the fish is lying on the bottom. "Well, take it out finally!" Goering urges.

"Why?" asks Hitler, looking meaningfully at his Propaganda Minister. "He still hasn't asked for help."

In Warsaw, jokes were told against Russia also, which Poles despised for abandoning them to Nazi Germany. This example comes from the end of the war:

Two ghosts meet in the Soviet Union in 1945.

"Where did you die?" the first one asks.

"1941, in Stalingrad. And you?"

"1943, on a collective farm."

A third apparition enters.

"Where did you die?" the first two ask.

"I'm not a ghost," the third form answers. "I just came from a Russian gulag."

A cabaret comedian in the Aryan part of Warsaw told the audience: "Now I know how to count in German."

He puts four piglets on the stage, and counts:

"Einer! Zweier! Dreier! Führer!"

He was thrown in jail for insulting Hitler.

Six months later, considered rehabilitated, he returned to the cabaret.

"Now," he said, "I indeed know how to count in German."

Again he puts the four piglets on the stage, and begins counting. "Einer! Zweier! Dreier!"

As he reached the fourth piglet, he waved a finger at him and said, "Uh, uh! You won't catch me this time."

Einer, Zweier, Dreier are German for first, second, third. Führer, Hitler's title, sounds like Vierer, fourth.

What is the difference between Luther, Hitler, Goebbels, and Schacht?

Luther says what he believes.

Hitler believes what he says.

Goebbels does not believe what he says.

Schacht does not say what he believes.

75

Hjalmar Schacht, Nazi economics minister, was a rival of Goering and a leading opponent of excessive expenditures on rearmament. He was acquitted of war crimes at the Nuremberg trials.

The definition of a German Christmas goose: Fat as Goering, cackling like Goebbels, plucked like the German people, and brown like the party.

Hitler, Goering, Goebbels, and Food Minister Herbert Backe are making war plans.

Hitler to Goering: "How many years' supply of airplanes and gasoline do we have?"

Goering: "Five years, my Führer!"

Hitler to Goebbels: "How many more years can the people's will be pushed by propaganda?"

Goebbels: "Ten years, my Führer!"

Hitler to Backe: "And how long can we still feed ourselves?"

Backe: "Twenty years, my Führer!"

With his usual energy, Hitler says, "Then we can still keep the war going for a long time!"

Shyly, Backe reports again: "I meant only for the four of us!"

Hitler and Goering are standing on the Berlin radio tower. Hitler says he would like to give the Berliners some joy. "Then jump off the tower," Goering says.

Hitler visits a church. He starts talking to the Christ figure on the crucifix. Kindred souls, Hitler says. Both are misunderstood,

76

both are punished for their deeds, both are suffering because of the Jews.

The figure on the cross looks down at the Führer. "Boy are you lucky," he says. "If my hands and legs weren't tied, I'd kick your ass."

The pastor was speaking from the pulpit. "Lies are limping through the land today, and truth is lost."

A Gestapo officer who had secretly listened to the sermon had the pastor summoned to the secret police headquarters. "Were your words referring to a particular personality in our government?" he was asked.

"Whom did you have in mind?" replied the pastor.

"Well, our Propaganda Minister certainly limps, as is well known."

"But doesn't he lie too?"

Hitler was renowned for his lengthy speeches, in which he often referred to the fourteen years of supposed German degradation between the end of World War I and his ascent to power.

Hitler needed an operation. During the anesthesia, he started roaring his usual rhetoric about "14"—"For 14 years we had to bear the shame," and so on. The physician looked at the nurse and said, "Nurse, I'm going to lunch now. I'll be back in two hours—he probably won't be ready before that."

Two Germans are talking about their postwar plans. "When the war is over, I'm going to buy a bike and ride through the whole country."

"Wonderful. And what will you do in the afternoon?"

Conversation between two German businessmen:
"How's business?"
"Thanks, much better than a month hence."

Hitler visits a woman on her 100th birthday and asks her to make a wish.

"I don't have any more earthly interests," she says. "My highest wish is to have my death announced in a great newspaper."

Hitler immediately promises her a half-page notice in the *Volkischer Beobachter*.

"No," she says, "not in the *Volkischer Beobachter*. Then no one will believe I died."

In the final months of the war, German troops and civilians sang this adaptation of a popular tune:

Es geht alles vorüber,
Es geht alles vorbei.
Und erst geht der Führer
Und dann die Partei.

Everything passes,
Everything goes by,
And first goes the Führer
And then the Party.

This version of the Little Red Riding Hood fairy tale was popular in Germany in 1937:

Once upon a time there was a forest in Germany that the work service still had not cleared: a wolf lived in this forest. On one beautiful Sunday there was a harvest festival. A small member of the League of German Girls went through the forest. She wore a red hood and wanted to visit her Aryan grandmother who was put up in a National Socialist old-age home. She carried a little basket in her hand with a donation for the German cause, and a bottle of wine.

There she met the angry wolf. His fur was totally brown, so that no one should notice at a glance that he was a foreigner. Little Red Riding Hood didn't suspect anything, because she knew that all parasites of the people were in concentration camps, and she believed that an entirely plain dog stood in front of her.

"Heil, Red Riding Hood," said the wolf. "Where are you going?"

Red Riding Hood answered, "I'm going to visit my grandmother in the old-age home."

"So," said the wolf, "bring her a couple of the flowers with which the Office for the Beauty of the Lumbering has spruced up the forest."

Red Riding Hood set out right away to pick a bouquet. But the wolf hurried to the old-age home, ate up the grandmother, slipped into her clothes, put on her Party decorations and lay down in bed.

Red Riding Hood came to the door, and asked, "How are you, dear grandmother?"

The wolf tried to imitate the grandmother's voice, and answered, "Good, my dear child!"

Red Riding Hood asked, "Why are you speaking so differently today?"

The wolf answered, "I worked too hard in the speaker's training course this morning."

"But grandma, what big ears you have?"

"So I can better understand the whispers of the grumblers."

"What big eyes you have?"

"So I can better see the subversive moles!"

79

"What a big mouth you have?"

"You know, of course, that I am in the Reich's Cultural Community!"

And with these words he ate poor Red Riding Hood, lay down in bed, fell right asleep without a care and began to snore.

The local hunter went by then. He heard the wolf, and thought, "Ah, how can an Aryan grandmother snore so un-Germanically?"

When he looked in, he shot the wolf dead at his own risk, although he had no hunting license for wolves. Then he cut the wolf's belly open and found grandmother and Red Riding Hood still alive. There was great joy! The wolf was handed over to the Reich Food Distribution Committee, and was made into meat in his own juice. The hunter could embroider a gold wolf on his uniform, Red Riding Hood was promoted to leader in the League of German Girls, and her grandmother took a recreation trip to Madeira on a new "Strength Through Joy" steamer.

Two Berliners meet.

"Why do you look so out of sorts?" the first asks.

"There will be war soon."

"Why?"

"Hitler gave a speech about peace today."

There is a blackout in Berlin. A man makes his way at night through the dark streets of the capital. Suddenly he hears a voice:

"Stop or I'll shoot!"

The man stops, and the aggressor comes closer and says:

"Give me your wallet right away!"

The man hands over his wallet and says with relief:

"You had terrified me—I thought it was the Gestapo."

What does life in Berlin look like?

The Germans rule the cellars, the foreigners rule the streets, and the British rule the air.

During the war, ten-foot-high slogans appeared at factories and workplaces throughout Germany. They read: "We can thank our Führer for being able to work here!" The slogan prompted this story:

> Everyone in the family comes home, one-by-one, and leaves a little note, "Sorry, won't be home for supper," before rushing off to their S.A., Hitler Youth or B.D.M. (League of German Girls) meeting. When the family finally gets home they find the apartment stripped by thieves who have left a note of their own: "We can thank our Führer for being able to work here."

German propaganda during the war:

First year of the war: We have won.

Second year of the war: We will win.

Third year of the war: We must win.

Fourth year of the war: We cannot be defeated.

At the end of the war, Roosevelt cables Hitler: N.S.D.A.P. K.D.F. U.S.A.

"*Nun suche deinen alten Pinsel. Kaufe dir Farbe und suche Arbeit.*"

81

[Look for your old brush now. Buy yourself some paint and get a job.]

The initials, ostensibly conveying concession in the German parlance, stand for the National Socialist German Workers' Party, and the Strength through Joy chapter of the U.S.A.

A woman looks out the window at her neighbor and sees that she is fanning the potatoes in her skillet with a swastika pennant. The woman goes over and asks her neighbor, "What are you doing with the pennant?"

"I have no fat, and I have to fry the potatoes for my husband, and because so many have become fat under this pennant, I'm trying it too."

During the war in Libya, Hitler calls Mussolini:
"Benito, have you already occupied Egypt?"
"I can't hear well," Mussolini answers. "Speak louder, dear Adolf."
Hitler speaks louder. Whereupon Mussolini says:
"Speak louder, Adolf, it's hard to hear well. Are you calling already from London?"

After the defeat at Stalingrad, Germans greeted each other with "Howl Hitler!"

What is naked and eats only grass?
The German people in one year.

A propaganda poster displayed in a Berlin street bore the legend:

"Under National Socialism People Live Longer."

One night someone wrote underneath this: "Perhaps it only *seems* longer."

In Paris, people told the story of Hitler's visit to Napoleon's tomb. He shouts down: "Napoleon, before you stands the man who has accomplished what you failed to achieve—the conquest of Europe!"

From the depths of the tomb comes a voice: "So you have conquered England too?"

"Not yet," replies Hitler.

"Then climb down, brother, and lie beside me," suggests the voice.

Hitler, who was superstitious and had his own astrologer-in-waiting, arranged a seance to summon the spirit of Moses. Moses duly appeared.

"How did you manage to divide the waters of the Red Sea?" Hitler asks. "I should like to use the same method for crossing the English Channel."

"Well," replies Moses, "all I had to do was touch the waters with my magic rod."

"And where can I find that rod now?" asks Hitler.

"In the British Museum," chuckles the spirit of Moses.

God is disturbed over the situation on earth. To find out what is wrong, he sends Methusaleh down. But Methusaleh comes back to Heaven after a few hours.

God asks, "Why are you back so quickly? You were supposed to investigate."

"Yes, I wanted to, but when I came to Germany, they tried to draft my age group right away into the civilian service, and I had to escape."

The crops were in danger from weeks of drought and the Catholic priest of the village fixed an intercession service for rain. Meeting the local Nazi leader in the street, he invited him to the service.

"What made you invite this enemy of God and the Church?" asked one of the congregants. "Why, it's because of them that we've been cursed with this drought."

"Think for a second," replied the priest, "the Lord *once sent a whole flood* because of people like them."

A German reports voluntarily to Army induction headquarters and is given his choice of assignments.

"I'd like to work in the Führer's headquarters," he says.

"Are you crazy?" cries the officer in charge.

"Why? Is that a requirement?" the German asks.

The Dutch had their own anti-Nazi jokes.

The Dutch would raise their own hands and call out, "Heil Rembrandt."

When challenged by the Nazis, they would say, "You have your painters, we have ours."

A Nazi officer is shown around Luxembourg by a local guide: "And this," points out the guide, "is our admiralty."

"Why do you have an admiralty?" asks the German. "Luxembourg hasn't got a navy."

"Isn't there a Ministry of Justice in Berlin?" replies the Luxembourger.

Picasso is summoned by the Nazi commandant of Paris and shown a reproduction of the artist's painting of Guernica's destruction by German bombers during the Spanish Civil War. "Did you do that?" the commandant asks.

"No," replies Picasso, "you did."

Several storm troopers enter an Evangelical Church on Sunday morning during services. The leader of the group walks up to the minister and says he must make an announcement.

"My fellow Germans," begins the chief storm trooper, "I am here in the interest of race purity. We have tolerated non-Aryans long enough and now we must get rid of them. All those whose parents are Jews are ordered to leave the church at once."

A number of worshipers rise from their seats and leave.

"And now I am ordering out all those whose fathers are Jews." More depart.

"One more announcement and I am through. All those whose mothers are Jewish please leave."

Upon hearing this the pastor jumps up, takes hold of the

crucifix on the pulpit, and says: "Brother, now it is time for you and me to get out."

During his brief stay in Paris, Hitler visited an elementary school and interrogated the children about their political views. Turning to a young boy, Hitler asked: "Now that you know where France stands, what would you like to be when you grow up?"

"A Nazi!" answered the boy. Elated with this reply, Hitler repeated the same question to another boy who happened to be Jewish.

"I am a republican," replied the boy. "It is my hope that France will once again be a republic."

"Why are you a republican?" inquired Hitler.

"Simply because my father, grandfather, and great-grandfather were all republicans," replied the boy.

"Is that so?" Hitler yelled. "Supposing your father were a murderer, would you be one too?"

"If my father were a murderer," replied the boy, *then* I would be a Nazi."

From New Year's 1942: "This year will henceforth be known as 1941A, because Hitler promised his people to end the war in 1941."

A saying in Berlin during the early 1940s:

"One can recognize honest men easily—they are those who have lost at least 10 percent of their weight since 1936."

An overworked laborer in Berlin, hungry and anemic looking, paused on a street corner and took another notch in his belt. "What are you doing?" a storm trooper barked at him. The worker looked at him sadly and answered:

"Nothing. I'm just having my breakfast."

"Why does Hitler sit in the front when he goes to a theater?"
"Because that is the only place he has the people behind him."

At an inn near Berlin a tourist asked the innkeeper how business was.

"Oh, fine," he replied.

"So it is true," said the tourist, "that business is better since Hitler came into power?"

"Yes," responded the proprietor, "things are wonderful now. One Country, one Leader, one Customer."

Physicians from different nations were discussing the advances in surgery during a banquet at an international surgeons' congress in Genf. "We have succeeded in removing a major part of the intestine," declared an American doctor, "and we can replace it by plastic surgery. As clinical experience proves, digestion functions quite normally after this operation."

"Very nice," agreed a Swedish physician. "But we have developed methods to set a nonbeating heart in motion through an operation. What do you say to that?"

A German surgeon responded. "All of that is nothing," he said. "We have removed the brain of most of the people, and no one has noticed a thing!"

An elderly man who was robbed and beaten up by toughs in a Berlin street one night yelled, "Help! Murder!" Rushing up, a policeman quieted the victim. "Shh! You must not discuss politics so loudly."

In Berlin two men were engaged in conversation on a street corner. One of them spoke his mind:

"This Nazi government consists of knaves and fools. It is starving the population, everything is going to rack and ruin . . ."

At that point a Gestapo man seized the rash one. The man's friend tried to save him:

"Don't take this fellow seriously, he is crazy, insane, and not responsible for what he says!"

"Huh!" snorted the secret agent, "if he is crazy, how does he understand the political situation so perfectly?"

"There's a German living in my house."

"Hush. If Hitler hears about it, he'll annex the whole district."

Hitler was to inspect an asylum. The inmates were carefully coached. As Hitler walked down the line, each lunatic gave the Nazi salute and shouted, "Heil Hitler!" But the last man stood stolidly at attention.

"Why don't you salute me?" shouted Hitler.

"Your excellency is making a mistake," came the polite reply. "I am the keeper."

One German physician, to a colleague: "Heil Hitler."
Second physician: "Why don't you do it?"

In German, "heil" also means "to heal."

While driving through the country, Hitler's car runs over a dog. His chauffeur stops the car, looks at the dog, and pronounces him dead. Hitler instructs the driver to inform the farmer of the accident and recompense him for the loss. The chauffeur enters the farmer's house, identifies himself, and announces, "The dog is dead."

"Wonderful," responds the farmer. "Let's drink to that good news."

Two Germans meet on a street corner.
"Can you lend me a cigarette paper?" asks one.
"Sorry," replies the other. "I used my last one to wrap up my meat ration."

A little girl in Germany told her schoolteacher that her cat had given birth to five kittens. "They are all darling little Nazis," added the girl. A month later a Nazi officer visited the school, and the teacher asked the little girl to repeat the story.

"Yes, Herr Inspector," she said. "My cat gave birth to five little kittens, and they are all darling little Social Democrats."

"What," shouted the teacher, "I thought you told me they were darling little Nazis."

"Yes, they were," replied the little girl, "but that was four weeks ago. Now their eyes are open."

89

A Gestapo agent questioned a small boy.

"Have you a picture of Hitler hanging in your house?"

"No."

"Have you one of Goering and Goebbels hanging in your house?"

"No," replied the boy, "but when my father gets out of concentration camp, he said he's going to hang them all."

Hitler's birthday. A teacher addressed her pupils:

"Our beloved Führer is more than just a leader; he is like our father. Now just suppose that he was really your father and you could have anything you wished. What would you want most?"

"I would want him to make me a general," shouted one boy.

"A *gauleiter,*" called another.

"A storm trooper," yelled a third.

"An orphan," shouted little Moshe.

A railway compartment in German-occupied France. A German officer, a young man, an old woman, and a pretty girl.

The train enters a tunnel. The passengers hear the sound of a kiss, a heavy blow, and a groan. When the train exits the tunnel, they see that the German is nursing a black eye.

"What a courageous girl to hit a German officer like that," thinks the old woman.

"Strange that the German kissed the old woman and not me," thinks the young girl.

"This Frenchman is not as stupid as he looks," thinks the German officer. "*He* steals a kiss, and I get the black eye."

The young man thinks: "I managed that well! I kissed myself

on the hand, gave the German a black eye, and got away with it without anyone knowing."

What is the difference between Communism and National Socialism?

Under Communism, if a man has a cow, it is taken away from him. Under National Socialism, he is allowed to keep the cow and feed it—only the milk is taken away.

What is the difference between Christianity and National Socialism?

In Christianity, one man died for everyone. In National Socialism, everyone has to die for one man.

What is the difference between Gandhi and Hitler?

In India one man goes hungry for all the people: in Germany all the people go hungry for one man.

In the late 1930s, a British diplomat visited Hitler's Berchtesgarden mountain hideout. The Führer tried to show the futility of Western resistance. "What can the British do," he asked, "against an army so devoted to me that they will go to their death at my nod? Do you see that soldier there? Soldier, jump out that window!"

At Hitler's command, the soldier leaped out of the window to his death. The British diplomat was stunned.

"I'll show you once more," Hitler boasted. "Soldier, jump out that window."

The second soldier jumped.

Hitler issued the command a third time. This time the diplomat seized the German soldier who was headed for the window, and demanded, "How can you abandon life so lightly?"

The soldier replied, "You call this a life?" Then he broke away and jumped.

A group of downed German pilots come to the gates of Heaven, but the guard refuses to let them in. The pilots are infuriated. How can this be?

The Führer assured them explicitly that the gates of Heaven would be open to anyone who comes from Germany.

The guard then shows them the communiqué from German military headquarters, which states explicitly that only three pilots had been killed in fighting. "How can you expect me to let you, more than a hundred persons, into Heaven when your communiqué states with certainty that only three were killed?" asks the guard.

A Swiss dog meets a foreign-born member of his species at the Basel train station.

"Where are you from?" the first canine asks.

"From Germany."

"But from what I read in the newspapers, you have everything there in abundance. So what do you want here in Switzerland?"

"To bark."

At a gathering of friends, one of them announces that a new song is being written:

"God keep Adolf Hitler . . ."

Adds a voice in the background: ". . . as soon as possible."

"I heard the Führer's new speech yesterday," the Nazi Party member excitedly told a man who didn't belong to the party. "And you?"

"I also heard it," he answered, "but it was a year ago."

A group of Germans are huddled in an air raid shelter during a bombing raid.

The shelter warden, still an enthusiastic Nazi, calls out: "And where would we be without our Führer?"

From a dark corner comes the answer: "In bed."

In 1944, it was said, it was easy to tell the difference between an optimist and a pessimist in Greater Germany.

The former learned Russian, the latter, Chinese.

Hitler died and went to Hell, where he met Mussolini and Hirohito. They immediately made plans for a new Axis—it would have an invincible army and one leader. "Give me a minute," Hitler said, jumping up. "I have to discuss a few things with the Almighty." After a few hours, he returned, visibly upset. "The Axis is all off. Imagine . . . *He* insisted upon being the leader."

A horse, cow, and goat reach Heaven and ask Saint Peter for permission to return to earth and observe how animals are being treated in the Third Reich.

First the horse visits earth. He returns in a short time and says, "There's no life for my kind anymore. They issue only autos now."

Then the cow descends. She too returns in a short time and says, "They think of nothing night and day but milk."

At last the goat makes the journey. She does not return immediately. After nearly a year, she comes back. Saint Peter greets her: "You must have been well pleased with things in the Third Reich."

"Pleased?" cries the goat. "Quite the contrary. I bleated once and they put me in a concentration camp."

Two Nazis meet in Berlin.

"How are things with you?" asks one.

"Very well, thank you. I have a fine job," says the other.

"What sort of job?"

"I sit on top of a steeple all day, and watch so I can report to the Führer when Germany has conquered the world."

"What is your salary?"

"Twenty marks a week."

"Well, that isn't much."

"That's true . . . but it's a lifetime job."

Winston Churchill sat on the African shore, fishing. Across from him on the Italian shore sat Mussolini and Hitler, also fishing. Churchill would cast in his line, get a nibble, and pull out a fish. Then he would bait his line, cast again, and pull out another fish. This kept on until Churchill had a basketful of fish.

In the meantime, Mussolini and Hitler had not a single bite. Finally, Hitler had enough.

"Hey Winston," he shouted, "why is it that you get a fish every time you throw in your line and we can't get a single bite?"

94

"Why? Simple," Churchill replied. "Over there the fish are afraid to open their mouths."

Once Hitler visited an insane asylum. He strutted up and down, asking the patients, "Don't you know who I am? Der Führer. I possess all the power. In fact, I'm almost as powerful as God himself . . ."

"Imagine," muttered a patient. "That's the way it started with me, too."

During the Weimar Republic, a professor at the German Academy whispered that at the next meeting a matter of great cultural importance would come up.

"What is that?" inquired his confidante.

"What else?" was the answer. "The translation of *Mein Kampf* into German."

A Norwegian villager visited his mayor, a collaborationist.

"But suppose Germany loses?" asked the villager. "What will you do then?"

"Germany can't lose," shrugged the Nazi mayor. "But if it did, I'd just put my hat on and . . ."

"Put your hat on?" growled the villager. "On what?"

Hitler, Mussolini, and Hirohito go to Heaven. They stand before the Lord on His throne. Mussolini approaches the throne, throws out his chest, raises his arm, and shouts "Ave Caesar!"

The Lord smiles, steps down from His throne, embraces Il Duce, wishes him a good day, and returns to His throne.

Then Hirohito steps before the throne, smiles, and bows.

Again the Lord smiles, steps down, embraces the emperor, and steps back on His throne.

Finally Hitler goose-steps forward, clicks his heels, raises his arm in the Nazi salute, and shouts "Heil Hitler!"

This time the Almighty smiles and waves affably—but remains seated on the throne.

After the visitors leave, Saint Peter asks: "Dear Lord, how is it that you stepped down from the throne and embraced the two dictators, yet for the third and most powerful of them all, you remained seated? Der Führer will be furious."

The Lord smiled patiently and put His arm around Saint Peter's shoulder. "My dear friend, you don't know that fellow. If I had left my throne for a second, he would have hopped up there and occupied it."

Hitler, convinced of his likeness to God, insists that his name be inserted into the Lord's Prayer. The Church resists for a long time, until it sees a way to fulfill his wish. "We include your name daily in our prayer," they inform him: "And deliver us from evil."

Charlie Chaplin is indignant. "I don't complain that Hitler has my small beard; it's all the same to me that Goebbels imitates my walk; but it makes me very angry that Goering gets more laughs than I do."

After the war a German goes to a kiosk and asks for *The National Socialist World* newspaper.

96

"Not available any more," the dealer says.

The German appears at the kiosk soon again, and asks for the newspaper again.

"Not available any more," declares the dealer.

A few hours later the German comes again, and requests the same publication. The dealer is fed up. "How often do I have to tell you," he declares. "*The National Socialist World* isn't here any more?"

The German apologizes. "Excuse me—but I can't hear it often enough."

At the end of the war, when there were bomb alerts every day and night, the citizens went into the air raid shelters at the sound of the alarm. If someone greeted the other people with "Good evening," it meant he had not slept yet. Some said "Good morning"—they had already slept. A few said, as was the custom throughout the war, "Heil Hitler"—those were still sleeping.

What is the city with the most warehouses?

Berlin. When you go through the city you are told: "Here were houses, there were houses."

Hitler asks a portrait of him on the wall, "How will the war end?" Answers the picture, "They will take me down and hang you."

An Allied soldier is shot down over Germany. He is injured and taken to the hospital.

The surgeons amputate his left leg. He asks the hospital to send his limb to his mother, to be buried in U.S. soil.

The soldier's other leg becomes infected and is also amputated. He has it sent back home, for the same reason.

The infection spreads. His right arm goes. His left arm, too. He makes the same request. The hospital refuses.

"We're wise to you," the head doctor declares. "You're trying to escape."

The German soldier has simple wishes: The clothing of the Russians, the nourishment of the English, the Italians as opponents—and Hitler as the Unknown Soldier of World War I.

Scene at inspection for the German Army. The chief physician is hard at work. "What do you have?" he asks the first recruit. "I am shortsighted," the young man answers.

"Baloney!" replies the doctor. "We all are shortsighted. I am shortsighted, the officers are shortsighted, and the Führer is shortsighted too. Nevertheless we must all fulfill our duty. Next!"

The second recruit asserts that he suffers from constant headaches.

"Fantasy!" growls the doctor again. "I also have continuing headaches, the officers likewise, and the Führer too. Nevertheless we all fulfill our duty. Next!"

The third recruit admits softly that he has stomach problems. "Nonsense," the doctor snorts. "I have stomach problems, the officers have stomach problems, and the Führer too. But everyone fulfills his duty."

The fourth recruit laughs and tells the doctor. "Don't waste your energy on me. I am feebleminded."

What is the difference between a missionary and the Reich Bishop?

The missionary makes the savages devout, the Reich Bishop makes the devout savage.

Bishops and other religious functionaries with official titles under the Third Reich were considered illegitimate Christians whose theology was tinged with Nazi leanings.

What is an Aryan?
The rear end of a Proletarian.

Hitler sat in a barber's chair. As hard as the barber tried, his shears kept sinking into the Führer's mop of hair. "My hair is too flat to comb," Hitler said. The barber laughed: "I have a good remedy for that. Allow freedom of the press again and you'll see your hair stand on end."

A washroom attendant was asked if the Third Reich had brought an increase in her business, as everywhere else. "Of course," she said. "It's very clear. Ninety percent sh— in their pants and 10 percent on the government."

A poem on the same theme in 1933, when Hitler's overthrow was still considered a possibility:

"Heil Hitler!" ist der Deutsche Gruss.
Die Reichswehe steht Gewehr bei Fuss.

Im Herbst, da gibt es grossen Krach,
Dann sagen wir wieder "Guten Tag!"

"Heil Hitler" is how Germans greet.
The Reich's army stands ready, rifles at feet.
In fall, there will be a loud bang,
Then we can say again, "Good day!"

This was a Third Reich adaptation of a popular children's song:

Ten little grumblers sat on a vine;
one imitated Goebbels,
then there were only nine!
Nine little grumblers, all did cogitate,
One's thoughts were noticed,
then there were only eight!
Eight little grumblers had written down their thoughts,
a search turned up what he had penned,
then there were only seven!
Seven little grumblers, they asked "How does it taste?"
One said, "It's fit for snakes,"
then there were only six!
Six little grumblers swore at the Hitler Youth,
one called them a pack of lice,
then there were only five!
Five little grumblers at the piano played a score,
one chose Mendelssohn,
then there were only four!
Four little grumblers, all knew Dr. Ley,
one had the goods on him,
then there were only three!
Three little grumblers, "Mythos"* is trash, they'd say,

---

*Alfred Rosenberg's "The Myth of the Twentieth Century" set the philosophical
tone for the Nazi movement.

Party member Rosenberg had two more hauled away.
One small grumbler, this verse to share had a yen.
he was brought to Dachau,
then there were again—ten.

An art dealer visits his best customer, a rich banker. The dealer warily opens an ebony chest he has brought and says, "Mr. Pfeffer, I've brought something very beautiful for you—a death mask of Franz Liszt." The banker studies the death mask for a long time, then asks: "Don't you have one of Hitler?"

What is the difference between a deathly ill person and Hitler? The former lives unfortunately, the latter unfortunately lives.

At the end of World War II, rations of everything were very short in Germany.

Jesus has come back to Earth and takes a walk down the main street of Berlin. Goebbels strolls near him, concerned about the precarious situation. When he sees Jesus, his eyes light up—he can ask for advice.

"Tell me, Jesus," he asks, "how did you feed 5,000 persons in your time without bread?"

"You ask me *that*?" Jesus replies in wonder. "How did you get 80 million people drunk without alcohol?"

Germany's high unemployment rate at the start of Hitler's reign and his bachelorhood were combined in one tawdry joke:

What does the Führer have under his shorts?
An unemployed one!

A gullible Bavarian goes to confession. He asks, "Is it a deadly sin if I have such rage at Adolf that I wish his death?"
"In this particular case, no!" replies the priest.

In the year 2000 in New York, a small kid asks his father, "who was Adolf Hitler, Papa?" The father doesn't know either. They consult an encyclopedia: "Hitler, Adolf—a German bandit at the time of Stalin the Great."

Hitler and Mussolini discuss which city will become the capital of the new Europe.
"Rome should become the capital, because the Almighty has already determined it," says Mussolini.
"When did I say that?" asks Hitler.

A little girl takes the streetcar for the first time and asks her mother several questions.
"Mama, what kind of man is that with the big leather pouch?"
"That is the conductor, my child."
"And the man up there who is turning the crank?"
"That is the Führer [driver]."
"Mama, is that the man Daddy is always swearing at?"

A man appears every day at a newsdealer, buys a newspaper, looks at the front page, and discards the the paper. One day the puzzled dealer asks the man what he is looking for.

"I'm looking for a death notice," the man answers.

"Death notices aren't on the first page," the dealer says.

"The one I'm looking for will be," says the man.

Variations of this joke have had Stalin, Brezhnev, and countless other dictators as the foil.

What is the difference between Adolf Hitler and the sun?

The sun rises in the east and sets in the west. Hitler's star goes up in the west and down in the east.

Actor Peter Lorre had become famous for his performance as a murderer in the film *M*. At the beginning of the Third Reich he went to Vienna. Goebbels, who did not know that Lorre was a Jew, tried to get the renowned performer to come to Germany. Lorre responded to the invitation with a telegram: "There isn't room in Germany for two murderers like Hitler and me."

Frederick the Great, Napoleon, and Hindenburg are in Heaven, discussing the modern management of warfare.

"If I had as many airplanes as Goering, then I would have ended the Seven Year's War in four months," Frederick declared.

Hindenburg said, "If I had as many Panzers as Hitler, then not a single Russian would have entered East Prussia."

"If I only had Dr. Goebbels," said Napoleon, "the French would never have found out that I lost the Russian campaign."

Hitler and Rohm are walking along the Spree River. A man jumps into the water to commit suicide. As the man surfaces and stretches his arm out, Rohm says, "That's your sign. Rescue him!"

The drowning man disappears under the water and surfaces again with his backside pointing up.

"*You* jump in, that's for you!" Hitler says.

Ernst Rohm, the first leader of the German forces until his assassination on Hitler's orders in 1934, was a known homosexual.

"Why are you here?" one concentration camp inmate asks another.

"On the 5th of May, I said 'Hess is crazy.' And you?"

"On the 15th day of May, I said 'Hess is not crazy.'"

Rudolf Hess made his controversial flight to England on May 10, 1944.

A German remarks, upon reading a newspaper report of Hess's flight to England, "Now we really know that Hess is crazy—he wants to return to Germany."

Hitler visits Hindenburg at Neudeck, the country estate of the Reich President. Hindenburg loses his handkerchief during a walk in the park. Hitler picks it up and requests it as a souvenir.

"I'd rather keep it," Hindenburg replies, "because it is the only thing I can still stick my nose into."

After Hitler's assumption of the Reich chancellorship, President Hindenburg was effectively shut out of the governing process.

What is the difference between National Socialism and Communism?

It's colder in Russia.

The schoolteacher asks, "How big is the Nazi Party?"

Little Fritz raises his hand and gives the unexpected answer, "Five feet, three inches!"

The teacher, who has expected the answer "Four million members," is perplexed. "Please explain that, Fritz."

"Very simple. My father always says, 'I've had the Party up to here,'—Fritz raises his palm shoulder high—and my father is 5' 9"."

A saver brings his money to the German Bank in 1939. He cautiously inquires if the bank can guarantee the amount of his deposit.

"Of course," says the cashier, "the bank vouches for every single deposit."

"But what if the bank goes broke?"

"Then Greater Germany will vouch."

"But what if Greater Germany is destroyed?"

"Well, your deposit would be worth that!"

A woman goes to a bookstore and says, "My husband is sick, I'd like to buy a book for him."

105

"Does he want a National Socialist book?" asks the salesman. "No, my husband isn't *that* sick," the woman replies.

A Nazi official visits a farmer and tells him he must sacrifice and donate even more. Whoever has two cows must hand over one; whoever still has two suits can do without one—for example, the natives in Africa don't need two suits.

"How long have the Nazis been in charge there?" asks the farmer.

"We have more submarines than you," brags an Italian soldier. "But we have more airplanes," says the German enlisted man. "Yes," retorts the Italian, "but we have the better allies."

Here is a German prayer:

Dear God, make me blind, that I find everything splendid.
Dear God, make me deaf, that I believe all of Goebbels.
Dear God, make me mute, that I don't come to Dachau.
Dear God, make me crazy, that I succeed in fleeing to Scotland.

Who is the biggest farmer in the world?
Adolf Hitler, because he has 80 million oxen.

After the Allied crossing of the Rhine, it was said: "Mother Germany has become very ill; she is lying in labor pains—a small Germany is expected."

All Berliners are of one mind that the Memorial Church on the Kurfürstendamm should be rebuilt again—but this time submurgible.

The towering Kaiser Wilhelm Memorial Church on West Berlin's main promenade, damaged by Allied bomb attacks, was left with a gaping hole in its spire after the war as a reminder of the cost of war.

There is a great swamp in Hell for liars. The more someone has lied, the deeper he sinks in the swamp. Mussolini, stuck in the swamp up to his nose, looks with astonishment at Hitler, who has sunk only up to his chest.

He asks Hitler, "Adolf, how is that possible? You told a lot more lies than I ever did."

Answers Hitler, "I'm standing on Goebbels' shoulders."

Hitler saw this in a dream: Seven fat and seven lean cows, tended by a blind man. Because he did not understand the dream, Hitler goes to a fortune-teller for an interpretation.

The fortune-teller ponders, then says: "The seven fat cows are your ministers and party bigshots, the seven lean cows are the German people, and the blind man, who doesn't see, that is you."

Hitler visits a village and is greeted by a large crowd. Suddenly a small girl appears and presents the Führer with a bouquet of daisies instead of the usual roses. Hitler accepts them, holds them out before the crowd, and asks the child, "Why don't you bring me roses, instead of daisies?"

"Because the people here say that if the Führer pushes up daisies, then Germany will get better."

Hitler decreed that his gravestone should state: "This is my last territorial demand."

Shortly after the Anschluss, two Viennese are talking.
"Tell me," says the first, "what do you think of the Nazis?"
"The same as you do," answered the second.
"Then you can be arrested immediately."

In occupied France, a Nazi invites a Frenchman to a meal. At the table, the Nazi asks him, "Do you want coffee or tea?"
Answers the Frenchman, "Tea—liberty—of course."

After the French government protested the Nazi excesses before the outbreak of World War II, a group of SA officers appeared at the French Consulate in Cologne and smashed all its window-panes. When the French press reported on this, an angry mob appeared at the German Consulate in Nancy, wishing to do the same to its windows. Before the first stone could be hurled, an old man spoke to the crowd:

"French patriots, don't do anything stupid. If you smash the windows in this building, then our government will have to pay for them. What's more, our government will have to apologize to the Nazis. I have a much better idea. The German Consul has a mistress here; she lives not far from here on Rue Victor Hugo. Go there and smash her windows. No one will have to apologize to the Nazis for that, and the damage will be paid for by the Nazi Consul."

One ambulance after the other arrives at a Warsaw hospital with wounded soldiers. Among the interested onlookers is a weeping woman. Someone asks her, "Why are you crying? These are Nazis, you know."

Sobbing, she answers, "Because there is space for six in the hospital, and they've brought only three Nazis."

There is an Independence Alley in Warsaw. A woman on a streetcar asks the conductor, "How far is it to Independence . . . ?"

Answers the conductor, "Not more than a year, madam."

Two Poles meet after a separation of several years.

"How are things, what are you up to?"

"Everything is fine, I have a position in the national administration."

"And your wife?"

"She also has a job in an office."

"And your daughter?"

"She is working in an office."

"And you can live from that?"

"No. Thank God my son is unemployed."

A German asks a Pole, "You Poles don't want us Germans to stay here in Poland forever?"

"Why not? You're very welcome . . . six feet under the earth."

A squadron of American bombers flies over Swedish territory. A Swedish transmitter sends the message, "Attention! You are flying over neutral Swedish territory!"

The Americans answer, "We know that!"

The Swedes send another message: "Attention. We warn you, if you don't leave our territory, you will be bombarded by our antiaircraft gun."

The Americans respond, "We know that!"

The Swedish cannons fire at the American aircraft.

The Americans send this message, "You are shooting 1,000 meters too low."

The Swedes respond, "We know that."

A stocky man with loose curls and an Austrian accent appears in the headquarters of the British intelligence service in May 1945, removes his stuck-on moustache, and reports: "Secret agent 51 . . . assignment completed . . . Germany totally destroyed."

4

Werner Finck and the Cabaret World

One should not fight dictators, one should ridicule them.

—Bertolt Brecht

Silence is golden, speech is Dachau.

—Proverb in World War II Germany

During the early 1930s, *Die Katakombe,* one of the most prominent political cabarets in Berlin, was closed by the Gestapo for a few days after the troupe ridiculed the Nazis. When the club reopened, with members of the Nazi secret police sitting visibly in the audience, *conferencier* Werner Finck walked onstage and declared: "Yesterday Die Katakombe was closed. Today it's open again. If we are open again tomorrow, we'll be closed again the next day."[1]

Finck's prescient quip about "open" satire jeopardizing his club's operations—Die Katakombe was eventually closed again, permanently—defined the precarious existence of political cabarets in Germany's major cities during the early years of the Third Reich. Operating openly, in the pattern of their halcyon days during the Weimar Republic, thinly veiling their mockery of the authorities, they flouted the prohibitions against antiestablishment criticism. Their intimate halls afforded the country's independent-minded, often-left-leaning citizens a brief respite from Reich propaganda.

113

"It is difficult for Americans to comprehend the importance of the theater in German intellectual life, much less the German political cabaret," wrote Harold Poor, a biographer of cabaret writer Kurt Tucholsky. During the first third of the twentieth century, strict government censorship "made the cabaret form necessary."

"In Germany and the Austrian Empire," Poor wrote, "the censorship continued through the First World War, necessitating the veiled criticisms of satiric innuendo and ironic symbol—forms which find their most effective expression in a live performance on stage. Writers and poets were able to get away with dissenting commentary and biting opposition impossible in books and journals."[2]

The cabaret shows were part political commentary, part musical satire. They were the precursors of North America's contemporary comedy clubs and improvisational troupes. The settings were nightclubs or smoke-filled cellars, where self-styled sophisticates sat at crowded wooden tables over food and drinks. The performers, often young and poor, were partial to tattered clothes and scuffed shoes. The *conferencier*—part comic, part master of ceremonies—was the star. His role, according to Lisa Appignanesi's study of the cabaret world, "was a complex and manifold one. Not only was he, like a master of ceremonies, to introduce acts and set the tone for performances which, in themselves, might be extremely modest; but he also had to be able to draw the audience into the spectacle and provide a quick repartee to any challenge it might make."[3] The ideal *conferencier* was versed in literature, history, politics, and other affairs of the day; Finck, for his part, was self-taught.

Each cabaret developed its own identity, from "amusement dives or strip clubs"[4] to "students' cabarets . . . and mixed agitprop, even street theatre, with a more traditional programme."[5] They all shared, however, a decidedly independent and critical tone. The same traits that attracted audiences to cabarets, their "imme-

114

diacy and topicality,"[6] the nuances conveyed by a wink or shrug or mispronunciation of a key word, earned the censure of police authorities.

Die Katakombe "continued the line of genuinely satirical and politically unaffiliated cabarets," Appignanesi wrote. "Though some of its performers . . . might be committed revolutionaries, the Katakombe's tone was never propagandist. Rather, it emphasized the battle against the increasing power of the National Socialists and their apocalyptic ideology of racial purity, and exposed the nature of internment camp existence, along with other aspects of Nazi terror."[7]

The Nazis tried at first to control the voice of the cabaret through prior censorship, temporary closings, and mandatory membership in the Chamber of Culture, or *Reichskulturkammer*. The chamber was initiated by Propaganda Minister Joseph Goebbels in 1933. Made up of seven divisions, it was designed to direct the work of creative artists and to stifle any deviation from the Party's "absolutely airtight control."[8] Naturally, Jews, the "so-called racially inferior and the politically unreliable were excluded."[9] No art show could be held without official permission; materials could not be purchased, professional groups could not be joined, commissions could not be received; a dreaded *Arbeitsverbot* [work prohibition] could bar an artist from working, even in the privacy of his own home. Chamber membership was mandatory for entertainers, authors, musicians, painters, sculptors, architects, and other professionals, and expulsion was tantamount to unemployment.

In time all the cabarets were closed. Many performers went into exile; some committed suicide; some were put into jail or concentration camps, where a small number died. The strictest punishments were meted out to the *conferenciers*, who shaped the public image of each club. "Nothing is more hated by such regimes than the political joke and its most visible representative, the conferencier," Finck declared in one of his memoirs three decades after World War II. He called the *conferencier* "a distinguished sniper, who shoots the birds from the ambush of double meaning. In contrast to the anonymous whisperers, he stands in public with his word and because of his word."[10]

Misdirection, the ability to make statements that ambiguously skirted the outer limits of the Riech's tolerance for irreverence, was the *conferencier's* stock in trade. Weiss Ferdl, a Munich colleague of Finck, would appear onstage with photographs of Hitler, Goering, et al., and ponder if he should hang them or line them up against the wall. Vienna's Fritz Grunbaum presented this explanation of Germany's "democratic" annexation of Austria: A dozen men in frock coats stand on an empty stage; an unmistakable figure with a toothbrush moustache speaks: "Party members, we are coming to a decision over the important issue of authorization for full emergency powers. Those for, stand up. Those against, sit down." Lacking chairs, the men remain standing; "Party members, the motion is unanimously accepted," the moustachioed man announces.[11]

Finck called his method "the suggestive pause: It made the point of attack invisible."[12] He and other "versatile cabaretists" were judged particularly adept at this "camouflage technique."[13] Even Nazi observers were unable, at times, to pinpoint the seditious character of Finck's act. Goebbels often sent loyal Party members to Die Katakombe. Hans Schwarz van Berk, editor in chief of Goebbels' newspaper, *Angriff,* who was dispatched by the minister to observe Finck one night, wrote in Die Katakombe's guestbook: "Dangerous or not dangerous! Carry on!"[14] Other observers' reports, Goebbels complained, were "entirely different" from one another. "While some of these old comrades were of the opinion that the humor was open to vastly different kinds of interpretation, the others recommended the closing of the cabaret."[15] The latter prevailed. But Finck's sheer bravado—"He couldn't hold his tongue or suppress a bonmot,"[16] one biographer wrote—and ubiquitous career after World War II made him the symbol of Germany's early anti-Nazi cabarets.

"Finck's technique of the half-sentence was even more than a stylistic whim, it was an expression of a trancelike understanding with those who listened to him,"[17] an obituary in a German newspaper stated. "It belongs to the entity of great satire that leaves the censor helpless in the end." His best lines of poetry and prose were branded *Finckenschläge*, "Finck strokes." His routines—both actual and apocryphal—are legendary. When he died in 1978, at age 76, one German newspaper called Finck simply "The Cabaretist."[18]

A shy man with a balding head, bushy sideburns, steel-gray eyes, bulbous nose, and prominent lips, he seemed an unlikely candidate to become a national figure. He grew up in Gorlitz, a small town in eastern Germany. His father, "a national liberal, East Prussian patriot, true to the Kaiser and Godfearing,"[19] was a druggist; his mother, a housewife. Young Finck studied arts and crafts in school and spent several years as a wandering teller of fairy tales. In 1929, at 27, after four years as an actor in a regional theater, he was "drawn to Berlin by the founding of a new cabaret."[20] He and three friends established Die Katakombe in the cellar—28 steps down—of an art hall in the "freest metropolis of the world,"[21] where some half-dozen cabarets already operated. Why did Finck name the club Die Katakombe? "Very simple," he explained. "Two thousand years ago the catacombs were the refuge of the first Christians. Today it is the refuge of the last ones."[22]

Only Finck remained at the helm of Die Katakombe after a few years of Nazi persecution: "Yes, I was entirely alone."[23] To friends' questions why he remained in Germany after 1933, Finck answered: "It did not occur to me then why I should straightaway leave. I always thought to myself: The others should go away. And in 1945 they did go away."[24]

From the start, the club immediately drew large and enthu-

117

siastic crowds; its building was soon sold, and Die Katakombe settled into new quarters near the center of Berlin. "Our guests had to climb up one story, instead of a story deeper in the cellar. The first case of a catacomb on the second floor."[25] Though Finck foresaw the cabaret's days growing more embattled under an increasingly stronger Nazi Party, Hitler's rise to absolute power seemed unlikely. All the cabaretists made a mistake, Finck wrote. "We underestimated Hitler: 'A lunatic.' As if that keeps you out of politics."[26]

Finck and his cabaret's entire troupe were Gentiles. "At our opening program we were without exception, by accident, what was called Aryan four years later."[27] This was a rarity in Europe's cabaret world, where "the Jewish element . . . was very strongly represented."[28] Finck, though an identified Christian, chose not to reveal his specific denomination or particular religious beliefs.

He was equally ambiguous about his political persuasions. "I was acquainted with literature to some extent, but I had no idea then about politics. I just knew that you had to be on the left in a cabaret. Then I was on the left, at least in the evening. My heart no doubt stood on the right, but my understanding stood on the left, when it didn't stand still."[29]

"There are people who assert today that I was against the Nazis," Finck wrote. "That is slander. What I must admit, of course, is something else: The Nazis were against me. That is really a difference."[30]

Not without reason were Hitler's sympathizers enraged by Finck. With apparently no concern for his own safety, he would bait Goebbels' omnipresent informers. "Gentlemen, am I speaking too quickly?" Finck asked one night. "Are you following me? Or shall I follow you?"[31] Another night, a Nazi follower shouted "Dirty Jew" at the *conferencier*. "I'm afraid you're mistaken," Finck retorted. "I only look this intelligent."[32] With sharp ears and quick pencils, Goebbels' spies pounced on his double-edged remarks, "especially if there was resounding laughter or stormy applause."[33]

118

"Can anyone here tell me the name of a German, famous the world over, representative of the Aryan race, and very intelligent," he would ask. "Here's a clue: The first three letters of his name are Goe . . ."

"Goebbels," shouted the audience.

"Well he's German all right, and famous the world over," Finck continued, "but I said representative of the Aryan race." Rumors abounded in Nazi Germany that the propaganda minister had Jewish blood.

The spectators tried again. "Goering!"

"Wrong. He's famous, representative of the Aryan race, but I said 'very intelligent.'"

The audience was stumped.

"I'll have to tell you the answer," Finck concluded. "I was referring to Goethe,"[34] the eighteenth-century German poet and novelist.

Of the coalition between the Catholic Church and the Nazis—the regime pledged to respect the rights of the Church, in return for the Church's acquiescence—Finck commented: "They will probably have to divide up the swastika." The German word for swastika is *Hakenkreuz* [cross of hooks]. "The Catholics will have the cross," Finck said, "and the hooks will be with the Nazis."[35]

Because a Nazi organization called the Front for German Culture had been established, Die Katakombe could form a like front for "Salutary German Humor," the *Kampfbund für den Deutschen heilsamen Humor*, or KfDHH, Finck would state. The final two initials, he stressed, did not represent "Heil Hitler," the Nazi greeting.

One of Finck's most celebrated routines featured a customer buying a suit at a tailor shop. *Einreihig oder zweireihig?* (single-breasted or double-breasted), the tailor would inquire. *Das ist mir gleich. Nur nicht diesreihig.* (It's all the same to me. Just not

119

this-breasted). Finck would pronounce the last phrase to sound like "Just not this *Reich*."[36]

Finck was not sure, he often said, if he was a timid hero or a brave coward. "I trembled. I had genuine fear. I thought, God willing, how will this end. It never held true, that I was an active opponent of the dozen-year Reich, otherwise it would probably not be possible for me to deny the rumors of my death. Passive resistance brought me enough unpleasantness."[37] Of Goebbels, Finck once said: "I was not afraid, because I long knew in advance that he would die. Because his motto was 'Win or die.'"[38]

Throughout his career, Finck received credit for routines he had actually never performed. Praise for a brilliant act came from those who were "convinced that they had personally experienced it somewhere on a stage."[39] Typical of this was the story of the crate:

> Two men come on a stage carrying a crate. Then they walk away. Another man opens the crate and takes out of it life-size busts of the Nazi top brass—Hitler, Goering, Goebbels, etc. After the busts are all set up, the man turns back to the crate, upon which he sees the inscription. "Caution, do not overthrow."

"This joke," Finck said, "which was always put on my shoulders with certainty, was never done by me. But even good friends of mine could not be dissuaded that they had seen it with their own eyes. Even after the war this version kept up, despite all my protests."[40] In time, he said, he had to share credit for his putative act; it was also attributed to Weiss Ferdl, his wartime colleague in Munich.

On New Year's Day in 1933, Finck, who had earlier earned a reputation as a "great poet,"[41] recited an original composition, "There blows a fresh wind, two, three":

Es weht ein frischer Wind, zwei, drei,
Wir wollen wieder lachen,
Gebt dem Humor die Strasse frei,
Jetzt muss auch der erwachen.

Der Löwe ist das Tier der Zeit,
Der Mars regiert die Stunde;
Doch die geliebte Heiterkeit
Geht langsam vor die Hunde.

Das aber soll dem Teufel nicht
uned keiner Macht gelingen;
Uns um das inn're Gleichgewicht
Und um den Spass zu bringen.

Drum lässt des Zwerchfells Grundgewalt
Am Trommelfell erklingen.
Wem das nicht passt, der soll uns halt
Am Götz von Berlichingen.[42]

There blows a fresh wind, two, three,
Again we want to laugh,
The roads for humor are now free,
Now it must wake up.

The lion is the beast of the time,
Mars rules the hour:
Yet the beloved cheerfulness
Will slowly disappear.

But the devil and no power
should succeed:
in killing our equilibrium
and our fun.

Therefore let the diaphragm's power
On the eardrum be ringing.
Our advice to whomever finds this sour
is Götz von Berlichingen.

The last line was an allusion to a well-known scatological reference in a Goethe poem. Finck's verse was removed from the cabaret program, on government orders, after the Nazi takeover in March 1933. From that point on, cabaret scripts were subject to government review. No more "pulling the leg"[43] of the Nazis. Interference increased until Goebbels ordered Die Katakombe closed in May 1935. Goebbels' explanation: "The reason for the closing lies not in the nature of the program, rather in the composition of the public, that gives an entirely different meaning to many points of the program."[44]

"In so-called political jokes," Goebbels stated in a subsequent official order that summarily closed Germany's remaining cabarets, "they openly or discreetly practice criticism of the leadership of the Reich's politics, economy or culture."[45]

The *Völkischer Beobachter* stated that Finck's troupe had "linked prostitution with the activity of collecting for the *Winterhilfswerk* [the Party's Winter Help Relief Organization], and aroused general opposition against collections. They mocked military and party uniforms, ridiculed the organization of the Party, and dragged the national service through the mud."[46]

Finck was taken into custody one night in May 1933 by two Gestapo officers and interrogated in Gestapo headquarters on Prince Albrecht Street. Accordingly to Finck, "The officials were very friendly, wanted autographs and seemed to be especially happy."[47] Finck thought he'd be set free in a half hour. Instead, he was taken to a prison across the street. An S.S. officer at the entrance asked Finck if had any weapons. "Why?" Finck asked. "Does one need them here?"[48]

122

Finck and two other members of the Die Katakombe troupe were soon sent to Esterwegen, a concentration camp near the Dutch border. They were interned with 1,000 men—500 political prisoners and 500 career criminals. "You should really say 580 or 590 career criminals, because the guards must also be classified somewhere."[49] He and other interned cabaret artists were pressed by the camp's commanders into putting on an impromptu performance one afternoon. His performance, "under the free heaven," was cheerful—"as my profession requires."

"Comrades," he told the prisoners, "we want to try to amuse you a bit today. Our humor will help us with that. We have kept it. Although we have never experienced humor and gallows so near to each other." He pointed to the barbed wire, the guard towers, and the prominent machine guns. "But these machine guns can not impress us, comrades. Because we have cannons with us, yes, cannons of morale." He yielded to Walter Gross, another performer. "Shoot away, Walter!"[50]

During another performance he addressed an obvious question: Why Finck and his fellow performers appeared so "lively and merry." His explanation: In Berlin they constantly feared being sent to a concentration camp. "And now, you see, we need not fear any more. We are, of course, in here."[51]

Camp guards observed every performance. "The guards doubled up with laughter," Finck wrote. Two S.S. officers took him aside one day and said, "You did your act first class. Real class! But why haven't you performed some of the things that brought you here?"

Thought Finck, "We wanted to swear that in Berlin we had said not a little more."[52]

Finck's incarceration lasted only a few months. The camp commander addressed Finck and a group of released prisoners on their last day. In a "rather undressed condition,"[53] wearing bathing trunks and revolver, he advised the prisoners to remain on good behavior. With Finck's release came a year-long ban on working; afterward, government permission would be needed. He sold his country house in Kuhfort, and accepted secret assistance from friends and the "circle of my public."[54] "I had a lot of free time then, unvoluntarily. What should I do? I got married."[55] He gives no more details about this personal side of his life.

Before the ban expired, Finck and a few out-of-work performers found themselves in front of a special Nazi court. "Obviously," he speculated, "an attempt to subsequently vindicate our concentration camp imprisonment." During the court's session on cabaret practices, young performers from the Tingeltangel Club were ordered to put on an "objectionable" sketch, "The Alarmist on the Men's Party," which was full of songs and allusions. "The indictment consisted nearly entirely of sketches, chansons, political jokes, and conferencier banter." The courtroom, which was not closed to the public, broke out in laughter at every line. The enraged president of the court finally commanded: "If the laughter does not stop, I'll have the room cleared. We're not in a cabaret here!"

When the noise subsided, Finck's turn came. His sketch, "Fragment from the Tailor," was under question. He was acquitted "for lack of proof."[56] The ban was repealed in April 1936. Finck's own club being still closed, he was invited to perform at Berlin's Das Kabarett der Komiker, the Cabaret of Comics, the city's largest club. His first night back onstage he delivered a lengthy speech on humor. He requested the audience's patience for his oratory—"I am not accustomed to speaking freely."[57] Finck went on to anger Goebbels by identifying himself as a "slightly throttled finch."[58] The phrase is a play on his name as well as on the verb *drosseln*, which means "throttled" but resembles the words for "thrush" and "throat."

As a guest performer, Finck repeatedly tested the propaganda minister's patience. Again, Finck lost. In 1939 he was expelled from the Chamber of Culture and forbidden to work in public.

Goebbels explained the expulsion in an article, "Do we still have humor?—Dr. Goebbels on the Finck case," in the *Volkischer Beobachter*. Wrote Goebbels: "Political jokemaking is a liberal leftover. In the past system you could still accomplish something with it. We know that the newspapers in Paris, London and New York that are hostile to Germany will champion our poor conferenciers."[59]

The Gestapo kept Finck under surveillance thereafter. When war broke out in September of 1939, Finck escaped the secret police by volunteering for the German Army. He was assigned to the front, where he served as a broadcaster. Though circumspect about his duties in the army, Finck apparently retained his independence. "Several times I came under suspicion of working for the enemy side because I threw our entire news system into disorder."[60] His army record: service in France and Russia; 10 months in detention: service in Italy until Germany's surrender.

After the war came successful cabaret work in Munich, Stuttgart, and Hamburg; scores of acting roles in theater, films, and television; tours of Europe and of North and South America; and prolific writing of books and newspaper articles.

Only one postwar part of Finck's career failed—an attempt to open a cabaret in Berlin. Following are cabaret anecdotes.

Finck crawled onstage on all fours, to loud laughter.

He raised himself with great precision, beat the dust from the creases of his trousers, and said: "You're laughing at me . . . but don't *you* crawl?"

At the end of one performance, Finck looked at his watch, and declared: "Please excuse me for talking about the time. I will stop. Because I don't want to discuss our time."

Cabaret artist Fritz Grunbaum was arrested by the Gestapo. During his imprisonment in Buchenwald, he asked an S.S. guard for some toilet paper. The enraged guard answered, "We don't have any toilet paper."

Retorted Grunbaum, "Whoever has no toilet paper should not be able to afford concentration camps."

This story is told about Finck, as well as about cabaret artists Weiss Ferdl and Karl Valentin:

A *conferencier* greeted the audience with the Hitler salute. The crowd laughed resoundingly. "Why are you laughing?" the host asked. "The snow outside is this *high*."

After the bogus Austrian referendum of April 10, 1938, Valentin met a friend.

"Did you hear?" the friend asked, "98 percent voted for Hitler!"

"That is remarkable," Valentin answered, "I keep meeting only the other 2 percent."

Karl Valentin walked briskly onstage one night, raised his arm in the Nazi salute, and shouted: "Heil . . ." —then scratched his head—"Dammit, now I've forgotten the name!"

Valentin told his audience, "This morning I saw a beautiful new Mercedes limousine stopping right in front of me. The door opened—and, you'll be surprised—it *wasn't* an S.S. officer who stepped out."

Valentin was severely reprimanded by the authorities. "Don't worry," he promised, "I'll put things right."

The next night he apologized to his audience for having misled them. "The truth was, it *was* an S.S. officer, after all."

Weiss Ferdl appeared onstage in Munich one night covered in jewelry. "What's the matter?" he asked his astounded audience. "Do you think I was asleep during Kristallnacht?"

One night Ferdl read this version of a well-known poem, replete with fictitious titles, which mocked the Nazi Party's slew of organizations:

Ein Baumlein steht am Waldesrand,
das ist organisiert,
es ist im NS-Baumverband,
damit ihm nichts passiert!

A tree strands in the forest,
it is organized,
it's in the Union of Nazi Trees,
so that nothing happens to it!

127

Ferdl spent some time in custody for spoofing the Nazis' organizational mania. Upon his return to the stage, he apologized to the public and read a "corrected" version of the verse:

Ein Baumlein steht am Waldesrand,
das ist organisiert,
ist nicht im NS-Baumverband,
—damit mir nichts passiert!

A tree stands in the forest,
it is organized,
it's not in the Union of Nazi Trees,
so that nothing happens to me!

Referring to the Nazis' Thousand-Year Reich, Ferdl said, "It's miraculous, how fast one can become 999 years old."

Ferdl came on stage, displayed a bunch of asparagus and cauliflower and asked, "What is this?"

"Asparagus and cauliflower" answered the audience.

"Wrong!" Ferdl scolded, "This is the past."

The next time he came on stage he displayed a pair of radishes, and asked, "What is this?"

"Radishes!"

"Wrong. This is the present."

When Ferdl appeared with a bunch of grass, the audience shouted: "The future!"

Ferdl shook his head and said, "How can you talk so dopey? If I had said that, I would end up in Dachau!"

Ferdl came on stage another time unshaven, dressed in a patched-up suit, frayed shoes, and a greasy hat. His old pipe smelled up the whole club.

The crowd laughed heartily.

"What's the matter," he barked, "I'm just two years ahead of the rest of you."

"I would really like to see a Nazi," Ferdl said one night.

"But you can have that pleasure any day," a compatriot said. "In the Party assemblies you see 500, 1,000, 10,000, 50,000, 100,000 Nazis."

"No, not a thousand, not even a hundred, rather just one single one . . . and I'd like to see him entirely alone."

Ferdl appeared on stage with three pigs, a piglet, a medium-sized pig, and a huge sow, which he introduced. "This is the daughter Mann, this is Mrs. Mann, and this is Mr. [Herr] Mann."

Laughter ensued.

Ferdl's allusion to the corpulent Goering got his cabaret closed down for three days. When the club reopened, he came on stage again with three pigs, whom he introduced: "Daughter Mann. Mrs. Mann." And, pointing to the third pig, "Because of this fat sow my place had to be closed for three days."

The Gestapo closed his club again.

5

Jewish Humor

A man is known by his laughter.

—Talmud, *Eruvin* 65b

Whoever has cried enough, laughs. Even the martyred peoples of Europe will find one day that unflinching serious acceptance would be too much honor for their tormentor.

—Heinrich Mann

"Jewish humor died with its humorists when the Nazis killed off the Jews of Eastern Europe."[1] Irving Kristol, social critic and author, made that observation in *Commentary* six years after the end of World War II. "The victims," he reasoned, "could not respond with the aesthetic freedom of Sholem Aleichem," short story preserver of the Pale. "Just as humor cannot mature in a life of utter religious faith, so it cannot survive a life of sheer nihilism."[2]

Kristol, like many others who view Jewish life in twentieth-century Europe from a postwar, trans-Atlantic perspective, over-looked one key fact about how humor functions. It requires not merely artistic and political freedom, but psychological freedom. The clearest manifestation of Arthur Koestler's paradigmatic "creative process," humor and wit grow where the mind is free of restraints; paradoxically, in prison, where there is nothing left to lose, the individual is in a way the freest. And Nazi Europe was a prison for its Jews.

"In the punishment cell I was inwardly a free man. I had to take everything that was dear to me, everything that had meaning in my life, with me to prison,"[3] wrote a recent Jewish prisoner, former refusenik Natan Sharansky, who spent nine years in the Soviet penal system for his dissident activities. He relentlessly baited his captors with wit and defeated them with faith. "The world I created in my head turned out to be more powerful and more real than the world of Lefortovo Prison . . . my inner freedom [was] more powerful than the external bondage."[4]

"In freedom, humor is a mere luxury," Sharansky says. "In prison, it's the only weapon. The moment you can laugh at them you are free."[5]

Humor clearly lived in Sharansky's world. If Jewish humor is moribund, as might be true in Kristol's contemporary America, the death blow was delivered not by persecution, but by assimilation; as Jews merge into the general society, they feel less marginal and less distinctive, conditions that molded the Jewish humor prevalent in the modern West.

The refuge of choice of the Chosen People, contemporary Jewish humor draws on ancient sources. In the Hebrew scriptures, the interplay of God and the early Israelites is seasoned with dashes of irony. Rabbi David Marcus, a biblical scholar at the Jewish Theological Seminary of America, has found "a tremendous amount" of irony, exaggeration, and satire in the Old Testament. The sources are Genesis, Numbers, Judges, Samuel, Kings, Isaiah, and Jonah, and other books of the Bible. "It's gentle humor," designed to "evoke in the reader contempt and humor,"[6] Marcus says. In the Talmud, the oral law, probing intellectuality is tempered by lighter moments. Rabbah, a third-century Babylonian scholar, would start each lecture with a few words of mirth.[7] His contemporary, Yirmiya, was known to pose foolish questions to his teacher, Zera, to draw a smile.[8] The Prophet Elijah, according to one of the Talmud's aggadic tales, ascribed reward in the next world to those who bring laughter to the depressed in this world.[9]

Humor surfaces in the biographies of prominent rabbis through the ages. It is a staple in the Chelm stories, set in a Polish *shtetl*, which illustrate the triumph of faith over naïveté. In pre-Holocaust Eastern Europe, the *badchan*, or jester, had an honored place at wedding celebrations, amusing the guests with clever rhymes and silly antics. Humor is a vital ingredient in the traditional folktales—first oral, then recorded—of Eastern European Ashkenazic Jews and of Sephardim, with roots in the Levant and northern Africa. In both cultures, Jews are educated and multilingual, and intellectual discipline is emphasized.

A medium between pious fanaticism and skeptical fatalism, "Humor even taught Jews, with wit sufficiently sharp and arms long enough, how to box with God," writes Joseph Dorinson, a historian and student of Jewish humor at Long Island University. "The laughter evoked helped to create a delicate balance between piety and complaint."[10]

As the comforting qualities of chicken soup have earned it the sobriquet the "Jewish penicillin," humor deserves the label the "Jewish novacaine." It is the ultimate Jewish painkiller, a remedy much needed in World War II. It can be imagined that humor helped the Jewish people survive a long series of tragedies through the ages—the Crusades, the Inquisition, the pogroms and expulsions. The wandering Jew never left his sense of humor behind. In 1935, in pre-Israel Palestine, the annual Purim *Ad Loloyada* parade (the Hebrew phrase "until you do not know " refers to the holiday injunction to imbibe until unable to distinguish between Mordechai the hero and Haman the villain) through the streets of Tel Aviv featured cars disguised as Nazi tanks and marchers wearing imitation Nazi uniforms. Though anti-Jewish persecution had already begun in Germany, and German Jews had started fleeing their homeland, the Reich was considered a fit topic for Jewish mockery.

The wry, cosmopolitan wit most associated with Jewish humor today was born near the turn of the nineteenth century. Its parents, proudly European, were political emancipation and religious enlightenment. "Wit, in its highest and most brilliant expression," writes Salcia Landmann, an authority on Jewish humor, "requires a combination of intellectual training and a profound insight into universal problems. Such a combination has been available among Jews ever since the age of Enlightenment when religion began to loosen its hold upon men's minds—minds which, however, still bore the impact of traditional religious training."[11]

The first such Jewish jokes were directed against "the hostile environment," but soon turned inward. Jewish humor matured under the czars, "where the Jews were persecuted, kicked around, looked down upon, yet remained convinced that they were no worse, not less valuable human beings, than their coarse, uneducated and corrupt oppressors."[12]

This trait has come full circle in Israel. Surrounded by hostile neighbors, subjected to war and terrorist attacks, the Jewish state's political humor—aggressive, even arrogant—bears little resemblance to the humor of Western Jewry. Israeli humor, shaped in large part by the generation that settled there after the liberation of Europe, reflects the survivors' uncompromising outlook. "The Israeli citizen of today," Landmann states, has no need for humor as a defensive measure, "since he can, and will, take up arms to defend himself. Humor is not a weapon of open combat," but rather "a means of expressing forbidden thoughts which weigh heavily upon us, and which we cannot even put into words—let alone convert into deeds."[13]

Jews were stripped of power and forced into isolation during World War II. The life of the spiritual descendants of Job was defined by marginality and separateness. As in the past, the principal victims of Hitler's genocidal campaign against the conti-

136

nent's *Untermentschen* [subhumans] strove against oppression with a humor "rooted in tragic optimism."[14]

The yellow star that Jews were forced to wear came to be known as Pour le Semite [For the Semite], patterned after Germany's well-known military order, Pour le Merité.

"Here was a human being who could laugh,"[15] Warsaw Judenrat head Adam Czerniakow wrote in praise of one Zofia Feigenbaum on November 6, 1941, noting in his dairy her death that day of typhus.

"The Jews had long been conditioned to assauge pain with the balm of humor," historian Richard Grunberger wrote. "Though impaired, this faculty did not desert them even in the Third Reich."[16] A Yiddish rhyme, sung in the Warsaw Ghetto to a Chasidic melody, bears this out:

> *Lomir zayn freylech un zogn zich vitsn,*
> *Mir veln noch hitlern shive noch sitsn.*[17]

Let us be gay and tell jokes,
We'll yet live to see Hitler dead.

One J. Hecht, who hid in the town of Zolkiev during the war, recorded these biting observations in his secret journal:

> March 25, 1943 . . . We are four; we wait for better times, and . . . Philippe M., the fifth tenant of our little "palace." This "palace" is inhabited by many diverse species. We, men—no, excuse me, Jews, we live in the bottom of building, underground; the ground floor is inhabited by two little pigs who cost 700 zlotys. There is also a rooster. The first floor is occupied by rabbits, who number four. In addition, we are also neighbors with a cow. Between all of us, that is to say the Jews, chickens, pigs and cow, we are living very well, that is to say, like Aryans.[18]

137

An unprecedented amount of humor—expressed in art, poetry, music, and underground theater—was created by the decimated Jewish population across Nazi Europe as forms of rebellious expression. It could be as simple as a group of Theresienstadt prisoners who organized a Passover seder in the spring of 1945 and defiantly recited, in the presence of S.S. officers, the traditional holiday declaration, "This year we are slaves, but next year free!"[19] In the death camps and ghettoes, of course, where even the semblance of judicial due process was absent, a joke against the Nazis could spell peril. One entertainer in the Kracow ghetto who braved the climate of intimidation by performing a satirical song on a nightclub stage one night was shot by German soldiers the next day.[20]

The Nazis' victims, from trained humorists to businessmen to beggars, turned to humor in every venue of oppression. This reaction was so common that a group of training-weary German storm troopers supposedly asked Hitler to let them tell jokes and make the Jews do the marching.

Across the Mediterranean, the endangered Jews of Nazi-occupied Tunisia also used humor to maintain their morale. Passover, the holiday of liberation from Egypt, should not be observed, they would propose; had the ancient Hebrews remained in Egypt, the Tunisian Jews explained, twentieth-century Jews would still be free. One Meyer, an olive oil merchant whose business took him from city to city in Tunisia, entertained his Jewish friends with the latest jokes. "What caused the American troops' delay in reaching Tunisia?" he would ask. "The MPs had posted speed limit signs everywhere, and the GIs were afraid of being arrested for speeding."[21] He told this popular story:

> Hitler has been defeated. He dies and goes to Hell. There, the Führer of the Great Reich feels so superior that he does not talk to anybody, not even to his closest accomplices, whom he accuses of having lost the war.

One day, from a great distance, he sees white-bearded Moshe Rabenu[22] and rushes in his direction. To everybody's surprise, the two men are seen engaging in a lengthy and animated conversation.

The stunned, pious disciples who have watched this unbelievable scene wait patiently for an explanation from their revered Prophet. They surround him and ask respectfully: "What in heaven have you been talking about?"

And Moses answers: "He was asking me how I had managed to cross the Red Sea."[23]

The joke was a reference to the Germans' unsuccessful attempts to reach and cross the Mediterranean.

Jewish humor in World War II was an escape from that particular pain, but it drew on memories of earlier catastrophes, especially with references to pharaoh, Haman, and the perpetrators of pogroms. Drawing on Jewish history, relentlessly mocking Jewish traits, Jewish humor clearly maintained its distinctiveness. The implicit historical feature of Jewish jokes, and their continuing stress on self-mockery, contribute to the uniqueness of Jewish humor.

During the Nazi period, Lefkowitz walks into a German police station, carrying a newspaper with a job advertisement circled in red.

"You've come about this job?" asks the desk sergeant. "You must be kidding. Can't you read? We need a young man, strong and hardy, a man who doesn't wear glasses. And look—the ad specifically mentions that we want an Aryan. You're obviously a Jew. So what are you doing here?"

"I've just come to tell you," says Lefkowitz, "that on me you shouldn't count."

"In the best examples of this kind of humor there is behind the comic facade not only something serious, which is present in the wit

139

of other nations too, but sheer horror,"[24] Theodor Reik wrote in *Jewish Wit*.

Psychoanalyst Reik, a Vienna-born contemporary of Freud who fled Europe in 1938, cites the story of two Jews sitting at a coffeehouse in Vienna a few years before Austria's annexation by Germany in 1938. Customers at the establishments would take several newspapers to their table, reading one after the other, inconveniencing other patrons who shared the same taste in reading fare.

"A Jew imagines that Hitler sits in a Vienna coffeehouse while a Jewish customer reads all the journals and puts them aside after he has read them. In the Jew's imagination, Hitler then comes to his table and politely asks: 'Please, is the *Wiener Journal* free?' The Jew will answer: 'Not for you, Herr Hitler!'"

"The point is not that the punishment for the criminal is so harmless," Reik explains, "but that the Jew cannot imagine a more cruel and exquisite torment than the withholding of the desired newspaper and the suffering of agonizing suspense of the loathed enemy."[25]

As the war progressed, much Jewish humor bore this tone. In summary, the Jewish humor from Nazi Europe was intrinsically Jewish. It was *by* Jews. It was *about* Jews, Jewish suffering, Jewish holidays, and Jewish ideals. It was often expressed in Yiddish, the Jewish argot, or at least hinged on Jewish expressions. It had a distinctive point of view. It contrasted in many ways with the general anti-Nazi humor that emerged at the same time. This "Jew's prayer," from Emil Dorian's diary in occupied Romania, was one, admittedly ascerbic, example:

"Dear God, for five thousand years we have been Your chosen people. Enough! Choose another one now!"[26]

The traditional foils of European Jewish humor, the matchmaker, the *shlmiel* [klutz], and *shlmazel* [fallguy], were largely absent from wartime humor. Other reference points were employed. Across the continent, Jews alluded to their holiday traditions to describe the all-encompassing poverty. "We eat as if it were Yom Kippur, sleep in *succahs*, and dress as if it were Purim."[27] (Yom Kippur is a fast day; *succahs* are the booths Jews dwell in during the seven-day autumn *Succot* festival; adults and children dress in all manner of costumes to celebrate Purim.) "Jews are now very pious. They observe all the ritual laws: they are stabbed and punched with holes like *matzahs*, and have as much bread as on Passover; they are beaten like *hoshanas*, rattled like Haman; they are as green as *esrogim* and as thin as *lulavim*; they fast as if it were Yom Kippur; they are burnt as if it were Hanukah, and their moods are as if it were the Ninth of Av."[28] (*Matzahs* are the unleavened wafers eaten on Passover, when bread is banned; *hoshanas* are myrtle leaves, which are beaten on the ground on *Hoshana Rabba* in symbolic expiation of sins; *etrogim* are citrus fruits, and *lulavim*, palm leaves, which are shaken during Succot; candles are lit each night during Hanukah, the festival of lights; the Ninth of Av is a day of mourning for the destruction of the Temples in Jerusalem.)

Jews wielded language as a weapon from the first days of Hitler's rule until his defeat in a Berlin bunker—in jokes, puns, rhyme, and wordplay. German Jews adopted Saint Olympiade[29] as their patron during the 1936 Olympic Games in Berlin, when the ubiquitous *Juden unerwünscht* [Jews not wanted] signs were removed for the sake of foreign visitors. Cynics in the Westerbork transit camp derided as *Austauschwitz*[30] a proposed exchange—a trade of Jewish prisoners in a special "safe" camp for German nationals in Allied hands. *Austausch* is German for exchange, *witz*, for joke; in other words, the hopeful prisoners would still end up in Auschwitz.

Jews in the camps would assure each other, "If we can survive for 21 days, we will be saved."[31] The 21 days: the 8 days of the Passover festival, the 8 days of Succot, the 2 days each of Shavuot

141

and Rosh Hashanah, and the single day of Yom Kippur. In other words, a cycle of the Jewish holidays, or a full year.

Musical creativity, which continued under Nazi persecution, employed humor in both lyrics and physical setting. There was the *Nichtarische Bach-Cantata-Gesellschaft* [Non-Aryan Bach Cantata Society], which proudly marked its first anniversary in 1936. It was a small chamber music group composed of accomplished Jewish musicians who banded together in Hamburg to play for friends after being barred by the Nazi racial laws from working with "Aryan" colleagues. The society played works of Bach and other Baroque composers in supporters' homes. Members, according to the group's bylaws, had to undergo a strict review to confirm their non-Aryan background. And they pledged to perform their cantatas in Hebrew, Japanese, Eskimo, and Swahili—apparently as preparation for whatever land would give them refuge.

Congratulatory letters poured in from around the world on the society's anniversary. Hitler sent best wishes, and expressed the hope that it would continue to uphold the reputation of German culture. Dr. Albert Schweitzer requested information on the society for a book he was writing on Bach. Other notes bore the signatures of theologian Martin Buber, conductor Leopold Stokowski, and *Der Stürmer* editor Julius Streicher. In Stokowski's note, the conductor of the Philadelphia Symphony Orchestra said he was sending a portrait of Bach as a gift to recognize "the incomparable artistic merits with which the *Gesellschaft* has won worldwide renown." He explained that the portrait, authenticated by Bach's own signature, was purchased about 1800 by a "Philadelphia Bach enthusiast, Mr. Zedekiah Bigbelly . . . we would not be able to find a more dignified successor in the ownership of this unique piece" than the society. The conductor's letter, like all the missives containing lavish praise for the group, was counterfeit, a creation of society members.[32] As conditions for German Jews quickly worsened, the

142

three founders of the group left; they immigrated in 1937 to the United States and Great Britain.

In the later years of Nazi rule, after the Kristallnacht riots in 1938 gave the Reich the West's *carte blanche* for persecution, after the Wannsee Conference in 1942 set the machinery of the Final Solution in motion, Europe's remaining Jews were packed into ghettoes or shipped to concentration camps. For them, and for those in hiding or in resistance units, humor took on added meaning as a form of psychological escape. It was bittersweet humor. The more bitter the situation, the sweeter the joke. Or the more needed the laugh.

Israel Kaplan, a Lithuanian Jew who survived several ghettoes and camps, complied captives' cryptic slang expressions in Hebrew and Yiddish. He called these code words the "voice of Jacob."[33] The phrase refers to the Old Testament patriarch who used subterfuge to gain the paternal blessing intended for his brother Esau.

"The expressions, mottoes and witticisms which were created by, and circulated among, the captives contained within them the power to comfort and encourage the broken-hearted," Kaplan wrote. "Even during the back-breaking work, with the guards standing over them, following every movement with hostile eyes, ears strained to hear every syllable which the mouth produced. In order to give expression to their innermost desires and thoughts, they created a secret way of talking, a sort of code, a language based largely upon Hebrew, the sacred tongue, especially as found in the prayer book, that faithful companion of the Jew from the days of his childhood in his father's house."[34]

Hebrew proved a more effective medium of secret communication around Nazi soldiers than Yiddish, a recognizable dialect of German. The generic term for a German was *Daled*, the name of the letter *d* in the Hebrew alphabet, standing for *Deutsch*. The approach of a guard would bring a call of *Yaale Veyavoy* [he will rise and he will come], from a silent prayer recited on holy days. A high-

143

ranking German, for whom the prisoners had to appear particularly hard-working, merited the appellation *Hallel Hagadol* [the great praise], the collection of psalms read on auspicious days. *Yoytsey* [he goes out], meaning that an individual had fulfilled the requirements of a particular commandment, was declared when a guard had left and the prisoners could let up. Extra work shifts were called *Toysfoys* [addenda], the name of a medieval commentary on the Talmudic scholar Rashi. The Nazi dream of A New Europe was rendered *kapore khadoshe*, a new scapegoat.[35] "After the Russian victory at Rostov" in 1941, Emmanuel Ringelblum's Warsaw Ghetto diary reported, "The Jews began to call the city *Rosh-tov*"—meaning, "a good beginning" in pidgin Hebrew.[36]

Among themselves, the Jews reverted to Yiddish. When admonished by an overseer that labor "makes life sweet," a worker would whisper under his breath, *Mir zaynen nit keyn nashers* [we're not snackers]. Someone viewed as unduly optimistic would be dismissed as declaring "The Messiah comes seven times a day." This was a particularly biting comment among a people eagerly waiting their deliverer's *first* coming. With the report of good news would come the question whether its source was YIVO, not the respected Yiddish research institute that was founded in Vilna and relocated to New York City, but an acronym for *Yidn viln azoy* [Jews want it like that]."[37] In the Lodz Ghetto, where horsemeat sometimes replaced the scarce meat of cattle, a Jew who saw someone running would comment, *Er est vishtsninove ferd* [he eats racehorses]."[38] A Judenrat, the Nazi-appointed Jewish council that controlled ghetto activities, at times to the detriment of the impoverished residents, was called the Yudenfarat, the betrayal of Jews.[39] In concentration camps, bombers were *feygelekh* [birdies], bombs were *kneydlekh* [matzah balls], and Soviet planes were *royte hiner* [red hens].[40]

"In camps we sang, we tried to tell jokes," says Israel Oppenheim, an Israeli Holocaust historian. "It's quite natural."[41] "In the ghettoes there were a lot of jokes, there was a lot of humor,"[42] says mime Zwi Kanar, a native of Skalbimircz, a Polish *shtetl*. A survivor of six concentration camps and a death march, he perfected his art while interned in the Werk c Skarzyt Camp.

In the Vilna Ghetto, formerly the seat of Jewish scholarship in Poland, a large part of the population disapproved of levity, no matter what the purpose, claiming, "A graveyard is no place for entertainment."[43] More typical was the Warsaw Ghetto resident who called humor "the only weapon in the ghetto . . . there is no other remedy for our ills. People laugh at death and at the Nazi decrees. Humor is the only thing the Nazis cannot understand."[44]

"Here's a joke that's making the rounds" of the Warsaw Ghetto, a resident wrote, sandwiching it between news of forced labor conscriptions and the latest count of Jews who sought conversion to Catholicism as a means of escape. "A woman was having a difficult labor. Nothing anyone did could help her. But the moment her friends left the house, the infant came crawling out of the womb to ask his mother: 'Mama, can I come out now, have all the *schleppers* gone?"[45] *Schlepper,* Yiddish for one who pulls or drags something, was a Nazi soldier in the ghetto parlance. Commenting on the abundance of emaciated, malnourished Jews in the blockaded ghetto, another inhabitant noted the residents' jokes that "they no longer have to travel to Carlsbad, for the spa has come to them."[46]

Yiddish folksongs, whose verses had traced Jewish suffering since the sixteenth century, multiplied during the Holocaust.

"Der Yiddisher Gelechter" [The Jewish Laughter] was written by Rikle Glaser, a prisoner in the Vilna Ghetto:

The Jewish Laughter
Contains so much pain.
When weeping is of no help,
One laughs as much as he can,
Although the heart would cry with pain.

145

We are laughing
As long as we will live
Let your laughter sound far.
So hope the time is near,
When you will laugh
From the depth of your heart always.[47]

In the Lublin Ghetto, humorous songs mocked collaborators.
In the Kovno Ghetto, slave labor brigades would sing:

We don't weep or grieve
Even when you beat and lash us,
But never for a moment believe
That you will discourage and dash us.[48]

In the Lodz Ghetto—where deportation notices were referred
to as "wedding invitations"—jocular musical compositions assumed
an editorial role, defining and satirizing the issues of public notice.
One song noted the malapropisms committed by the newly arrived
German Jews. *Es Geht a Yeke Mit a Teke* [A German Jew Goes With
a Briefcase], a popular song to the tune of an army song, "The
Machine Gun," made fun of the *Yekes*, as they are known in Yiddish
slang. According to the song, the *Yekes* are forever hungry,
searching for food, and the locals take advantage of the newcomers'
naïveté.[49] Jankele Herszkowicz, a ghetto troubadour and former
tailor, composed a song entitled "Rumkowski, Chaim," about the
chairman of the Judenrat, the Nazi-appointed council that nomi-
nally ran ghetto activities. One verse alleged:

Rumkowski Chaim gives us bran-a,
He gives us barley, he gives us life.
Once upon a time, Jews too ate manna,
Now each man is eaten by his wife.[50]

146

Herszkowicz earned a living for several months by performing that song—the chairman himself anted up 5 marks. Herszkowicz teamed up for a while with a Karol Rozencwajg, a former traveling salesman from Vienna who played the guitar or zither. They enjoyed "great success with the populace," one ghetto journal declared. "The duo sometimes ends up with 6 marks to share after a full day's work, a tidy wage indeed."[51]

In the Lodz Ghetto, the dominant humor was "typically Jewish—sarcastic and critical," one resident wrote in his journal. "You can't die either these days,"[52] complained a woman who had come to the mortuary office to arrange her mother's burial and encountered a delay of several days.

"Food, of course, is the paramount theme" of humor in the Lodz Ghetto, the same journal stated. "Lately, the abominable food situation has begun to be reflected in people's outward appearance. The sight of people swaying as they walk down the street has given rise to macabre humor. With tears of laughter in his eyes, a ghetto Jew will remark in jest: 'Before the war we ate ducks and walked like horses, now we eat horses—and waddle like ducks.'"[53]

Humor was a popular pastime in the Warsaw Ghetto, largest of the involuntary enclaves. "Nalewski Street looks like Hollywood nowadays," it was said there. "Wherever you go you see a star."[54] Jews in the ghetto were required to wear an armband bearing the six-pointed Star of David.

Verses recited around Warsaw concerned Adam Czerniakow, chairman of the ghetto's Jewish council, which replaced the former Kehilla, or community council:

When the chairman is a nitwit,
The whole Kehilla is a shit.
Prexy Czerniakow, the fat pot,
Gets his chicken soup hot.
How so? Just dough!

Money is a dandy thing.
Madam Czerniakow is sure to get her hair done,
She takes her tea with sugar and bun.
How so? Just dough!
Money is a dandy thing.[55]

In the Warsaw Ghetto, as elsewhere, secret plays with undisguised allusions to the political situation were presented on Purim, the springtime holiday that celebrates the Jews' victory over Haman, anti-Semitic prime minister of ancient Persia. In one instance, new words were put to an old tune:

Listen here, Haman you,
Jews will live to even scores,
You will get your comeuppance.
Jews have lived and will endure.
But Haman, you will go to hell.[56]

An undated Purim play from the Nazi era, in Yiddish and German, centered on a German police officer looking for a certain Jew. In the end the Jew, bowing to the German's boasts, concedes that Hitler will indeed get his due—including *ein Miese Meschine*,[57] a violent death. The expression is an especially gruesome curse, in a language rich with curses. A children's *Purimshpil* in the Warsaw Ghetto would end with "a disgraced Hitler"[58] being led to the gallows, echoing Haman's fate. Throughout the Holocaust, Jewish humor linked Hitler to Haman. "In the expressions, jokes, sayings and parables of the day, one could easily see the influence of the Purim scroll, the Megillah."[59] A cabaret character boasted that he was "the old Haman."[60] A Purim verse in the Vilna Ghetto spoke of *Hitlertashen*,[61] a contemporary version of the three-cornered, fruit-filled *Hamantashen* pastry eaten on the holiday. A popular joke had a similar theme:

Hitler made one of his famous speeches, in the days before he became chancellor. In the front row sat a little Jew who during the whole speech shook his head and smiled. After the speech Hitler had the little Jew brought to him, and asked him why he behaved as he did.

"I was only amazed," replied the Jew, "and asked myself some questions."

"About what?" snorted Hitler.

Said the Jew: "To remember Pharaoh and the exit from Egypt, we celebrate Passover and eat matzahs. To remember Haman, and his plans to kill the Jews of Persia, we celebrate Purim and eat hamantashen. I wonder what holiday we will celebrate, and what we will eat after your exit."

This joke points up a Jewish tendency to mock foes not only through humor, but through gastronomical allusions. "While nations in general remember their heroes, we remember our enemies," wrote Oscar Teller, historian of Europe's Jewish cabarets. "And we do it not through curses, songs of hate or other customs of derision, rather through pastry."[62]

During the early days of the occupation in Poland, Nazi authorities permitted a wide range of cultural activities in the Warsaw Ghetto, including vocational courses, Hebrew schools, choral groups—and cabarets. One group of cardplayers raised the money in the ghetto to engage a favorite Warsaw singing comedian. The idea proved so popular that "impresarios could make a living by handling artists' bookings and fees." Performances were given in private homes, cafés, and public kitchens. The acts included "comic patter . . . farce or satire on ghetto bureaucracy, and buffoonish or melodramatic one-acters."[63] Farcical adaptations of Russian songs were especially well received. "However poor the talent and trashy the content," Lucy Dawidowicz wrote in *The War Against the Jews 1933–1945*, this "improvised entertainment heightened ghetto morale simply by releasing the audiences for a brief span from their day-to-day anxieties."[64]

Five theaters opened eventually in the Warsaw Ghetto, two performing in Yiddish and three in Polish, all concentrating on comedies and revues. The police showed up sometimes and "broke a few heads."[65] Mary Berg described one such café theater in her Warsaw Ghetto dairy: "Gas lamps were burning in every corner of the crowded cabaret. Every table was covered by a white tablecloth. Fat characters sat at them eating chicken, duck, or fowl. All of these foods would be drowned in wine and liquor. When I came in, M.Z., the renowned Polish actor, played the role of a comic character, eliciting lots of laughter. Within the walls of the cabaret one could not sense the tragedy taking place a few yards away. The audience ate, drank, and laughed as if it had no worries."[66]

Outside the theaters, humor cropped up in even the most grotesque situations. One jester would go up to a corpse, empty the pockets, and ask: "Did you remember to turn in your ration card, comrade?"[67] Ber Mark, historian of the Warsaw Ghetto Uprising, tells of "a simple Jew named Baruch . . . a *shlmazel*, a misfit," who was part of a group of fighters who smuggled weapons from the Aryan side through a sewer. Baruch was the slowest member of the group.

> "Remember," one of Baruch's compatriots teased, "it's all over with you if you continue to creep that way—I'll kill you myself."
> "Good, it's better you kill me and end my troubles," Baruch answered.
> "I'm ready to carry out your wish, but first you have to pay me 100 zlotys for your bullet."
> "Baruch began to bargain in earnest—he could only pay 50 zlotys: 'I can't afford any more,' he pleaded."

Everyone burst into laughter, the only heard in those gruesome hours.[68]

Elie Wiesel's classic *Night* contains a sardonic passage concerning a rumor that the Red Army was approaching:

> We were already accustomed to rumors of this kind. It was not the first time a false prophet had foretold to us peace-on-earth, negotiations-with-the-Red-Cross-for-our-release, or other false rumors. . . . And often we believed them. It was an injection of morphine.
>
> But this time these prophecies seemed more solid. During these last few nights, we had heard the guns in the distance.
>
> My neighbor, the faceless one, said:
>
> "Don't let yourself be fooled with illusions. Hitler has made it very clear that he will annihilate all the Jews before the clock strikes twelve, before they can hear the last stroke."
>
> I burst out:
>
> "What does it matter to you? Do we have to regard Hitler as a prophet?"
>
> His glazed, faded eyes looked at me. At last he said in a weary voice:
>
> "I've got more faith in Hitler than in anyone else. He's the only one who's kept his promises, all his promises, to the Jewish people."[69]

This sense of futility and a knowledge of the fate that awaited millions of Hitler's victims is reflected in these quips:

> In Treblinka, where a day's food was some stale bread and a cup of rotting soup, one prisoner cautions a fellow inmate against gluttony. "Hey Moshe, don't overeat. Think of us who will have to carry you."[70]
>
> Also from Treblinka: The consolation to friends upon leaving was, "Come on, cheer up, old man. We'll meet again some day in a better world—in a shop window as soap." To which the friend would reply, "Yes, but while they'll make toilet soap from my fat, you'll be a bar of cheap laundry soap."[71]

151

> A newcomer to Auschwitz asks a veteran about getting out. The old timer points to the smokestacks and says, "That's the only way out."[72]

> Residents of one ghetto, where the Nazis pledged to keep some Jews off the trains to the death camps, would ask, "What is a protected list?"
> "A collection of the names of the Jews who will be deported next."[73]

This is a postwar example, which shows the suspicion in which Jews held the non-Jewish world, even those non-Jews who offered help during the war:

> Two Poles are talking in the early 1950s. One notices that his neighbor is living quite comfortably—new car, nice clothes, annual vacations.
> "What gives?" the first Pole asks.
> "I have a family of Jews living in my basement," the second answers. "They're well off, and they give me money every week."
> "They must still be frightened to stay in hiding so long."
> "No. I never told them the war is over."

Understandably, the darkest humor during the Holocaust came from Poland, from ghettoes and death camps, where conditions were arguably worse than in the other conquered areas. The difference in tone is especially apparent among the Jewish jokes. Those set toward the West in Germany and Austria, where violent pre-Nazi displays of anti-Semitism were relatively rare and Jews drifted toward assimilation with their non-Jewish neighbors, were relatively mild and optimistic.

Theresienstadt—Terezin in Czech—the Potemkin Village established in a former Czechoslovakian garrison town, was one of the richest sources of humor during the Holocaust. A variety of cultural

activities took root there—music, theater, and libraries. A cabaret
was formed two days after the second Jewish transport arrived in
December 1941. A variety show took place the same evening in hall
Number 5 of the Sudeten barracks. Subsequent transports swelled
the ranks of the cabaret participants; performers came from among
trained poets, actors, musicians, and directors in the camp. Cabaret
performances became known as *Kameradschaftabenden*, evenings of
fellowhip. The revues included songs, skits, and jazz. To amuse the
infirm and bedridden, the performers would do their sketches in the
infirmaries. Their work received the blessing of Rabbi Erich
Weiner, spiritual leader of the prisoners who viewed the cabaretists'
efforts as a form of ministry. Weiner "observed the effect and
recognized that the prisoners' courage to live grew by means of the
cabaret, that it gave them moral support and strengthened their
will to survive as well as infused their power to resist."[74]

Alfred Kantor, an artist interned in Theresienstadt, recalled
later "how we gathered at night in a cramped storage cellar to watch
Karel Svenk's *Cheers to Life* . . . stinging political cabaret."[75]
Svenk, the cabaret's founder and manager, "the sad clown par
excellence,"[76] was a cabaret veteran who had started his career in the
Club of Wasted Talent in Prague. His routines "reflected all the
irony, all the mockery, all the distortions of ghetto life."[77] In
general, the cabaret material was upbeat. It elicited memories of the
"good old times" in Berlin, Prague, and Vienna; no reminders of life
in prison were needed.

In one variety show, Svenk prepared a satirical sketch on a lost
food card, a topic dear to the hearts, and stomachs, of the prisoners.
His "Terezin March," coupled with a catchy marching melody,
quickly became the inmates' anthem, which was incorporated into
following cabarets:

Everything goes, if one wants,
United we'll hold our hands.

153

Despite the cruel times
We have humor in our hearts.
Every day we go on
Moving back and forth,
And can write letters in only thirty words.
Hey! Tomorrow life starts over,
And with it the time is approaching,
When we'll fold our knapsacks
And return home again.
Everything goes, if one wants,
United we'll hold our hands.
And on the ruins of the Ghetto we shall laugh.

At first a Theresienstadt prisoner stood guard at the cellar door in case an S.S. man approached. When it later suited the Nazi propaganda purposes, the guards turned a blind eye to the cabaret performances. "It sounds unbelievable, but it is a fact," according to Ulrike Migdal, a German researcher who has documented the camp's cultural life, "that since the culture operation was officially ordered, there was not the trace of censor in Theresienstadt, regardless of the program's design. Everything could be played and presented."[78] Works by Jews or with Jewish themes were allowed. Veiled references to Hitler were featured.

Better satire than insurrection, was the commandant's apparent reasoning: "Let them have their fun, they'll all be dead tomorrow anyhow."[79]

"The SS was generous; you could laugh," another Theresienstadt historian wrote. "But it was a bitter laugh."[80]

Most of the cabaret texts presumably perished with their creators; one surviving poem about life in the camp ended with this verse:

Alle Sorge sind vertrieben
Hier an diesen schönen Fleck

154

Und nur eine ist geblieben:
Wie kommt man hier wieder weg?

All worries away are sent
In this lovely spot of land,
And only one is still present:
How does one come back here again?[81]

Its composer, Leo Strauss, a resident of Theresienstadt who composed many of the cabaret's lyrics, also wrote this paean to his prison home:

Ich kenn ein kleines Stadtchen,
Ein Stadtchen ganz tiptop,
Ich nenn es nicht beim Namen,
Ich nenns die Stadt Als-Ob.

Nicht alle Leute dürfen
In diese Stadt hinein
Es müssen Auserwählte
Der Als-ob-Rasse sein.

Die leben dort ihr Leben,
Als ob ein Leben war,
Und freun' sich mit Gerüchten,
Als obs die Wahrheit war.

Die Menschen auf den Stassen,
Die laufen im Galopp—
Wenn man auch nichts zu tun hat,
Tut man doch so als ob.

Es gibt auch ein Kaffeehaus
Gleich dem Café de l'Europe,

Und beii Musikbergleitung
Fühlt man sich dort als ob.

Und mancher ist mir manchem
Auch manchmal ziemlich grob—
Daheim war er kein Grosser,
Hier macht er so als ob.

Des Morgens und des Abends
Trinkt man Als-Ob Kaffee,
Am Samstag, ja am Samstag,
Da gibts Als-ob-Haché.

Man stellt sich an um Suppe,
Als ob da etwas drin,
Und man geniesst die Dorsche
Als Als-ob-Vitaman.

Man legt sich auf dem Boden,
Als ob das wär ein Bett,
Und denkt an seine Lieben,
Als ob man Nachricht hätt.

Man trägt das schwere Schicksal,
Als ob es nicht so schwer,
Und spricht von schönrer Zukunft,
Als ob schon morgen wär.[82]

I know a little city,
A place which is terrif',
I don't call it by its name,
I call the city As-If.

Not all people may
Live in this place,

They must be chosen members
Of the As-if race.

They live out their lives there,
As-If there was a life,
And amuse themselves with rumors,
As-If they were the truth.

The people on the streets,
Who run at a fast clip—
Even when they have nothing to do,
They still do it As-If.

There is a little coffeehouse
Just like the Café Europe,
And when the musical should start to play,
Inside they feel As-If.

They hang around with others
With people rather coarse—
At home, though no celebrity
They make out here, As-If.

In the morning and in the evening
They drink coffee, As-If,
On Saturday, yes on Saturday
There is As-If ground beef.

They sit down at their soupbowl,
As if something was therein,
And they enjoy their codfish
As an As-If Vitamin.

They lie down on the ground,
As if it was a bed,

And think about their loved ones,
As if they had some news.

They bear the hard fate,
As if it weren't so hard,
And speak of a beautiful future,
As if it were already tomorrow.

Strauss died in Birkenau, part of the Auschwitz compound, where he was shipped during the last weeks of the war.

Ohne Butter, Ohne Eier, Ohne Fett [without butter, without eggs, without fat], a poem about Theresienstadt's physical deprivations by an anonymous author, concluded with this salute to Jewish eternity:

Sterne gab es schon so lange unsre Welt besteht,
Ohne Butter, ohne Eier, ohne Fett.
Wir sind stoltz auf diesen Stern,
Weil er nie untergeht,
Ohne Butter, ohne Eier, ohne Fett.
Wenn auch knapp hier die Achile,
Einmal geht es doch zu Nile,
Ohne Butter, ohne Eier, ohne Fett.
Frei sind wir von Schuld und Fehl,
Ewig lebt "Schma Jisroel"
Auch ohne Butter, ohne Eier, ohne Fett.[83]

There have been stars as long as our world exists,
Without butter, without eggs, without fat.
We are proud of this star,
Because it never perishes,
Without butter, without eggs, without fat.
Although now the food runs low,
This will end one day, we know,

Without butter, without eggs, without fat.
Free of guilt and blame are we,
"Shma Yisroel" will live eternally
Also without butter, without eggs, without fat.

Another Theresienstadt prisoner, Willy Rosen, wrote a poem entitled *Der Pojaz* [a clown or fool], from the Slovak term for an outsider:

Everywhere there's one,
who's laughed at by the folks,
Everywhere there's one
the one who makes the jokes,
One is designated,
his job's to play the fool,
His whole life, he is fated,
it starts, at first, in school.
He must wander through his life,
as the eternal clown,
Oh, the people like to laugh
At somebody's expense:
Everywhere there's one,
who's laughed at by the folks,
Everywhere there's one,
Who for you, makes the Pojaz.[84]

Alfred Kantor, the Prague-born artist imprisoned for three years in Theresienstadt, Auschwitz, and Schwarzheide, weaved satiric references into the 127 pages of drawings he completed during a "two-month frenzy of creation" in a Bavarian displaced persons' camp after liberation. A sketch of a Theresienstadt inmate dragging a piece of luggage into an overcrowded attic is entitled: "How to get 70,000 into a city built to accommodate only 3000." In another drawing, a sign dominating a drawing of an Auschwitz

159

latrine, where men and women sat on opposite rows of wooden planks, proclaims: *Sauberkeit ist deine Gesundheit!* [Cleanliness is your Health.] A sketch of Schwartzheide, in flames after an Allied bombing raid, contains the sign: "Caution, inflammables. Smoking forbidden."[85]

Humor figured in the creations of other Jewish artists in areas under Nazi occupation. One whose works satirized daily life in Theresienstadt was Pavel Fantl, a Czech-born physician. Early in the war he was pressed by the Nazis into doing office work at Gestapo headquarters in Czechoslovakia; he sabotaged their files and smuggled food to Jews held by the secret police. In 1942 he was imprisoned at Theresienstadt. There he produced several paintings which were smuggled out and hidden by a Czech friend until 1945. His works showed Hitler in a clown's costume and gawky, goosestepping German soldiers. Fantl, his wife, and his son died in Auschwitz.[86]

Bertalan Gondor, a Hungarian lithographer who was conscripted into forced labor service under the Nazis, sent a series of illustrated postcards to his wife in Budapest. Each carried a "reassuring, innocuous message" designed to escape censorship. In one drawing he trudges under a heavy backpack; "Don't worry about me," he wrote. "I am well, and as you can see my sense of humor has not disappeared."[87] One inmate in a French labor camp made simple sketches of conditions there, including one showing a bent-over Jew, with the inscription, "The mood in the camp is excellent."[88]

Humor in the death camps themselves had a particularly sardonic quality. "I remember a kapo joking with us, 'Behave properly, because yesterday a man was *even killed* for not behaving,'" an Auschwitz survivor says. "We thought it was very funny, the irony of such a warning in Auschwitz."[89]

One Buchenwald survivor described his initiation to the concentration camp in eastern Germany. "When we arrived at

Buchenwald we were sent to the showers, and by that time news of the gas chambers had filtered out, so we thought that we were being sent to our deaths. I can still picture the scene now: a vision of Bedlam, naked men, some weeping, some praying, some even joking."[90]

The Exodus from Egypt, a playlet staged in private by Romanian prisoners in the Transnistria area of the former Austro-Hungarian Empire, was replete with obvious allusions to the Jewish enslavement.[91] For a while, Dutch prisoners presented a cabaret in Auschwitz. They told jokes and made music. "The S.S., for unknown reasons, gave it their stamp of approval," according to a study of the death camps. "The prisoners and the S.S. roared in approval during the performances."[92]

In Auschwitz as in other camps, prisoners who were put to work by the Nazis making signs and posters were permitted to do their own work, "if it was not offensive to the authorities, after the fulfillment of their prison assignments."[93] At risk to themselves, the artists recorded the horror of camp life, and sometimes managed to smuggle the works out of the camp. Joseph Czarnecki, a Polish photojournalist, stumbled upon these overlooked drawings and sketches during his visits to Auschwitz. He noticed, and photographed, "drawings in latrines and washrooms and storage attics; murals in the children's barracks; here and there strange scratchings, paintings, inscriptions, decorations." The art included "shafts of grim humor"; a painting of a distraught and quite possibly drunk apothecary; one of a mocking chimney sweep; caricatures of Hitler and Mussolini; renditions of elegant bathroom mirrors that mocked the camp's stark reality.[94]

At the war's end, as the liberating Allied armies confirmed the Jews' confidence in Germany's ultimate defeat, humor emerged from the shadows. One survivor of Buchenwald, who escaped from a death march in the final days of fighting, tells this story:

161

We teamed up with a couple of liberated prisoners-of-war from the camps that had been around Dresden—an Englishman and a big, black American, who used to get our food for us. This is how he did it: when we approached a village, he'd strip naked and march into the village with a huge kitchen-knife clenched between his big white teeth—and he'd march into a farmhouse and shout COCOROCOO!—meaning that he wanted a chicken. We were always given food—more than enough. The Germans were quite terrified. And we were just dying of laughter. It was just incredible, the way we laughed then. I know I will never be able to laugh like that again.[95]

From the Warsaw Ghetto

In the sewers two friends meet.
"Have you heard the one about . . . It goes like this:

It was the end. Only two Jews were left,
ropes about their necks, waiting to be hanged.
"Cheer up, it could be worse.
"Listen, they've been saying that since
the ghetto walls began to rise."

"I know, but haven't you thought
why they're hanging us; why we're not shot?
They haven't any ammunition left, you see;
the joke's on us, even when we die."[96]

Judith Friedlander, a member of a Chasidic family who spent her childhood in hiding from the Nazis, relates how a sense of humor, expressed through practical jokes, became a means of disciplining others in hiding:

162

Friedlander and her family were among 200 Jews kept by a Hungarian general in his Budapest apartment. Food, taken to them surreptitiously, was scarce. At one point, several Jews in the apartment noticed that their meager rations of bread were missing. They immediately suspected one man, a nudge who found many ways to shatter people's nerves. A group of Jews conspired to leave their pieces of bread in plain sight, where the suspected man would be sure to see them. Sure enough, the bread quickly disappeared. That night, they stole back all of the man's bread. He went hungry for several days. He never took anyone else's bread again.

All the residents of the apartment slept on the floor at night, except for one man, a loud snorer, who insisted on making a bed for himself out of a pair of chairs. Two young men in the apartment once loosened the legs in the chairs. When the man slept in his ersatz bed that night, the chairs wobbled and his body slowly sagged. He awakened, frightened to find himself in an unusual position, and shouted, "Sh'ma Yisroel, I'm dying." The subterfuge was revealed to him. Chastened, he henceforth joined the other Jews on the floor at night.

When the general's apartment building was gutted by Allied bombing, Friedlander and her family found refuge in one of the homes under the protection of Swedish diplomat Raoul Wallenberg. With them were a father and daughter, estranged, who would curse at each other and yell, "I want to see you in a coffin." Somehow, a casket was slipped into their apartment. A few young men placed the daughter in the wooden box after she fell asleep one night. She woke up, saw her surroundings, and thought she was dead. "You're not dead, you're talking to me," the father assured the hysterical girl.

Father and daughter made peace.

One man in hiding, who fancied himself particularly brave, would try to calm the others during bombing raids by observing, "Well, we all have to die once." A fatalist partial to hats, he had the premonition that he would meet his end while wearing a hat. A piece of shrapnel tore through his hat during one British raid. The man was convinced he was dead. Only the concerted effort of the people in the apartment convinced him otherwise. "It took three hours to convince him that he was not dead," Friedlander says. "I tell you, people were hysterical."

After that, the man was more understanding of others' fears.[97]

Jokes that circulated from 1933 to 1945:

In the early years of the Nazi movement, an SA officer is killed in a street fight with the Communists. His comrades want to organize a solemn burial. They go to a funeral home to find out how much it will cost. The firm demands 200 marks for its services. But the soldiers don't have enough money, so they go to another funeral home. The undertakers there ask for 150 marks for the burial. That is still too much money, but the SA men, wherever they ask, find no undertakers who request less than 100 marks. Finally they find a small firm: they explain who they are, and ask for a price to bury their comrade. The owner answers, without thinking it over, that he is ready to bury the SA officer for 10 marks. The SA men are astonished and happy at the same time:

"How did you arrive at that cost—the other firms want no less than 100 marks?"

"You see, we are a Jewish firm. For 100 marks I'd be ready to bury your entire SA."

A Jews walks along the street of Berlin and mutters: "Damn the Führer . . ." A storm trooper stops him. "How dare you . . ." The man replies, "I didn't mean *your* Führer. I mean ours. If the damned fool hadn't let us out of Egypt, we would all have a chance of becoming British subjects."

Emigration quickly became an option for the Jews of Germany under the Third Reich. "Are you an Aryan?" one friend would ask another, "or are you learning English?"

A German walks into a Jewish grocery store in Berlin and asks for a Hitler herring. The grocer's wife, not knowing what the customer wants, shouts to her husband: "This man wants a Hitler herring. Do we have it?"

"Sure," says the grocer. "Give him a Bismarck minus a head."

A Jew is on a train from Berlin to Frankfurt. Opposite him sits a Brown Shirt who fixes a fierce look at his traveling companion. The Jew becomes uneasy and begins to repeat, "Long live Hitler. Long live Hitler."

"Shameless Jew!" yells the Brown Shirt. "During the Weimar Republic, you shouted 'Long live Rathenau!' and now you have the audacity to shout, 'Long live Hitler!'"

"Well," asks the Jew, "is Rathenau alive?"

A German-Jewish war veteran, who had been wounded in the trenches of World War I, succeeds in getting an appointment with Goebbels, and appeals to the Propaganda Minister for a job.

"I'll tell you what I'll do for you," said Goebbels. "I am going to have a sign made with the following inscription: JEWS GET OUT! YOU HAVE BEEN HERE LONG ENOUGH! MAKE ROOM FOR THE ARYANS! If you will carry around this sign, the Propaganda Office will pay you 400 marks a month."

The Jew consents to the arrangement and calls the following day for the sign. At the end of the month, he comes for his pay.

"You are not entitled to any money," says Goebbels. "My men did not find you anywhere with the sign."

"Your men looked in the wrong places," replies the Jew. "I carried the sign around the Jewish cemetery."

After the Nazis had set the date for the official boycott of the Jews, the mayor of a small town in the German hinterland dispatched the following wire to Goebbels: "Rush a couple of Jews at once. Otherwise our boycott will be a flop."

The defendant is on trial in accordance with the new German laws, which decree that any punishment must be doubled if the offender is a non-Aryan. Personal particulars are therefore important.

"How old are you?" asks the judge.

"Thirty-three."

"What year were you born in?"

"1900," replies the defendant.

"But then you're 39 years old. Why do you say 33?"

"Do you call the last six years living?"

A Jew stands on a busy corner in Berlin, distributing handbills. Two storm troopers knock him down and call for the police. When the officer arrives, he notices that the handbills are only blank sheets of paper.

"Are you crazy?" shouts the policeman. "Nothing is written on these sheets."

"The Jews know what is on them," answers the offender.

A Brown Shirt collecting funds for the Nazi cause walks into a crowded restaurant. To his disappointment, no one pays attention to him. Finally, he confronts a guest: "Please drop a coin."

"Why should I contribute to the Nazi Party?" the guest says. "I am a Jew."

"It is certainly strange," says the Brown Shirt. "Jews are persecuted in the Third Reich and yet everyone claims to be a Jew."

Bauer and Katz had been neighbors in Düsseldorf for years, but with the advent of Hitler, Bauer became sarcastic.

"You Jews don't know the meaning of patriotism," Bauer says. "I'll bet that in the Great War your son was interested only in the few marks a month that he received, while my son fought for German dignity and honor."

"What's wrong with that?" asks Katz. "Don't we all crave what we don't possess?"

"What is the meaning of Nazism?" asks the teacher in a Berlin public school. To her chagrin, nobody knows the answer.

"I am ashamed of you," scolds the teacher. "Don't you know what your Führer, who saved your country from degradation and ruin, and his great Party stand for?"

Nobody says a word. After a while, little Isaac raises his hand.

"What is it?"

"I think I know the answer," says the Jewish student. "Nazism stands for beauty, purity, and sacrifice."

"Excellent," exclaims the teacher. "How did you, of all people, know the answer?"

"The credit should go to my mother," explains Isaac. "Only last night I heard her say that she hoped Hitler would be a *schoene, reine kapore*."

In Yiddish, "schoene, reine kapore" means a beautiful, pure sacrifice.

A Jewish father in Nazi Germany is teaching his son how to act properly in public. "In present-day Germany," says the father, "the correct form of grace before meals is 'Thank God and Hitler.'"

"But suppose the Führer dies?" asks the little boy.

"Then you just thank God."

A German Jew was speaking to another Jew who was very ill and had visited the doctor.

"What did the doctor say?" asked the first Jew. "Did he give you any hope?"

"Well," replied the the second, "he told me to expect the worst—and in Germany *that means I'll live*."

Nazi Finance Minister Hjalmar Schacht is addressing a group of London bankers on the subject of a German loan. He points out how this step will help all Europe. "All your money is perfectly safe," the financier explains. "Please remember that in spite of anti-German propaganda, we are still a stable country. Underground we have mines with untold treasure. Above ground we have our great and incomparable Führer."

One of the bankers whispers to Lord Rothschild, asking the Jewish banker's opinion of Schacht's proposition.

"If the guarantees were reversed, I would be in favor of the loan," Rothschild replies.

Shortly before World War II, a British travel bureau takes a number of men and women on a tour of Germany. The party includes an English Jew. While in Dresden, the group visits Schiller's study.

"Here the great German national poet expressed the soul of his people," says the Nazi guide.

"Pardon the correction," says the Jew. "Schiller was not a national, but an international poet. You know that he wrote *Marie Stuart* for the English, *The Maid of Orleans* for the French, and *William Tell* for the Swiss."

"Hasn't he done anything for the Germans?" asks the Nazi indignantly.

"Schiller did not neglect you," replies the Jew. "For the Germans he wrote *The Robbers*."

The Jews in the Warsaw Ghetto said their troubles stemmed from disobedience of the "11th Commandment: Thou shalt choose for thyselves the proper grandparents."

Churchill invited the Rabbi of Ger, a Chasidic leader reputed to have mystical powers, to consult him on how to defeat Germany.

"There are two ways," the rabbi said, "the natural way and the supernatural way. The natural way would be for a million angels with flaming swords to attack Germany and destroy her. The supernatural way would be for a million Englishmen to make a landing in Germany and annihilate her."

A German Jew called on Hitler in 1936 and said to him, "My Führer, you remember me. I'm Saul Kohn. I served in your company during the Great War. We were together at the front for two years. Think of our experiences together and let me move to Vienna with my family and my belongings."

"Very well," replied Hitler.

After the annexation of Austria in 1938, the Jew visited Hitler in Vienna and said:

"My Führer, we were together at the front for two years. Think of our experiences together and let me move to Prague with my family and my belongings."

"Very well," replied Hitler.

A few months later, after the annexation of the Sudetenland, Kohn appeared before Hitler again and repeated his little speech: ". . . at the front together . . . our war experiences . . . let me move with my family and belongings to Warsaw."

"No, not Warsaw, definitely not Warsaw!" exclaimed Hitler, wrinkling his brow. Then he added:

"Look here, why don't you go far, far away? I don't want to see you every week."

The German Army invaded Poland on September 1, 1939.

A tiger escaped from the Berlin zoo and created havoc among the farms on the city's outskirts. Notices were put up offering a prize for its capture, "dead or alive." Two Jews read the notice and suddenly one paled and whispered to the other:

"I think we ought to escape before we are shot."

"But why?" asked the other, mystified. "We're not tigers."

"I know," stammered the first Jew. "But can we prove it?"

A badly frightened Jew stood before a German court.

"The charge against you is very serious," intoned the judge. "You are accused of maligning the Nazi Party—the government itself."

"B-b-but your honor," stammered the Jew, "I was referring to the Communists, not the Nazis."

"Don't lie to me," yelled the judge. "The indictment accuses you of using the words 'murderers, gangsters, and thieves.' The court knows exactly whom you meant."

A judge in Nazi Germany was unusually depressed. "Why so glum?" asked a colleague.

"I had a very difficult case today," sighed the judge. "A Nazi Party member stole 1,000 marks from a Jew and I was forced to sentence him to a whole day in jail."

"That's not so bad," said the other soothingly. "After all, you had to keep up appearances."

"It wasn't that part of the case that really bothered me," the first judge explained. "I was forced to sentence the Jew to only five years in a concentration camp for putting temptation in the Aryan's way."

An elderly Jew was released from a concentration camp. "What happened to you?" asked a friend. "Your teeth are missing, your arm is twisted, you walk with a limp, your face looks as if it

171

went through a meat grinder, and you weigh less than 70 pounds."

"Nothing happened," the Jew responded. "I am just another atrocity lie."

Goebbels was touring the German schools. At one, he asked the students to recite patriotic slogans.

"Heil Hitler," shouted one pupil.

"Very good," said Goebbels.

"*Deutschland über alles*," another called out.

Goebbels beamed. "Excellent. And how about a stronger slogan?"

A hand shot up. Goebbels nodded, and the little boy declared: "Our people shall live forever."

"Wonderful," exclaimed Goebbels. "What's your name, young man?"

"Israel Goldberg."

Kohn is sitting in a Berlin teashop, waiting for the glass of milk he had ordered. Someone bursts in from the street and gasps out that Hitler has been assassinated.

"Waitress!" cries Kohn, "I want black coffee instead of milk . . . I'm mourning!"

A Jewish immigrant wants to be spared from working. He declares, "I am lame."

"Are you *meshugenah*?" his friend says. "Unless you want to be discovered as a fraud, you'll have to be lame your whole life."

"Of course not!" answers the immigrant. "If I change my mind, I'll just go to Lourdes!"

Two Jews in Berlin are discussing their plight.

"Terrible," says one. "Persecutions, no rations, discrimination, and quotas. Sometimes I think we would have been better off if we had never been born."

"Sure," says his friend, "but who has that much luck—maybe one in 50,000."

Pfeiffer, a staunch Nazi, went to the barn one morning, only to find that his prize ox was sick, unable to rise from its bed of straw. He called the only Aryan veterinarian in the community, but the ox grew even more ill. Pfeiffer recognized that the animal needed immediate treatment. He secretly called Fleischmann, the Jewish veterinarian.

Fleischmann took one look at the animal, forced some medicine down its throat, and whispered in its ear. Immediately, the ox leaped to its feet.

The Nazi farmer was astounded. "What did you say to the ox?"

"I just used a little animal psychology, Herr Pfeiffer," said Fleischmann. "I whispered the name 'Hitler' in its ear. There isn't an ox in all Germany that won't leap to its feet at its mere mention."

Two Nazi judges were discussing why their courts were nearly always empty.

"I haven't had a case in over a month," sighed one. "I can't understand it."

"Well, I can," grumbled the other. "We haven't any work because a Jew will not sue another Jew, and he is afraid to sue an Aryan. An Aryan will certainly not sue a Jew because it would advertise the fact that he had business dealings with a Jew."

173

"What you say is true," acknowledged the first judge, "but still, one Aryan can sue another Aryan."

"No, they won't do that either," explained the other. "Where would they get Jewish lawyers to defend them?"

A history professor in Germany asks his students to recite the reasons for the Nazi losses.

"It is the fault of the Jews," responded one student.

The professor beamed. "Very good, but can you tell the class what the Jews did to bring about this catastrophe?"

The student remained silent, but another spoke up. "There are too many Jewish generals."

The professor was shocked. "That simply is not true. There isn't a single Jewish general in our whole army."

"I know, sir," the student answers. "I was referring to the American and British armies."

A teacher asked his pupil, "Tell me, my little one, why did we lose World War I?"

The child answered, without hesitation, "Because of the Jewish generals, sir."

"But there weren't any Jewish generals in the German army," the teacher said.

"That's why we lost."

A Nazi policeman swaggers down the street with a large Saint Bernard on a leash.

"That's a fine dog you have there," says a Jewish passerby. "What breed is it?"

174

"He's a cross between a mongrel and a Jew."

"Aha," says the Jew. "Then the dog is related to both of us."

A Jew is walking down a street in Berlin when he accidentally brushes against a storm trooper.

"Swine," roars the Nazi.

"Epstein," says the Jew, bowing.

Moshe Greenspan read an advertisement that a publishing house in Berlin needed a proofreader, and he applied for the job.

"We don't employ Jews here," said the foreman. "No Jew will ever be employed by this firm as long as I'm alive."

"I'll wait," said Greenspan.

In the early 1940s, an elderly Jew in New York decided to surprise his wife on her birthday with a gift of intimate apparel. He went to Macy's and began looking through the lingerie section. Finally, he settled on a display of brassieres.

"Can I help you, sir?" asked a young salesgirl, but the old man was so embarrassed he could hardly talk.

"Do you know your wife's bra size?" she asked. The old man merely shook his head.

"Well, then," she said softly, "tell me this: are they big?"

With an obvious sense of relief, the man replied, "Hoo boy, are they big! Hitler should have them for tonsils!"[98]

An old, bearded Jew managed to find his way into Hitler's inner sanctum. Facing the old man, the Führer was caught off guard.

175

"I'll grant you anything you wish," declared Hitler, "but please tell me—just how did you get in here?"

"It was simple," said the Jew. "I just told them I was Goebbels' father."

Throughout the Nazi era, rumors abounded that the Semitic-looking propaganda minister had Jewish blood.

At the beginning of the Hitler era, Blumenthal travels to Berlin. When he returns home, he tells a friend: "I saw Goebbels. He looks like Apoll . . ."

"Are you mad," the friend says. "That cripple!"

"Let me finish speaking. He looks like *a Pol*ish Jew."

Early in Hitler's Reich, when Jews could still travel by train, an old Jew sat by himself in a compartment. His gaze fell on a propaganda poster: "A German does not lie." He repeats to himself, "A German does not lie." Then he thinks, reflectively, "A lousy percent for 80 million."

A religious Jew was traveling on a train and put on his *talith* and *teffilin* to recite his morning prayers. A Nazi officer was in the same car. The officer took off his leather belt, wound it around his dog, and addressed him: "Dog, I have made you a Jew."

The Jew exclaimed: "Poor dog, you will never be able to become an officer of Hitler."

176

An elderly Jew sat on a train across from a storm trooper with a large dog.

Each time the Nazi spoke to his dog, he addressed the canine as "Moses."

The Jew tried to ignore this, but the Nazi persisted in calling "Moses," each time in a louder voice.

The old man could not contain himself any longer.

"What a pity your dog has a Jewish name!"

"Why?"

"Well, having a Jewish name these days is quite a handicap. Without it, he might go far. He might even stand a chance of becoming a storm trooper."

During Hitler's early days in Munich, a group of young boys stood in front of Jewish stores yelling "Jew! Jew!"

One Jewish tailor, fearing a loss of business, approached the boys. "Any day you yell 'Jew' at me, I'll give each of you ten pfennigs."

The boys were delighted.

After a few days, the tailor went up to the boys again. "I'm sorry, but my business has fallen off. I can no longer afford to pay you."

One of the boys shouted angrily, "You expect us to stand here and yell 'Jew!' for nothing? Nothing doing."

And they left.

A popular wit in the Warsaw Ghetto said, "I had a *groschen*, but lost it: I had a *tsvever*, but lost it; I had a *grayer*, but lost it. Only the *firer* I can't seem to lose."

A groschen is a coin; a tsvever is Yiddish for a two-groschen piece; a grayer is Yiddish for a three-groschen piece. Firer, a four-groschen piece, is a pun on the Yiddish pronunciation of Führer.

During the early stages of the Nazis' anti-Jewish persecution, a squad of Gestapo agents raided a farm on the outskirts of Berlin. The husband, a Jew, was taken to a concentration camp. His wife, a Gentile, remained behind. She was able to smuggle a few letters in and out of the camp.

In one letter she complained that she was unable to plow the field and plant her supply of seed potatoes. Her husband considered the problem for a few days, then openly mailed a letter in which he ordered her to forget about plowing the field. "Don't touch a single spot," he wrote. "That's where I buried the rifles and grenades."

A few days later, several truckloads of Gestapo agents again raided the farm. For a week they dug in the field, searching each shovelful of earth for a trace of the guns and grenades. Finally, finding nothing, they left. Confused, the wife wrote her husband another letter, describing the raid. "The field," she related, "has been sifted from one end to the other."

The husband wrote back: "Now plant the potatoes."

After 1933, the Jewish pessimists went into exile; the optimists went to concentration camps.

During the early days of the Hitler regime, Goebbels maintained that the Jews were really clever people, and that Hitler was making a mistake by being so hard on them. "On the contrary," Hitler said, "they're quite dumb." Finally, to settle the argument, the two men disguised themselves and went downtown. Entering a china shop run by a German, Goebbels asked, "Do you have any left-handed teacups?"

The poor German had never heard of such a thing. He stammered, apologized, and finally admitted flatly that he had none.

Next, Goebbels and Hitler went to a shop run by a Jew. The Jew scratched his head, smiled, and said:

"What a lucky thing! I have just a few left-handed teacups left . . . naturally, I carry them in stock, although they're very hard to get. And, you understand, being so rare, they are a little more expensive than ordinary teacups."

Goebbels paid and picked up the package. "Anytime you want more, I'll be glad to order them," the Jew called after them. As they reached the street, Goebbels turned triumphantly to Hitler.

"There, didn't I tell you? The Jews are lot smarter."

"What do you mean smarter?" Hitler retorted. "He was just lucky—he had some in stock."

A band of Nazis stops a Jewish-looking man on Berlin's main street. After questioning him they discover he is an Egyptian diplomat. The leader of the Nazi band apologizes. "Excuse us, excellency. Of course, this won't happen in the future. For soon all the Jews will be exterminated."

Responds the diplomat: "We Egyptians said that 4,000 years ago—and you see what the result was."

Blumenthal meets Rosenstock, who was recently released from a concentration camp. Blumenthal inquires about the experience.

"Thank you, very pleasant," Rosenstock says. "We rose at 9 o'clock, and had a good breakfast. Then we went hiking—we read a little, played cards, and enjoyed a splendid lunch. After lunch we slept a couple of hours. In the evening we had a delightful dinner followed by chess."

Blumenthal stares, then says:

"That puzzles me. Yesterday I met Levy. He told me an entirely different story."

"Yes," says Rosenstock, "and he's back there again today."

One Nazi sees another walking out of a rabbi's home. "Why were you in a Jew's home?" he asks.

"I'm having the rabbi teach me Yiddish," the first Nazi answers. "That way I can listen when they are talking and discover their devious plans."

"That's really clever of you."

"Yes," boasts the linguist, pointing to his head. "That's using my *tochis*."

Tochis is Yiddish for one's derrière.

There is a raid on a Jewish home at breakfast time.

"Who are those men?" a frightened boy asks his grandmother.

"S.S., mein kind."

The Yiddish command "Ess, ess mein kind" {Eat, eat, my child}
has come to be the motto of the concerned Jewish grandmother.

Levi and Hirsch cross paths by chance deep in the jungle, each with a rifle slung over his shoulder, leading a caravan. They

180

embrace. "How are you, what are you doing here?" They exchange stories of safaris, of hunting for crocodiles and elephants. "And how are things with our old friend Simon?" "Oh, he's had a real adventure. He's stayed in Berlin."

Rosenstein was on the way to the market in Munich with a chicken under his arm. He was accosted in the street by a Nazi bully who demanded, "Jew, where are you going?"

"I'm going to the market to buy some feed for my chicken."

"What does he eat?" the Nazi asked.

"Corn," replied Rosenstein.

"Corn? The nerve of you people. German soldiers go hungry while you Jews feed your chickens on native German corn." He then slapped Rosenstein and continued on his way.

A moment later another Nazi stopped Rosenstein.

"Where are you going, Jew dog?"

"To the market, to buy some feed for my chicken."

"What does he eat?"

"Perhaps some wheat."

"Wheat? Of all things. The Jew's chicken eats wheat while German children go hungry." And he promptly knocked Rosenstein to the ground.

Rosenstein picked himself up and continued on his way, when he was accosted by yet another Nazi.

"Where are you going, kike?"

"To the market, to buy some feed for my chicken."

"Feed for your chicken? What does he eat?"

"Look," said Rosenstein, "I don't know. I figure I'll give him a couple of *pfennigs* and he'll buy whatever he wants."

Two Jews manage to escape from a concentration camp near the Dutch border. The Dutch border guards commit a major offense by rescuing them. The pair are fed, consoled, and then, at the changing of the guard, taken to safety in the countryside.

As the Jews trek along with the Dutch troops, one turns to the other and declares nostalgically, "And they call *this* marching. Not compared with *our* S.A."

A Swiss visitor asks a Jewish friend in Germany, "How are you managing under the Nazis?"

"Like a tapeworm: I wriggle my way night and day through the brown bulk, and wait until I am expelled."

Three immigrants met in New York. Says the first, "You won't believe this, but back home in Berlin I was the biggest clothing manufacturer in the entire city."

Says the second. "You won't believe this, but at home in Vienna I had a palace."

The third immigrant, whose dwarf terrier is sitting in his lap, says, "As for me, I was a poor devil back home just as I am now. But my terrier back there was a Saint Bernard."

A letter from Nazi Germany that passed the censor without fuss:

"Dear Cousin Shlomo,

"Everything is going splendidly for us. Everything that the American newspapers report of the mistreatment of Jews is pure horror propaganda. We wouldn't wish to live anywhere else—except maybe Aunt Sarah, *zichrona l'olam!*"

The Hebrew expression zichrona *{*zichrono *for a male}* l' olam *{May her memory last forever} is a traditional way to honor a deceased loved one.*

Here is a similar letter from Nazi Germany:
"Dear Yossel,
"All is going well for us. Everything your newspapers write about the mistreatment of Jews is lies.
P.S. We've just come back from the burial of Jankew Katz, who asserted the contrary."

In 1938, when all the Jews in Germany still had not grasped how dangerous the situation was for them, a Jewish representative of a foreign pharmaceutical firm came to a German doctor.
"Aren't you afraid of the Nazis?" the physician asked.
"Why?" asked the representative. "We came through the Red Sea, we can come through the Brown Excrement too."

Erich Maria Remarque, "Aryan" author of a pacifist book about World War I, had to emigrate during the time of Hitler.
Asked if he didn't feel homesick, he replied, "Why? Am I a Jew?"

During the Nazi era, it was almost impossible for Jews in Eastern Europe to get a visa for the United States.

A teacher asked a student, "Moritz, do you know why Columbus has become so famous?"

"Yes. Because he came to America without a visa."

On Kristallnacht the furniture was thrown out of a window onto the street from a high floor. Kohn stands in front of the house, looks at the scene, and laughs.

A man in a Nazi uniform recognizes Kohn as a Jew and yells at him, "That is a Jewish residence."

"Yes, that is my apartment," Kohn says.

"So why are you laughing?"

"Well," he says. "I'm still living in a furnished room."

There was a miracle rabbi in Romania. When Romania, an ally of Nazi Germany, was attacked by Russia, a young Christian woman came to the miracle rabbi. "Rabbi, I've heard many great things about you, and now you are our last hope. My husband was sent directly to the front and can fall at any moment. Please help us, please help us!"

The rabbi takes two days to think over the matter, then hands the woman a small package. He tells her, "Add this package to the other things you send your husband. And, you will see, God will bring your husband back home."

And that happened—two days later, the man came home. What happened?

When the packages for the soldiers arrived at the front, they were opened as usual and inspected. The small package from the rabbi was opened too. What was inside? Two Jewish prayerbooks.

The officer in charge screamed, "Private Muller is really a Jew? Send him back home!"[99]

During the war Hitler hears of a miracle rabbi who can foretell the future. He has the rabbi brought to him, and asks: "Who will win the war?" The rabbi answers, "For that I have to flip a coin." He explains: "If the coin lands with the eagle side facing up, then the Soviet Union will win. If the other side faces up, England will win. If the coin stands on its side, then France wins. But should God perform a miracle and the coin remain hanging in the air, then Czechoslovakia will win."

What is the difference between a judge before and after the Nazi takeover?
Before, the judge thought: "He is a Jew, but he is innocent."
After, he thinks: "He is innocent, but he is a Jew."

"How goes it?" a Berliner asks his friend.
"As with a Jewish attorney, I can't complain."

An S.S. trooper sits on a bench reading the anti-Semitic newspaper *Der Stürmer*. A Jew sits down and the S.S. man reads aloud the paper's motto, "The Jews are our misfortune!"
"Hopefully," says the Jew.

Moses Abraham wrote a letter about conditions in his concentration camp:

185

"We get up at 8 o'clock. Breakfast is at 9—coffee, tea or cocoa, bread, butter, sausage or marmalade. Then a little exercise. Whoever wants to can do a little light work. Lunch is simple but plentiful—soup, meat, vegetables, and potatoes. Then two hours of rest and a little more light work. After a hearty dinner you can go to the theater or the movies. There's a well-stocked library as well."

The letter ended with one short postscript: "Josef Levy, who did not believe all of this, was shot trying to escape."

In school the children are supposed to write an essay about the Jews. Little Hans writes: "The Jews wanted to bleed Germany, but Hitler beat them to it."

A man is standing before a judge in Germany. "Are you a Jew?" the judge asks, "or previously convicted of some other crime?"

A Jew's house is being searched in Berlin. The Gestapo officers find a ledger and hope to discover black market dealings. But as they leaf through it, they find on the first page:

God keep Adolf Hitler!

On the second page:

God keep Hermann Goering!

On the third page:

God keep Dr. Goebbels!

The soldiers joyfully return the book and leave, convinced of the man's loyalty.

"God of mercy," the man says to his wife, "what luck that they didn't turn to the next page!"

He shows her the fourth page, on which is written:

God keep Ernst Rohm!
And added underneath:
Already kept on June 30, 1934.[100]

June 30, 1934, was the date on which Rohm, an early follower of Hitler, was killed on the Führer's orders.

6

The Flavor of Humor: Anti-Nazi, Pro-Victim

A new joke acts almost like an event of universal interest: it is passed from one person to another like the news of the latest victory.
　　　　　　　　　　　　　　　　　　　—Sigmund Freud

The monuments of wit survive the monuments of power.
　　　　　　　　　　　　　　　　　　　—Francis Bacon

In humor's multi-front attack on the Brown Terror, jokes were the most common weapon used by both Jews and Gentiles. Their sheer volume and variety allowed for the most nuance, the subtlest shades of meaning. The humor was cerebral, requiring some knowledge of the time or of the human condition. But they were not elitist—they were understood by everyone then, as they are today. Puns, plays on words, arcane allusions were rare. Few jokes dealt with sex or scatology. There was little talk of suicide, none of the "sick" exploitative humor that surfaces with regularity in America. Surprisingly, the jokes reflected virtually no yearning for physical revenge or punishment. Retribution was described as in the future, in God's hands.

It is in a sense a misnomer to call the humor of the persecuted *anti-Nazi*. True, Hitler's followers were depicted as brutish, simplistic, and opportunistic. And the Führer and his close advisors

191

were seen as vile, duplicitous, mendacious. But those characteriza-
tions are the medium of rebellion. The underlying message of the
jokes was decidedly *pro-victim*. Unlike the so-called Holocaust jokes
at the expense of the Jews and other Nazi victims—disseminated in
Nazi organs like Julius Streicher's *Der Stürmer,* shared by Nazi
sympathizers then and periodically experiencing a limited revival in
certain European circles—the humor of the oppressed was as not as
much a weapon of attack as an instrument of defense.

Political jokes enjoyed particular popularity among Jews.
Throughout Europe, Jews made and shared hundreds of jokes,
providing a virtual textbook on the Chosen People's fortunes and
misfortunes, on the ebbs and flows of the war, and on differences
among various groups of Jews. An overview of Jewish jokes provides
a vivid contrast to the humor that developed in the general
population under the Third Reich. The differences highlight
contrasting perspectives on World War II.

Jokes made by Gentiles—at least those tales with no discernible Jewish content or authorship—tended to focus on the conduct
of the war (who was winning?) and its immediate effect on the
populace (what consumer goods were in short supply?). Margarine
was euphemistically known as "Hitler butter" because of the fat
shortage in Germany. Such humor treated the Nazi leaders be-
nignly, if not sympathetically. Under the jokes' surface, an under-
current lingered that Germany, or the other subjugated and
complicit nations, were still the victims' lands, though the leaders
had strayed.

Much of the period's Jewish humor, on the other hand, dealt
with the causes of the war (racist Nazi ideology and legislation), its
effect on individuals (from anti-Semitic slurs to the gas chambers),
and the war's aftermath (Allied victory was a certainty). In the
words of a popular statement, "God forbid that the war lasts as long
as the Jews are capable of enduring." The venality of the Nazi

leadership was stressed in Jewish jokes, though the humor was not vicious.

Jews distanced themselves in their jokes from the society that produced the enveloping madness. Only German Jews continued to maintain their patriotic identification. "Despite all they went through in Germany, they still talk about *unsere Führer* [our leader Hitler] and still believe in German victory," Emmanuel Ringelblum wrote of the German Jews who were shipped to the Warsaw Ghetto. "They are certain, despite everything, that they will return to Germany."[1]

The indigenous brand of humor that developed in response to the Nazi persecution and genocide veered from the accustomed path of Jewish jokes. Absent were the stereotyped figures, the *schnorrer* [beggar], the *shadchan* [matchmaker], the *shlmiel* [klutz] and the *shlmazl* [fallguy], and the bookworm rabbi. In lieu of familiar characters, historical or fanciful, Jewish jokes from the Holocaust period featured any number of protagonists who represented the fate of all: an Abraham or a Rudenstein or simply "a Jew."

Victimized Jews, in their jokes, painted themselves as victors, but Jewish traits, particularly the tendency to avoid confrontations with the powers-that-be, were held, as always, up to ridicule. This classic example has surfaced in other settings:

> Two Jews are about to enter the gas chamber in Auschwitz. One of them turns to the S.S. guard to make a last request for a glass of water.
>
> "Shah, Moshe," says his friend. "Don't make trouble."

Jokes were made about every facet of life—and death—in the Nazi era. No target, including God Himself and His prophets, was out of bounds. Starvation, disease, beatings, murder, propaganda, and every form of persecution were grist for the victims' joke mill. A representative selection follows.

193

God

Horowitz comes to the Next World. He sees Jesus in Paradise. "Hey, what's a Jew doing without an armband?" "Let him be," answers Saint Peter. "He's the boss's son."

Hitler

Freudenheim was walking down the street in Nazi Germany in 1934, when suddenly a large black limousine pulled up beside him. Freudenheim looked up in astonishment and terror as Hitler himself climbed out of the car.

Holding a gun to Freudenheim, Hitler ordered him to get down on his hands and knees. And pointing to a pile of excrement on the curb, Hitler ordered the Jew to eat it.

Freudenheim, putting discretion before valor, complied. Hitler began laughing so hard that he dropped the gun. Freudenheim picked it up, and ordered Hitler to undergo the same humiliation. As Hitler got down on the sidewalk, Freudenheim ran from the scene as fast as he could.

Later that day, when Freudenheim returned home, his wife asked him, "How was your day?"

"Oh, fine dear," he answered. "By the way, you'll never guess who I had lunch with today."

A compact social commentary is conveyed here: Hitler's very act of degrading an ordinary citizen signifies the public's low opinion of the Führer's overall *modus operandi*; the final reversal of roles in the victim's retelling shows the certainty of Hitler's eventual defeat; and the very recasting of the event, with no mention of the antagonist by name, indicates the contempt in which the Reich was held.

Anti-Semitism

A German entered a streetcar and, because there were no other seats available, had no alternative but to sit beside a Jew.

"I can see by your nose that you are a filthy Jew," said the German. "Every thought in your head is concentrated on defiling blond Aryan girls."

The Jew ignored him, studiously fixing his gaze in another direction.

After a few minutes, the German broke the silence. "What time is it, Jew?"

The Jew did not answer.

"I asked you a question—what time is it?"

No reply.

"Listen, Jew, I'm asking you for the last time—what time is it? What's the matter with you, are you deaf?"

"No, I am not deaf," the Jew answered at last. "But if you can tell my sexual preferences by looking at my nose, you certainly should be able to tell the time by looking at the watch in my pocket."

Anti-Semitism, in Romania

A scene on the streetcar. A Jew stands up and offers his seat to an old man.

"I'm not going to take a seat that has been occupied by a kike," the old man announces fiercely.

Another Gentile, standing near the old man, asks him: "You don't want to sit down?"

"I certainly don't."

The second Gentile takes the seat offered by the Jew. After two minutes he gets up again.

"There, you can sit down now," he addresses the old man, "the seat has been Romanianized."[2]

195

Emigration

The purser of a British liner had to visit the cabin of a Jewish refugee. On the table was a photograph of Hitler.

"Hey," said the purser. "What are you, a refugee, doing with the Führer's portrait?"

"Oh," said the refugee. "It's to prevent homesickness."

German Justice

Two Nazi judges meet and exchange experiences.

"Do you know," says the first judge, "I had a difficult case today. I was forced to sentence a Nazi to eight years imprisonment only because he stole one thousand marks."

"And I had a much more difficult case than that," says the second judge. "I was forced to let a Jew go free today only because he was innocent."

A furious Hitler orders that the person responsible for the deluge of caustic wit be brought before him. A few weeks later the police arrest Kaufman, a Jewish comic.

"What's your name, Jew?" asks Hitler.

"Kaufman."

"And are you responsible for the joke about me and the pig?"[3]

"Yes," says Kaufman.

"What about the joke in which whenever I die will be a Jewish holiday?"

"Yes, that one's mine."

"What about the joke in which I'm saved from drowning and when I offer the Jew who saved me a reward, his request is simply that I don't tell anyone what he did?"

"Oh yes, that one is also mine."

"Jew, how dare you make these jokes? How dare a Jew be so impudent? Don't you know who I am—the leader of the Third Reich, which is destined to last a thousand years?"

"Now wait a minute," says Kaufman. "Don't blame me for that joke—I've never heard it before."

The lineage of a particular joke is of course difficult, if not impossible, to trace. At best, the time and place of origin can be estimated by a reference to a particular event, a battle or a well-known personality, or by the tone. There is, of course, the rare case—"Altmann and his secretary were sitting in a coffeehouse in Berlin in 1935,"[4] starts one joke—that easily lends itself to tracing. Most don't, but here are some that do:

Two German Jews, Schwartz and Levy, were sitting on the yellow painted bench for non-Aryans in the public park. Schwartz was reading the Zionist weekly *Jüdische Rundschau*, while Levy was perusing Julius Streicher's infamous *Der Stürmer*.

"How can a Jew read such vile stuff?" asked Schwartz.

"This journal brings me encouragement!"

"Encouragement!" exclaimed Schwartz. "How is that possible?"

"Let me explain," replied Levy. "When I read the *Rundschau*, I am told of pogroms in Poland, of discrimination at home and abroad, of terrorism in Palestine—and I am greatly depressed. On the other hand, when I read the *Stürmer*, I am told that Jews are international bankers, that they control the press, that they dominate business—and I feel greatly relieved."

This comes from Germany, evidently from the early years of the Reich, when Jews felt able to appear in public in relative safety.

Leo Praeger, aged Jew of Vienna, was reading a newspaper item describing an airplane disaster in which six passengers had been killed.

"These certainly are critical times," remarked Praeger. "The air is getting to be just as unsafe as the street."

This is probably from the late 1930s, after the Anschluss—Germany's March 1938 annexation of Austria—and the subsequent anti-Jewish Kristallnacht *riots in November of that year, and before the deportations to concentration camps began in the early 1940s.*

A German asks a Jew to lend him 300 marks. The Jew immediately takes out the sum of money from his pocket and hands it over to the German. The latter is astounded. "How come? You don't know me and yet you trust me for such a large sum of money?"

"I have the highest confidence in the German," answers the Jew. "You took Stalingrad and gave it back. You took Kharkov and gave it back. Therefore, I am sure you will also return the 20 rubles."

This is evidently a joke from the early 1940s, after the German Army's unsuccessful push into Russian territory.

Political jokes in Germany during the early days of the Third Reich had a tone that seems naive in the light of history. Humor painted the Nazis as brutish thugs, but gave little hint of the horrors they would wreak. "Die Bonzen," the Nazi bigshots and their quirks, became targets of popular wisecracks, as did the Nazi Party's anti-Jewish and anti-democratic policies. "The Germans represent a medical miracle," it was said. "They are able to walk around upright in spite of having a broken backbone."[5]

The ubiquitous acronyms of government organizations took on new meanings. BDM (*Bund Deutscher Mädchen*), the patriotic League of German Girls, was quickly turned into the *Bund Deutscher Matratzen* (League of German Mattresses) with the attendant lascivious allusions. The motto *Kraft durch Freude* (Strength through Joy), or KdF, was rendered *Kind durch Freund* (Child through a Friend).

Many jokes were made about Hitler's liking for astrology and about Goering's girth. It was reported that Goering was going to wear a cellophane uniform so the ration-conscious Germans "could see some meat again."

A round of jokes made the point that a large part of the population, including Germans in uniform, were hostile to the Nazi cause. The ranks of Nazi opponents were said to include the 8 million Social-Democrats and the 5 million Communist sympathizers who had cast ballots in Germany's last free elections.

> A Berlin worker applies for a job at a labor exchange, where preference is given to "veterans" of the Nazi movement. He is asked if he qualifies as an "old fighter." "All I can say," he replies, "is that I already carried the red flag before they put a swastika on it."

> "What do a storm trooper and an English beefsteak have in common?" "Both are brown outside and red inside."

> A man becomes tired of living and totally indifferent. He wants to challenge fate. He disrupts a large Nazi rally. Standing on the street, he raises his fist in the air and shouts "Heil Moscow!" as a column of SA soldiers march by.
> The leader of the column urgently whispers to the man: "Shut up, man. There's a Nazi in the last row."

Within months of Hitler's appointment as chancellor, his grandiose plan to revitalize the German economy spurred cynicism in the population, which continued to face shortages in basic foodstuffs. This gravestone inscription was proposed for Hitler:

> *Hier ruht Adolf der Befreier*
> *Von Milch, Butter, Käse und Eier.*

> Here rests Adolf the Liberator,
> Of milk, cheese, eggs and butter.

One story had the Führer shopping at a grocery store:

> "Do you have butter?"
> "No."
> "Do you have eggs?"
> "No."
> "Do you have coffee?"
> "No."
> "Then what do you have?"
> "We still have a lot of these cards that say: 'Germany feeds itself.' "

The financial hardships of the lower middle class in the Reich's early years brought the story of a murderer sentenced to death by hanging. "A swift death is too good for a criminal like that," Hitler admonishes Goering. "He ought to be made to starve to death slowly and agonizingly." Goering replies: "How about opening a small store for him?"

Corruption among Nazi officials inspired the tale of two party officials taking a stroll. One finds a 50 mark note in the gutter. "What will you do with it?" his friend asks. "Donate it to the Winter Relief Fund." "Why do it the long way round?" the friend asks. Bureaucratic incompetence brought a round of cynical definitions—the appointment of a qualified applicant in place of an unsuitable party worker was "sabotage," and the occupant of a lucrative post coveted by a Nazi was a "reactionary."[6]

The introduction of the Nazi race laws in 1935, barring Jews, gypsies, and other non-Aryan aliens from German citizenship, brought a flood of jokes about the search for "Aryan grannies"— proof of one's pure genealogy. In a revision of Little Red Riding Hood, the fairy tale's heroine meets the big bad wolf in the forest. "Where are you going?" asks the wolf. "I'm looking for my grandmother," answers Little Red Riding Hood. Sighs the wolf, "Aren't we all?"

Jokes about German Jews trying retroactively to "baptize" their grandparents in a frenzied grasp for Aryan status were common; some Jews actually went so far as to claim that their parents weren't really their parents. One wartime resident of Berlin remembers, "Never before have there been so many marital infidelities, and so many daughters and sons ready under oath to assert their mothers' vagaries."[7]

As the war dragged on, bringing losses on the battlefield and shortages at home, the results of Nazi rule became the topics of jokes.

> A man wants to commit suicide. He buys a rope with which to hang himself, but the quality is so poor that it breaks. He tries to drown himself in the river, but the wood fibers in his ersatz clothing keep him afloat. He gives up trying to take his life and starves to death after four weeks on normal rations.

> "Are we going to lose the war?" one German asks another. "Yes," says his friend, "but when?"

> Hitler, not being a religious man, was inclined to consult his astrologers about the future. As the tide of war worsened, he asked, "Am I going to lose the war?"
>
> Answered affirmatively, he then asked, "Well, am I going to die?" Consulting their charts, the astrologers again said yes.
>
> "When am I going to die?" was Hitler's next question. This time the answer was, "You're going to die on a Jewish holiday."

201

"But when . . . on what holiday?" he asked in agitation.

The reply: "Any day you die will be a Jewish holiday."

It is not surprising that redemption—spiritual, economic, or military—found its way into wartime humor. This messianic tone—*when* the war is over, *when* the Nazis lose, *when* the Jews and other victims come out on top—characterizes much humor from the time. Throughout the period, Jews and Christians searched biblical verses, numerology, mysticism, and other obscure sources for signs of their messiah's imminent arrival. "Such is the imagination of a despised people which has nothing left but imagination," observed Chaim Kaplan in his Warsaw Ghetto diary. "The downtrodden masses are waiting for a miracle; the ground is ripe for Messianism. Every stupidity finds a listening ear. Healthy common sense is gone."[8]

Though few jokes then actually incorporated a messianic figure—Jesus, the prophet Elijah or the long-awaited Jewish redeemer—in a wartime setting, many centered around such religious themes as eternal reward and punishment. Where religion and humor met in jest, humor triumphed; a theological bent was only the vehicle for a sardonic message. But this grouping of jokes bore an implicit theme: final judgment.

A Jew comes to Hell. He wants to learn a little about his new surroundings, and he looks around. In the corner stands a writing table, cool and comfortable. There sits Hitler, working.

The Jew opens his eyes in wonder and asks in horror:

"This is supposed to be Hell?"

"Take it easy," another Jew reassures him. "He has to translate *Mein Kampf* into Hebrew."

Hitler dies and goes to Heaven. He behaves so well there that Saint Peter tells him he can go back to earth again as a treat, for a week. After 24 hours, he's back, hammering at the pearly gates to get in.

"What's the matter, Adolf?" asks Saint Peter. "You've got six more days."

"Let me in, let me in!" cries Hitler. So Saint Peter unlocks the gate, lets him in and sits him down.

"Now, Adolf," he says, "what's the matter? Didn't you enjoy it?"

"Enjoy it?" says Hitler, "Enjoy it? Everyone's gone mad down there since I left. I come back and what do I find? The Jews are fighting and the Germans are making money."

The fact that jokes from Nazi Europe depicted Jews in Hell— and more incomprehensibly, Nazis in Heaven—demonstrates only that humor is not necessarily bound by politics or logic.

Hitler, Goering and Goebbels die and knock on Heaven's gate. "Before I can accept you, I have to examine your life's behavior," declares Saint Peter, turning to Goering: "How often did you lie?"

"Five times," Goering answers hesitantly.

"For your punishment, run once around the Milky Way," Saint Peter determines, and turns to Hitler. "How often did you lie?"

"Fifty times," Hitler answers in an unexpected moment of truthfulness.

"For your punishment, run ten times around the Milky Way." While Goering and Hitler set out to begin their conviction laps, Saint Peter asks, "Wasn't there also a small fellow with you?"

"He's gone back to get a motorcycle," the pair answer.

A mild joke. Many, though, were equally benign. Does such a tale, which mocks Goebbels' diminutive physical stature and enormous capacity for prevarication, diminish his evil? Did any humor about Hitler's inferno mask the horror? Or was humor merely a filter that screened the awful truth from teller and listener?

203

Humor's facility at administering reality in tolerable doses was evident in two other common categories of wit from World War II—accommodation jokes and questioning jokes. Only the one grouping, bitter humor, which was expressed in a relatively small number of jokes, presented the oblique, unvarnished truth.

Accommodation jokes bespeak a grudging acceptance of the world's collapse, while achieving some small measure—if only verbal—of victory nonetheless. Just as messianic humor focuses on the victims' *post*-Holocaust triumphs, accommodation jokes reflect the certainty that good will defeat evil in *this* world.

> A Jewish peddler of seafood is shouting his wares from a stall in Berlin. "Fish for sale! Fresh fish! Nice fat fish—as fat as Goering!"
>
> A Gestapo officer hears the raucous chant and drags the peddler off to the People's Court, where the judge sentences him to a year in a concentration camp.
>
> After serving his term, the Jew returns to his business, and again loudly announces his merchandise in the same sing-song voice: "Fish for sale! Fresh fish! Nice fat fish as fat as . . ."
>
> "As fat as what?" snarls the voice of the same Gestapo officer who has sneaked up behind him.
>
> ". . . as fat as last year," finishes the peddler.

A quick-thinking merchant could save his neck and his honor; the earlier allusion to Goering's girth remains intact.

> During the Second World War, after three months of waiting in Casablanca, Lowenthal had almost given up hope of getting a visa for America. The American consulate was constantly filled with refugees, and it was virtually impossible even to get an interview with an American official. Finally, Lowenthal was able to make an appointment.
>
> "What are my chances of entering your country?" he asked.
>
> "Not very good," said the official. "Your country's quota is completely filled. I suggest you come back in ten years."

"Fine," replied Lowenthal impassively. "Morning or afternoon?"

This joke is a crossover; technically a questioning joke, its punch line is a query, capturing the best spirit of accommodation humor. The world is cold, but it will get warmer. Only a confident—or naive, considering the eventual fate of European Jewry—man could assume he would be alive a decade hence to apply again for a visa. For sure, he thinks, the Nazis will not be victorious. This joke, incidentally, is uniquely German, showing the teutonic penchant for precision. Only a *Yeke*, a punctilious German Jew, would inquire about the time for an appointment ten years away, taking at face value the response the official undoubtedly meant as a categorical brushoff.

Questioning humor. This form is especially common among Jews, who tend to answer one question with another—usually rhetorical—question.

Why?

Why not?

Jewish jokes are especially likely to end in questions—sarcastic questions. Which is how Jews think. As soon as the ancient Israelites became a nation, trapped by the advancing Egyptian army against the shores of the Red Sea, they confronted their leader Moses: "Weren't there enough graves in Egypt?"[9] This Jewish partiality for making statements or answering a question with another question has several explanations. Among them is the give and take of Talmudic argumentation. In the Aramaic text, which has no punctuation, an assertion is not immediately discernible from a query. Even among members of the community with tenuous ties to the legalistic debates over points of the oral law, the trade in questions in place of definitive answers is familiar. Like the apocryphal Wandering Jew consigned to eternal travel, a people unsure of their place in a society fear planting psychic roots. A

205

question may be an evasive answer, but it is less vulnerable to refutation or attack.

In the time of the Nazi barbarism, when life was precarious and the future ambiguous—why is this happening? Can we stop it? What does tomorrow hold?—this propensity for questioning was often expressed through jest. These jokes' unspoken theme: for some questions, there may be no answers.

During the onset of Nazi terror, an elderly Jew was walking down the street in Berlin when he was stopped by two storm troopers.

"Halt, Jew!" they cried, and proceeded to interrogate him.

"Who is responsible for all of Germany's troubles?" they demanded.

The Jew looked at them and said, "Why, the bicycle riders and the Jews."

"Bicycle riders?" they snorted. "What foolishness. Why the bicycle riders?"

"Why the Jews?" replied the old man.

For a generation whose faith was shaken, for whom there were no absolutes—where was God, where was man?—the most sensible answer was often a question.

Shortly after Austria's annexation by Nazi Germany in 1938, a Jew goes to a travel agent in Vienna. He inquires about emigration.

The clerk brings up the names of several countries, which are promptly discounted. One land requires an exorbitant amount of money for entry, another needs a labor permit, an Austrian passport is not recognized in yet another, still another does not admit any immigrants, and so on.

While the two men are reviewing their options, they twirl the globe near the desk. Finally, the Jew asks, "Haven't you got another globe?"

This is possibly the ultimate nihilistic joke. The desperate Jew denies the reality of his own experience—he is unwelcome everywhere, there *is* no other globe—but refuses to concede that there is no way out.

A widely heralded circus is scheduled to appear in Berlin during the Third Reich. The featured attraction which everyone awaits with keen interest is to be a wrestling contest between a man dressed in a lion's skin and a wild, man-eating tiger.

But the man who is to do battle with the tiger becomes ill and so the promoters, unwilling to lose their main attraction, advertise for a substitute. For three days they advertise, with not a single applicant for the job, but on the fourth day they are more successful: A sad-faced little man, wearing the yellow Star of David on his arm, applies for work.

"We hadn't thought of giving employment to a Jew," the promoters say.

"But what else is there for a man of my religion?" the applicant replies bitterly. "All other employment is closed to me."

"You realize you may be killed," the circus entrepreneurs tell him. "Even though you are only a Jew, you should know that the tiger is dangerous."

"My wife and children haven't eaten in three days," the Jew says wearily. "I have no alternative."

So, on opening day, before a capacity crowd, the Jew dons the lion's skin and, his teeth chattering, he enters the tiger's cage.

"I have only one chance for survival," he says to himself. "If I can only frighten the tiger, or at least make him a little cautious, I might leave this cage alive."

Desperately, he drops to his hands and knees, and, crawling on all fours, he roars like the king of beasts he is supposed to be. The tiger crouches, as though to leap, his cruel green eyes blazing.

"I'm going to die," the poor man thinks. "This is the end." And in his last moment of anguish he cries out the Jewish creed that is recited when death is imminent.

207

"*Shema Yisroel*! Hear O Israel . . ."

"*Ad-onay Elo-kenu, ad-onay echad*, The Lord our God, the Lord is One," recites the tiger fervently, completing the phrase.

"Wh-wh-why, you're not a real tiger at all," gasps the pseudo-lion. "You nearly scared me to death."

"*Landsman*,"[10] the tiger admonishes irritably, "what makes you think you are the only Jew in Germany who's working?"[11]

Does the ersatz tiger symbolize the false strength of the Nazi state? Is the Jew in the tiger skin co-opted, a fraud bought by a paycheck? Is such a tale complete if it raises more questions than it answers? One more example is set much later:

A Jew survives the gas chambers, having lost every one of his relatives.

The resettlement officer asks him where he would like to go.

"Australia," he replies.

"But that's so far," says the officer.

"From where?" asks the Jew.

This might be the same Jew who requested another globe. The attitude surely is the same—the world known to the European Jew has been reoriented, if not rejected outright. The resettlement official, well-meaning representative of Gentile society though he was, had not learned that Europe was no longer the epicenter of the world—certainly not of a survivor's world.

Finally, bitter humor, a distinct minority in the war. There is cynicism in the jokes, for sure, but little bitterness or condemnation. Only persons with a healthy sense of ironic detachment could refer to Nazi soldiers as "men of valor,"[12] the custom in the Warsaw Ghetto: "At the beginning of the ghetto period, *men of valor* tore down the *mezuzoths* [small containers with scriptural excerpts] from the doorposts of Jewish apartments and shops."[13] The handful of jokes that convey despair, resignation, and hostility are from the later years of the war, when Europe's bloodletting seemed not to have an end, and the fate of the continent's Jews was becoming known.

> Meeting the worried and abstracted Goldstein, Kohn tells him that Davidsohn has died. Goldstein shrugs his shoulders. "Well, if he has a chance to better himself . . ."

Most examples in this category are short, a quip or rapid-fire question and answer, such as the verse in the Vilna Ghetto: "Let's be joyous and tell our jokes, we'll hold a wake when Hitler chokes." It may simply be that despondent people did not make the effort to construct or tell a fuller joke. Or those who employed humor in the worst times may simply have lacked the means to preserve their comments.

In this group of jokes is a tale, found in the archives of the Warsaw Ghetto, but repeated at other dark times with other protagonists:

> A police officer comes into a Jewish home and wants to confiscate the possessions. The woman cries, pleading that she is a widow and has a child to support. The officer agrees not to take the things, on one condition—that she guess which of his eyes is the artificial one.
>
> "The left one," the woman guesses.
>
> "How did you know?"
>
> "Because that one has the human look."

> Two Jews in Berlin discuss their plight.
>
> "Terrible," says one. "Persecutions, discrimination, no food, quotas . . . now Hitler. Sometimes I think we would have been better off if we had never been born."
>
> "Sure," answers his friend. "But who has such luck? Maybe one in twenty thousand."

As was the case with general anti-Nazi humor, Jewish humor turned darker as the setting moved east and the war grew longer. This example, set in Germany early in the Nazi reign, had an almost whimsical spirit:

It was the first year that the Stein family had been living in Germany, and the father wanted his little boy to shine at his studies. Mr. Stein asked for Max's report card.

Reluctantly, Max showed it. Mr. Stein was angry, and scolded the boy for his poor grades.

"Well, Papa," said Max. "The other boys in my class are Nazis. They know I'm Jewish, and they bother me so I can't study. That's why I got such a bad report card."

Mr. Stein relented. "All right, my son," he said. "Anything for your future. I'm converting you into a Nazi; then you won't have any more trouble."

So Max had no more trouble in his class. But at the end of the next term, he came home with another terrible report. Mr. Stein was furious. "What's your excuse now?" he yelled.

"Well," Max said. "You know, Papa, we Nazis don't learn as fast as those Jewish boys."

Another joke, same time, same place, drew on the memory of Helmuth von Moltke, the respected nineteenth-century field marshal who reorganized the Prussian Army:

An old Jew stops at the statue of General Moltke, where a young Prussian officer is already standing. The old Jews ask the Prussian—with a strong Yiddish accent:

"Excuse me, Lieutenant, is this General Moltke?"

The officer replies, imitating the man's ugly accent.

"Yes . . . this is General Moltke."

The old Jew asks him, reproachfully:

"Why do you imitate *me?* Imitate *him.*"

During the Norwegian campaign in 1940, ghetto Jews boasted:

> Hitler has captured another piece of territory—the bottom of the sea.

In 1940, Jews in Warsaw were still confident of the Nazi defeat:

> Thousands of hammers from America have arrived. Their purpose: to drive dreams of London [winning the war soon] out of peoples' heads. [14]

In Eastern Europe, where Jews had lived apart from their countrymen in *shtetls* for centuries, where they had grown accustomed to the ever-present threat of pogrom, jokes had a harsher tone.

> A Jew laughs, then yells in his sleep. His wife wakes him up. He's mad at her. "I was dreaming someone had scribbled on a wall: 'Beat the Jews! Down with ritual slaughter.'"
> "So what were you so happy about?"
> "Don't you understand? That means the good old days have come back! [Our] Poles are running things again."

Only under the Nazis would the Jews long for the "good old days" of the Cossack pogroms.

A story recorded by Shimon Huberband, Emmanuel Ringelblum's assistant in the Warsaw Ghetto archives, described the inadequate sanitary conditions:

> No garbage was permitted to be taken out of the ghetto. A Jewish ghetto administrator appeared before his German commissioner to request permission to remove the garbage accumulating in

211

his home. When the Jew came into the commissioner's office and did not raise his arm in the Hitler salute, the commissioner became furious and threw him out of the room.

A few days later, the Jewish administrator appeared a second time in the commissioner's office. The commissioner was certain that this time the Jew would salute him by raising his arm. And indeed, the Jew entered the room, raising his arm. So the commissioner addressed the Jew, "This time, *Jude,* you acted correctly by raising your arm in the Hitler salute."

"No, Mr. Commissioner," the Jew answered. "I just wanted to show you how high the garbage has gotten."[15]

The Judenrat councils and the Nazi-appointed Jewish civil servants were lampooned by residents of many ghettoes. "Why do you think I've lost my drive?" one Jew asks another in Lodz. Answers his friend: "In the ghetto, if you don't have pull, you don't have drive."[16] "The jokesters have made up a new prayer," Chaim Kaplan recorded in his Warsaw diary. "Let us fall into the hands of Gentile agents, only let us not fall into the hands of a Jewish agent."[17]

The Führer asks Hans Frank, governor-general of Poland, "What evils and misfortunes have you brought upon the Jews of Poland?"

"I took away their livelihood; I robbed them of their rights; I established labor camps and we are making them work at hard labor there; I have stolen all their wealth and property."

But the Führer is not satisfied with all these acts.

So Frank adds: "Besides that, I have established Judenraten and Jewish Self-Aid Societies."

The Führer is satisfied and smiles at Frank. "You hit the target with the Judenraten, and Self-Aid will ruin them. They will disappear from the earth."[18]

7

Outside the Walls,
after the War

By making our enemy small, inferior, despicable or comic, we achieve in a roundabout way the enjoyment of overcoming him—to which the third person, who has made no efforts, bears witness by his laughter.
                                                               —Sigmund Freud

As to Hitler being funny, I can only say that if we can't sometimes laugh at Hitler then we are further gone than we think.
                                                               —Charles Chaplin

Nazi Germany, personified by its mustachioed Führer and his goosestepping followers, became a target of jocular derision even before Adolf Hitler became Reich Chancellor in 1933. A decade earlier, despite the failure of Hitler's beer hall *putsch* in Munich, the nascent National Socialist movement conducted a campaign to establish a niche among Bavaria's serious political forces. Its first efforts, however, were met with sarcasm. Political cartoonists, reflecting the public mood, found the Nazis' deportment and rhetoric a "broad and clearly visible target."[1] Nazi threats ensued. Indeed, writes Zbynek Zeman in *Heckling Hitler: Caricatures of the Third Reich,* art and esthetics, rather than politics, were at the center of some of the earliest clashes between Hitler and his opponents. "It was Hitler's misfortune that he and his movement

215

originated in Munich, the capital of Bavaria—but the art of caricature benefited from that chance connection."[2] In 1932, during Hitler's unsuccessful bid for the Reich presidency, a cartoon by Thomas Theodor Heine in the satirical magazine *Simplicissimus* showed the Nazi leader trying on an ill-fitting suit. The salesman advises Hitler, who earlier in his life had failed to land a police inspector's job: "Don't worry about that, Adolf. Being ridiculous is not fatal in Germany. If you could not become a police inspector you can always try to be the Reich President."[3] Heine went into exile, first to Prague, then Sweden, after the one-time postcard artist took power in Germany.

After 1933, as more of Europe's sharpest wits were likewise driven into exile, lampooning of the Nazi movement intensified in many corners of the world. Cabaret comics, native editorial cartoonists, American filmmakers and Allied propagandists found the Nazis an easy target. Derisive caricatures of Hitler appeared in newspapers and magazines throughout the world. A slew of jokes about Hitler and other top Nazis made the rounds of Allied lands, stoking the fire of populations at war with the Reich. The winning entry in a G.I. magazine contest that solicited postwar punishments for Hitler was this proposal from a Jewish soldier stationed in Italy: "He should live with my in-laws in the Bronx."[4] Books of anti-Nazi jokes were published in several Western countries. British dramatist George Bernard Shaw was credited with this *bon mot*: "There are three factors today in Germany—German intelligence, German honor and National Socialism. The three factors are to each other as follows: If a German is a National Socialist and honest, then he is not intelligent. But if a German is intelligent and a National Socialist, then he is not honest. And if a German is honest and intelligent, then he is not a Nazi."[5] Especially popular, abroad and in some German circles, was the quip "There are two kinds of Aryans—non-Aryans and barb-Aryans."[6] Like-minded individuals, ranging from a farmer in upper New York State to a couple in a southern French village and Communists in Russia, saluted the Führer by bestowing his name on their pet dogs. In displaced persons camps after liberation, refugee Jews used humor as a means of adjusting to their new free-but-shattered lives.

In the decades after World War II, movies, plays, and novels continued to throw a satirical light on the most grotesque facets of German rule. As the Holocaust became an accepted area of academic study a generation after the war's end, European scholars documented examples of humor in localized settings under occupation. A book of political humor from wartime Germany was divided according to these historical periods: "The first 500 years" [1933–1939] and "The second 500 years" [1940–1945].[7]

From its earliest days in Weimar Germany, ridicule of the Nazi movement increased with the movement's own growth. Confined in its formative years to politically conservative Bavaria, it drew satiric attention mainly among the region's cartoonists, whose works in the still-dominant newspapers and magazines played an important role in shaping public opinion. As the Nazis' popular and electoral success spread to other parts of Germany during the 1920s—and outside Germany after 1933—so did cartoonists' attacks. Hitler's increasing abuses of power brought correspondingly blunt attacks from cartoonists abroad. "The subtleties of the earlier portraits"[8] gave way to frontal attacks on the Nazi carnage. The overseas artists, both refugees and native cartoonists, drew strength from their geographic separation from Nazi retribution. *d'Orient,* a Dutch-language magazine published in Indonesia, carried a cartoon in 1936 that pictured a street scene in Germany: babies and daschunds sporting ersatz Hitler moustaches, swastikas on women's dresses and men's ties.[9] *"Oyfgang"* [Ascent], a literary journal produced by German refugees in Havana, featured an impaled Hitler above a field of skulls, with the accompanying label, "Made in Germany," on one 1934 cover.[10]

One of the clearest voices raised against the growing Nazi

strength belonged to John Heartfield, a Berlin-born artist, publisher, and set designer with Communist sympathies. A pacifist, he changed his name from his given Helmut Herzfelde during World War I as a protest against German nationalism. Heartfield was a pioneer in use of photomontage, a collage of photographs with editorial titles. During the 1920s he produced hundreds of montages that satirized German society. The Nazis, and their supporters, were frequent targets. "Millions stand behind me—the meaning of the Hitler Greeting," depicts a saluting Hitler, open palm raised over his head, accepting a handful of marks from a capitalist backer. In "His Majesty Adolf." Hitler is pictured in a medal-bedecked nineteenth-century military uniform adorned with a swastika armband and streamers incongruously flying from his helmet. Under the photograph is Hitler's boast, *"Ich fuhre Euch herrlichen Pleiten entgegen"* [I lead you toward magnificent disasters]. The words are a play on Kaiser Wilhelm's statement, "I lead you toward a magnificent era."[11]

Heartfield designed the last election poster for the Communist Party in March 1933. His apartment was raided by storm troopers, and much of his work was destroyed. His works appeared in two Nazi-sponsored exhibitions in Mannheim that year entitled "Horror Chamber of Art" and "Cultural Bolshevism." In 1933 Heartfield fled to Prague, which became the first port of safety for German political refugees. In the first five years of the Reich, Prague became the home of some 10,000 "registered" German refugees, including writers, actors, composers, and set designers. Czechoslovakia boasted a democratic government, a tolerance for dissident voices, and a circle of German cultural and educational institutions.

Heartfield continued his work on the newspaper *AIZ* (Arbeiter-Illustrierte-Zeitung). His *AIZ* collages mocked Nazi economic policies, propaganda, and militarism. During the next few years, his creations were exhibted in Prague, Paris, London, and New York. In 1936, a room at an international photography exhibition in the Czech capital was devoted to Heartfield's work. A German minister protested; some of the artist's work was confiscated by the police. Two years later Germany sought to extradite Heartfield. Czechoslovakia declined, and Heartfield escaped to London. After the German occupation of Czechoslovakia in 1939, five boxes of Heartfield's work were thrown into the Vitava River. In London, Heartfield was interned as an enemy alien, and released because of a serious illness and intervention by the House of Commons. After his release, he worked as a freelance designer for several publishers before returning to East Germany after the war, where he died in 1968.

The shapers of Germany's political cabarets suffered a similar dispersion after the Nazis took power. Threatened with censorship and imprisonment, the leading *conferenciers* and actors scattered around the globe. Some ended their days in concentration camps. "The cabaretists could be killed, but not the cabaret,"[12] wrote Reinhard Hippen in "Satire against Hitler: Cabaret in Exile." The transplanted cabaret "lived on in more than 20 lands of asylum. First in Prague, Budapest, Amsterdam, Paris, Sweden, Denmark, Norway, and Switzerland, later London, New York, Shanghai, Mexico City, Sydney, Caracas, and Palestine. Most of the cabarets, regardless of their new site, performed in German, boosting morale of the immigrants, continuing the battle against fascism and, through word of mouth, exposing the local population to the true horrors of Nazism. The cabarets, with their small overheads and exclusive audiences, often operated with a freer hand than the established local theaters that were subjected to budget cutbacks and government pressure."[13]

Der Liebe Augustin [Dear Augustin], a cabaret founded in Vienna in 1931, offered critiques of Austria's "political and cultural relationship to Germany [and] its burgeoning right wing." Similar clubs opened in subsequent years, including Die Stachelbeere" [Gooseberry] and "Literatur am Naschmarkt" [Literature at the

219

Nibbler's Market], which prophetically was playing its final program, "The Viennese Goes Under," when Germany annexed Austria in 1938.[14]

Frederick Brainin, a Viennese-born patent translator who left Austria in 1938 and served in the U.S. Army during World War II, wrote satirical poems about aspects of life in Europe. One work, published in a small American literary journal, was the "Ballad of Leo Slezak," which was based on a true story:

Sachs, a cobbler in Nazi-Vienna,
his arias chased his wife's blues . . .
But Leo Slezak, famed tenor,
was never in his shoes.

Jan Sachs, cobbler, in Nazi-Vienna,
made a stitch between lines in the news
when Wagner satire's penner
had Sachs work on Goebbels' clubbed shoes.

Jan Sachs was arrested in Vienna
by jackboots with other Jews—
like Rothschild, *Herr Doktor* Renner!—
who were now in his shoes.

They made him lie down in the gutter;
he listened to steps of the goose,
its man's skin made drum, *schmeisser's** stutter,
dead toenails grow long in their shoes.

He covered a grating for hours
(deaf to the autopsy of boos!)

---

*Brand of pistol used by the S.S.

Ice-cold in the sun, burned by showers
his soul hid in his shoes.

Shipped east (a reluctant survivor!)
he couldn't well refuse
his Treblinka-*Lager* slave driver
to save him for his shoes.

His genitals were frozen
(his barren wife's grief seemed obtuse!)
He *kapo*-clerked: one of God's chosen
accountants who filed mounds of shoes.

A marsh in Eastern Poland
with dawn's red sky did fuse:
He jumped into its hole and
escaped without his shoes.

At labor camps in Siberia
(where time's stitch heartbreaks glues!)
PWs from Styria
let him repair their shoes.

    L'envoi
Jan Sachs, he's back in free Vienna,
repatriated by Zeus:
His odyssey calls for a tenor . . .
but who can fill Slezak's shoes?[15]

Kurt Egon Wolff's Ping Pong cabaret, established in Berlin in
1930, moved to Amsterdam in 1933. Its takeoff on Hamlet
featured the protagonist and Ophelia, bound for Monte Carlo for
their honeymoon, proclaiming:

Sein oder Nichtsein—sage mir
Prinz Hamlet, wer ist heutzutage

221

Jud oder Nichthjud', das ist hier
Die sogenannte Rassenfrage.[16]

To be or not to be, tell me
Prince Hamlet, who is nowadays
Jew or not a Jew, that is here
The so-called question of race.

Erika Mann, politically conscious actress and publicist, daughter of Thomas and Katja Mann, object of Nazi hatred for a 1931 speech before the International Women's League for Peace and Freedom, was co-founder of the Peppermill, a cabaret in Munich. The club's "bitter, passionate protest against the brown shame"[17] moved to Zurich when Mann left Germany in 1933. The troup also performed its revues in Czechoslovakia, Holland, Belgium, and Luxembourg, giving a total of 1,034 performances.[18] In its Swiss setting—part nightclub, part beerhall—the Peppermill took steady but camouflaged shots at the German government, despite Switzerland's tenuous neutrality, which did not countenance direct attacks on its powerful neighbor. Germany's ambassador in Bern protested the performances; Nazi sympathizers in Switzerland tried to disrupt the shows by planting stink bombs and creating bomb scares. Mann kept improvising one night while police searched the premises for a bomb. Nazi supporters shouted "Out with the Jews" and "We don't need any Jews in Switzerland" during performances. The Peppermill performances continued, for a time, under police protection. Finally, Swiss authorities withdrew the cabaret's permit. Though the Peppermill ended, it planted the seeds for the Cornichon, a cabaret run by Swiss citizens and exempt from the regulations banning foreigners from appearing in political productions. The Cornichon lasted through the war.

Pianist Victor Borge, while touring with a revue in Sweden under his original name of Borge Rosenbaum in the mid-1930s, would openly taunt the Nazis. "What's the difference between a Nazi and a dog? . . . A Nazi will lift his arm."[19] Borge ended up on the Nazis' wanted list—No. 1, he brags. He was attacked on the street, had to hire a bodyguard, and finally had to flee for his life.

Besides making references to the situation in their homelands, the exile cabarets dealt with the problems of employment and acculturation in the immigrants' adopted lands. A sketch in New York in 1940 by two refugees, Karl Farkas and Armin Berg, spoofed one colleague's success:

> Farkas: Armin, how long have you been in America?
>
> Berg: For three years.
>
> Farkas: Well, and how are the poor immigrants managing?
>
> Berg: Wonderful, no problems at all. I even know one man who has become a millionaire here in America now. He was a poor beggar in Vienna, who came over here on the same ship as me.
>
> Farkas: Magnificent. How did he do it?
>
> Berg: In the first year he was a shoeshine boy, in the second a dishwasher, in the third a newsvendor . . .
>
> Farkas: Well, and? . . .
>
> Berg: . . . and then his aunt in Switzerland died and left him two million marks.[20]

Immigrant writers Egon Larsen and Frederick Gotfurt organized a theater collective under the name of Four and Twenty Black Sheep in London in 1939. Sketches by members of the collective were mixed with poetry by Bertolt Brecht. A revision of the fairytale "The Emperor's New Clothes" featured Hitler and Mussolini as central characters. But, working at a deficit, the troupe eventually had to disband. Many of its members joined the Little Theatre, a group subsidized by the Free German League of Culture. The league was based in a villa in London's Artists' Quarter bought from the Church of England. One song, performed in French,

German, and English—so-called Emigranto—by young actress
Agnes Bernell, portrayed the plight of refugees:

This region is familiar to me.
So are Montmartre's cabarets to me.
When one's rich, Paris is just grand.
As a refugee, it's not worth a damn.

In Cuba they wouldn't let us land.
Spain felt like home, or just about.
When the mine exploded in the sand,
A handsome sailor fished me out.

I know the world. It leaves me cold.
I'm now all of twenty years old.

As a child, travel was my dream.
On windy seas, I longed to roam.
Now there's one spot of which I dream,
One city, and that's called home.

I wish I could see it once again.
Hear how German sounds from where I stem,
Understand when I'm being addressed . . .
But that's all over now, I guess.

I know the world. It is so cold.
I'm now all of twenty years old.[21]

Another popular production of the group was "Mr. Gulliver
Goes to School," which brought Swift's peripatetic character to
contemporary Europe. Produced in German with explanations in
English, the musical was performed before audiences in Leicester
and Guildford as well.

In 1944 the group performed "My Goodness, My Alibi," a harbinger of the Nuremberg trials, which featured Sherlock Holmes producing evidence against a variety of "enemies of the people."[22]

The Lantern, an exile cabaret in London created by Austrian refugees, put on topical satirical sketches: "From Adam to Adolf" and "No Orchids for Mr. Hitler." The refugees produced plays such as "The Good Soldier Schweik," as well as a version of Wagner's *Rheingold* that depicted conditions in Germany and refugee problems abroad. Veteran actor Martin Miller performed in "The Führer Speaks," a Hitler parody which "reproduced minutely all the peculiarities of Hitler's diction and gesture."[23] On April 1, 1940—April Fool's Day—Miller's version was carried on the BBC, Hitler promising "to show his love for America by proclaiming a protectorate over it and making it a blossoming garden."[24]

Said Miller's dictator:

> Party members, men and women of the German Reich Convention, when in 1492 the Spaniard Columbus undertook his now well-known journey over the distant ocean, using German-made instruments and the results of German science, there could have been no doubt that with the success of this daring enterprise, Germany had to have some part in the achievement which this voyage of discovery was to result in . . .
>
> Ever since 1492 I have remained silent and left this problem untouched in the interests of peace. But now my patience is at an end.

The speech went on to recount Hitler's "heroic and self-sacrificing" rise to power and his recent "protective" policies. Finally:

> I hereby firmly declare that I have now made my last territorial demands in Europe, but beyond that I now have to state certain claims of a maritime nature . . . There are in America national

minorities closely connected by race and tradition with the German Reich. In Chicago alone, there are 324,000 Czechs, and they keep asking themselves, "Why can't we come under the Protectorate?" In the well-known city of New York, there are 476,000 Poles . . . They have a right to be protected by Germany and I shall enforce that right. . . . [25]

The address was interspersed with the relevant "bravos," "heils," and "pfuis." According to some reports, listeners in Britain, and CBS officials in the United States, were fooled.

Humor over the Allied airwaves, aimed at both the domestic listeners and captive populations, played an important role for Britain and the United States. The humor meant for German ears was fashioned to fit popular German tastes and relied heavily for its credibility on intelligence reports. The humor exploited the Germans' own despair. One Erich Weinert read satirical poems over Radio Moscow. Radio Luxembourg, under the auspices of the Allied supreme military command, broadcast a German-language program, "Corporal Tom Jones." It was made up of the comments of a typical American soldier who ended each program with an anti-Nazi joke. During the last year of the war, a *Soldatensenger* (soldiers' broadcasting station}, purportedly run by disaffected German soldiers somewhere in northern France, operated as a joint effort of the U.S. Office of Strategic Services and the British Political Intelligence Department. It featured supposedly captured mail sent to and from German soldiers.

Some of the BBC's most effective German-language programs were written by immigrants who had cabaret backgrounds. The BBC's satirical broadcasts to Germany, often productions lasting only a few minutes, were designed to portray the real conditions in Germany, expose the lies of Nazi propaganda, and weaken the morale of the German soldiers. One writer was Robert Lucas (real name Ehrenzweig), a native of Vienna, a pharmacist by training, and a veteran of Vienna's Jewish Political Cabaret. He came to England in 1934, found work as a newspaper reporter, was called to the BBC as a translator, and worked up to chief scriptwriter. He considered the ability to laugh at Hitler's regime, "in the middle of the hellish noise and hysterical shrieks of the Nazi propaganda . . . a liberating experience."[26]

Lucas created *Hirnschal Briefe,* letters from a front-line private in the German Army to his wife at home. The program placed critical observations about the war effort and the occupied populations into the mouth of a true believer. By 1942, letters arriving in London via neutral Switzerland and Sweden indicated that Hirnschal's letters had earned an eager following among German listeners. Wrote one listener: "According to my experience, broadcasts containing a touch of humor are important, for on account of their humor they are listened to by people less interested in politics, whereas the political part of the listeners is simultaneously won over."[27]

"Listening to the BBC," wrote Egon Larsen in *Wit as a Weapon,* was, "of course, strictly forbidden in Germany, and the German-occupied countries—but it was done all the same, despite savage punishment if one was caught."[28] One German woman, Larsen wrote, was brought into court in the winter of 1940–41. She was charged with listening to broadcasts from Britain. "She defended herself quite innocently: we were told, weren't we, that the Führer would speak from London in October—I've been waiting for that ever since."[29] Nazi authorities distributed signs, to be attached to German radio dials, which stated: "Think about this. Listening to foreign broadcasts is a crime against the national security of our people. By order of the Führer, it is punished with the most severe punishment of hard labor."

Larsen (real name, Lehrburger), who had a hand in cabaret productions in London, wrote for the BBC *"Im Gasthaus an der Isar"* [In the Inn on the Isar River], *"Politik im Hofbrauhaus"* [Politics in

227

the Pub], and *"Blockleiter Braunmuller"* [Blockleader Brownmuller].
Asked once if satire was an appropriate weapon against the Nazis,
Larsen answered: "What kind of question is that? What then? What
can you do, if not satire?"[30] Bruno Adler, another immigrant
writer, created "Frau Wernicke," monologues by a fictional-yet-
typical inhabitant of a small German village, and "Kurt und Willi,"
conversations between a loose-lipped Nazi propagandist and a
coffeehouse pal.

Over its German service, the BBC would play back, verbatim,
the speeches of German leaders foretelling the Reich's total victory.
A 1940 speech by Goebbels claiming England's defeat was carried
three years later, when the tide of war had turned against Germany.
An editorial note to the broadcast added that England seemed to be
"alive and kicking." Another 1940 speech by Goering, in which he
stated "we shall not allow a single enemy bomb to fall on the Ruhr,"
was rebroadcast after the Royal Air Force nearly obliterated Essen in
1942. Hitler's speech in 1941, boasting that "the Soviet Union is
already destroyed and will never rise again,"[31] was played back after
the 1943 German defeat at Stalingrad. The speech was followed by
detailed figures about German casualties in that pivotal battle.

The BBC drew a growing clandestine audience in Germany.
Goebbels, angered that the propaganda instrument he had mastered
a decade earlier was now being turned on him, disapproved of the
broadcasts' popularity. "It is for a civilian as despicable as for the
soldier who commits self-mutilation,[32] said he. Severe penalties
were imposed for those caught listening to Allied broadcasts.
German-manufactured radios were redesigned to receive only one or
two German stations; lacking shortwave capabilities, the sets could
pick up the BBC with difficulty on medium wave. The Nazis briefly
considered confiscating all radio receivers in the occupied countries,
but then reconsidered—such a move would cost the Germans a tool
for their own propaganda.

A German attempt to turn the tables on the Allies backfired in 1941. Over their English-language service, the Nazis asked American listeners to submit, by collect radio messages to Berlin, suggestions for "further propaganda broadcasts."[33] The offer drew an unwanted response. The cable office was "swamped"[34]—and of the hundreds of messages, a large proportion were sarcastic, asking for the broadcast of "such information as the bombing of Hitler's chancellery in Berlin or a description of Hitler's funeral."[35]

Artists in the Allied countries also joined the war effort, using their pens to attack, and mock, the Axis. The most-noted cartoonist was David Low, the New Zealand-born employee of the London *Evening Standard*. Fearing that "the wrong Germans"[36] would gain power in Germany, as early as the 1920s he criticized British politicians for not supporting the Weimar Republic. Misled by Low's attacks on British leaders, Hitler in 1930 asked the cartoonist, as one artist to another, for a few original sketches to hang in Nazi Party headquarters in Munich. Low's response is not known. As the Nazis grew stronger, his work took on a bolder anti-Nazi tone. By 1930, following the publication of the cartoon "It Worked at the Reichstag, Why not Here?" the *Evening Standard* and all papers carrying Low's cartoons were banned in Germany. The Reichstag cartoon implied that Hitler "was capable of destroying the League of Nations in the same way as he destroyed the Reichstag"[37] in an arson fire in 1933. Unlike some cartoonists who portrayed Hitler as a windbag, focusing on his moustache and forelock, Low's drawings pictured the German leader and his actions as dangerous. Low was also careful not to feed Hitler's self-image—or Mussolini's—by picturing the Axis leaders as blood-thirsty tyrants. That "only gratified their vanity,"[38] he reasoned. What piqued them, he felt, "was to be depicted as clowns, or as what they were, upstart plebians."[39]

Low remarked of Hitler:

I assumed that he would do just as he said and made my comment accordingly, earning for myself a cheap reputation as a prophet of remarkable insight when now and then I got in a cartoon about an event well before it happened.[40]

Sympathetic to the Jewish cause in Palestine, Low was critical of the British Mandate Authority's restrictive immigration policies. A 1937 cartoon, "Standing Room Only," showed a Jew standing on a small circle of sand on the shores of the Mediterranean marked "Jewish National Home." That year, Goebbels berated Lord Halifax during the British Foreign Secretary's visit to Germany. On his return to London, Halifax invited Low to lunch and conveyed Goebbels' sentiments. Low asked whether Britain would "find it easier to promote peace if my cartoons did not irritate the Nazis personally?"[41] Yes, said Halifax. Low temporarily softened his attacks on the Nazi leaders. But Germany's invasion of Poland in 1939, and Britain's declaration of war on Germany, allowed the cartoonist to resume his work as before, now with the government's blessing. "Lebensraum for the Conquered," a 1940 cartoon, showed piles of Jews at a railroad loading. They are stacked like boards of wood, bound together, with the shipping label, "To living hell Lublin." Drawings later in the war mocked Nazi brutality, and the Reich's Final Solution for Europe's Jews.

"If Hitler has not succeeded in establishing his 'New Order' in Europe," Low wrote in 1944, "certainly he has established the United Nations of cartoonists. Today throughout the free world the work of graphic satirists bears a recognisable family likeness. Now, despite tags and titles in foreign script (which can be guessed at, usually), the cartoons of the civilised nations have become virtually interchangeable . . . they reflect the common approach to the one subject-matter of the day—war against Nazi Germany."[42]

In Russia, caricatures in the pages of the popular *Krokodil* magazine—where Goebbels was shown as Mickey Mouse with a swastika tail—and posters on public buildings took aim at the Third Reich. Some two hundred artists worked on the posters, which were distributed throughout Russia. Drawings of a pair of Russian hands around a German throat expressed confidence in the Red Army. A leading artist in the United States who took up his pen against the Nazis was an illustrator named Arthur Szyk, a native of Poland who had studied art in Paris, and who spent World War II in England and America. His mocking pictures of the Nazi leadership appeared in newspapers and magazines, and were collected in a book, *The New Order*. One work, "Enemies of the Third Reich," showed a scowling Hitler, dagger at his side, pointing to a family of tattered Jewish refugees.

Another emigré, Bertolt Brecht, playwright, poet, and dedicated Marxist, fled his native Germany in 1933, on the day after the Reichstag became a victim of Nazi arson. His books were among the first to feed the flames. The author, "high up in the Nazis' liquidation lists"[43] as early as 1923 for his sarcastic treatment of the German soldier in *The Legend of the Dead Soldier*, was stripped of his German citizenship. He escaped, via Vienna, to Denmark, Sweden, Finland, and the United States, all the while writing poetry, drama, and screenplays, much with an anti-Nazi bent. In 1940, while waiting in Finland for an American visa, he wrote a play that was to be his ticket of admission into American culture. *Der Aufhaltsame Aufstieg des Arturo Ui* [The Resistable Rise of Arturo Ui] set the rise of a Hitlerlike figure in the world of Chicago's gangland wars. Brecht was inspired by the gangster films he had seen on an earlier visit to the U.S. The parable, written in three weeks, was an expression of Brecht's philosophy: "The great political criminals must be thoroughly stripped bare and exposed to ridicule."[44]

The play focuses on Ui's rise to power, rather than on the bloody consequences of his power. Ui is a self-pitying mediocrity who ruthlessly wrests control from the "backers" who helped establish him.

231

His impressive oratory is acquired from an out-of-work actor. He is
introduced by the play's announcer in the prologue:

> And lastly Public Enemy Number One
> Arturo Ui. Now you'll see
> The biggest gangster of all times
> Whom heaven sent for our crimes
> Our weakness and stupidity![45]

In succeeding scenes, Ui expounds on his feelings and philosophy:

> Nobody talks about me any more.
> This city's got no memory. Short-lived
> Is fame in such a place. Two months without
> A murder and a man's forgotten.

> I have been very much maligned, my image
> Blackened by envy, my intentions disfigured
> By baseness. When about fourteen years ago
> Yours truly, then a modest, unemployed
> Son of the Bronx, appeared within the gates
> Of this your city to launch a new career
> Which, I may say, has not been utterly
> Inglorious, my only followers
> Were seven youngsters, penniless like myself
> But brave and like myself determined
> To cut their chunk of meat from every cow
> The Lord created. I've got thirty now.

> I'm a quiet man. But
> I won't be threatened. Either trust me blindly
> Or go your way. I owe you no accounting.

232

I never smoke and have no use for liquor.
. . . Of carnal inclinations I have none.
. . . I am a Christian. That will have to do.
. . . My social views are balanced, clear and healthy.
What proves it is: I don't neglect the wealthy.[46]

In the final scene, Ui, who has risen to absolute power through a protection racket among Chicago's greengrocers, declares his intentions for future conquests:

For Chicago and Cicero
Are not alone in clamoring for protection!
There are other cities: Washington and Milwaukee!
Detroit! Toledo! Pittsburgh! Cincinnati!
And other towns where vegetables are traded!
Philadelphia! Baltimore! St. Louis! Little Rock!
Minneapolis! Columbus! Charleston! And New York!
They all demand protection! And no "Phooey!"
No "That's not nice!" will stop Arturo Ui![47]

Brecht's expectations for the play were unfulfilled. Its parallels between Hitler's Europe and Ui's Chicago were too obvious for a European audience and too arcane for Americans. *Ui* was not staged during Brecht's lifetime. Its first production, in Berlin in 1959, came three years after his death.

R. F. Patterson, a British poet, attacked Hitler in a lighter vein. His vehicle was *Mein Rant: A Summary in Light Verse* of Hitler's prison-produced manifesto, *Mein Kampf*. Patterson called his 1940 work, "more compressed and palatable . . . than the original text."[48] Hitler's work, the poet wrote, "has neither rhyme nor reason, while my abridgement undoubtedly has rhyme."[49] *Mein Rant* began with an author's preface:

233

Because I did a spell in prison
The ensuing volume has arisen;
I found my temporary fetters
Conducive to the craft of letters.

Here I've described, in prison pent,
My personal development,
Reducing thus to nothingness
The inventions of the Jewish press.[50]

The parody conveyed Hitler's obsession with Jews:

I underwent a course of cram,
And sat a most unfair exam;
For, though my genius cried aloud,
I ignominiously was ploughed.

[The examiner, the dirty dog,
Was member of a synagogue,
Or else, as I indeed surmise,
Was Mr. Churchill in disguise.]

The Marxists wouldn't hesitate
To overturn the German state,
Or ruin Europe altogether
Their own Hebraic nests to feather.

I learnt, moreover, that the throng
Abhors the weak and loves the strong,
And that a man, though vile and truthless,
Succeeds if he's completely ruthless.

I also learnt the curious news
That all our enemies are Jews,
That Destiny, when mischief *she* brews,
Has as her instrument the Hebrews.

234

My voice rose to a shrill falsetto
When speechifying on the Ghetto;
My words were full of sound and fury
When I denounced the crimes of Jewry.

The poem covers Hitler's other favorite topics, from propaganda to foreign relations, and concluded with the epilogue:

Behold the volume I have writ,
A masterpiece of style and wit;
I make my soldiers carry it,
Like iron rations, in their kit.

O readers, who have read, in rhyme,
My gallant deeds, my thoughts sublime,
You'll all agree with me that I'm
The greatest German of all time.[51]

Of all the media that cast a satiric eye on Nazi Europe, films, plays and novels were furthest removed from the actual events—the cinema, by geographic distance, fiction, by years. Hollywood, especially after America's entry into World War II in 1941, found the country's chief European enemy a natural target. Movies with the Nazis in sinister roles were entertaining, profitable, and effective propaganda for the Allied cause. While most of the productions were dramas, a good sampling incorporated humor. The same was true for war songs—most, in the tradition of songs from World War I, were serious or maudlin; but some, typified by Spike Jones' "Der Führer's Face," mocked the Axis. The novelty tune, which was written by composer Oliver Wallace and recorded by studio musician Jones to round out a last-minute recording session in 1942, became an instant hit and boosted Jones's career. His recording mocked German music with exaggerated vocals, tacky trombone blasts, imitation oom-pahs and frequent Bronx cheers. Here is one stanza:

> Ven Der Fuehrer says
> "Ve iss der Master Race,"
> Ve Heil [phbbt!]
> Heil [phbbt!]
> Right in Der Fuehrer's Face.
> Not to luff Der Fuehrer
> iss a great disgrace,
> So ve Heil! [phbbt]
> Heil [phbbt!]
> Right in Der Fuehrer's Face.[52]

Capitalizing on the recordings's popularity, Walt Disney changed the name of his studio's unreleased cartoon, tentatively titled "Donald Duck in Nutziland," to "Der Fuehrer's Face."

The pace for the entertainment industry's satirization of the Nazis was set by Charles Chaplin's 1940 production *The Great Dictator*. By the late 1930s he envisioned the plot for a film about a mustachioed Jewish barber mistaken for the Führer. Even before the film came out, the German consul in Los Angeles complained, and United Artists, the releasing company, was informed by Hollywood's self-policing Motion Picture Producers and Distributors of America—the so-called Hays Office—that Chaplin "would run into censorship trouble."[53] German sympathizers threatened to vandalize theaters showing the film and set off stink bombs in them.

Jewish studio heads, who held a virtual monopoly of Hollywood's major production lots, were especially reticent about fanning the flames of domestic anti-Semitism. Humorous treatment of the Nazis, more than drama, the moguls apparently felt, would reveal a premature anti-Nazi tilt or susceptibility to Jewish fears in

236

America. The American public, according to a Gallup Poll taken in 1939, the year World War II began, was strictly isolationist, opposing America's entry into the war.[54] In addition, anti-Nazi films, Hollywood feared, might create problems for Jews in Germany. Chaplin, who wrote the unusually intricate 300-page script, invested $2 million of his own money, and directed and starred in the production. "I was determined to go ahead," he said, "for Hitler must be laughed at."[55]

A potential roadblock in Great Britain, a British Board of Film Censors regulation that no living person could be portrayed on screen without the subject's written consent, was averted with the outbreak of the war in 1939. When *The Great Dictator* opened the next year in London, at the height of the Nazi bombing, "The British seemed to delight in Chaplin's ridicule, with none of the reserve felt by the Americans."

Chaplin's work earned the Nazis' wrath. His name was banned from the German press by one of Goebbels' *Sprachregelungen* [language rulings]. Political pressure had the film banned in Argentina. In Chile it was heavily censored, and thieves stole the reels in Paraguay. Only after the war, when the extent of the Nazi genocide was revealed, did Chaplin express reservations about making *The Great Dictator*. "Had I known of the actual horrors of the German concentration camps," he said, "I could not have made The Great Dictator; I could not have made fun of the homicidal insanity of the Nazis."[56]

The Great Dictator opened the door for cinematic mockery of Nazi Germany. Within a few years of Pearl Harbor, when three out of ten Hollywood films were about the war, humor had earned a respectable, if not unquestioned, place. Some critics, sympathetic to the Nazis' European victims, continued to raise questions about humor's propriety.

A 1940 Three Stooges short, "You Natzi Spy," subjected the Reich to the trio's usual brand of heavy-handed farce. One of the

237

trio's first productions to reflect a current political theme, it satirized Hitler (Moe was cast as Hailstone), Goering (Curly was Gallstone), and Goebbels (Larry was Pebble). The plot: three dimwitted paperhangers in the land of Moronia are duped by a group of rich businessmen into fronting as the country's dictators. Moe, effecting a Hitlerish moustache with a piece of misplaced electrical tape, imitated the Führer's mannerisms. In the film, the Stooges usual sequence of puns and sight gags ends with them fleeing for safety into a courtyard, where they meet their fate as dinner for three lions.[57]

By the last years of World War II, satire had spread to cartoons. "Confusions of a Nutzy Spy" featured Porky Pig as a detective following the trail of a spy, and Daffy Duck starring in "Daffy—The Commando," as a paratrooper fighting the "Gestinko Gestapo." "Der Fuehrer's Face," the Disney cartoon that cast Donald Duck as an oppressed worker on a munitions assembly line, won the 1943 Academy Award as best animated feature. The cartoon's poster shows Donald Duck pelting Hitler in the eye with a ripe tomato. "Der Fuehrer's Face" was translated into German and smuggled into Germany, "much to the chagrin of the Nazi Party."[58]

Among dramatic films, especially controversial was *To Be or Not to Be*, Ernst Lubitsch's 1942 release. The comedy spy thriller, which starred Jack Benny and Carole Lombard, was about a Shakespearean troupe in occupied Warsaw. The actors engaged in an ongoing—and ultimately successful—battle of wits with the Nazis. The film, which was made and released when the American public was privy to facts about actual conditions in Europe, was attacked for conveying an "irresponsible attitude toward war by using the invasion of Warsaw as the backdrop for a comedy."[59] One critic asked whether audiences should "laugh at some broad anti-Nazi satire while we are weeping over the sad fate of stricken Poland."[60]

The most inflammatory line was spoken by a Nazi colonel

about Benny's performance—as actor Joseph Tura, a preening egoist—as Hamlet: "What he did to Shakespeare we are now doing to Poland."[61] Some movie critics considered the line insensitive; others praised it as the funniest scene in the film, contrasting the Nazis' callousness with an actor's harmless posturing. Audiences accepted that line as well as the film, though *To Be or Not to Be* did not have the popular success of *The Great Dictator*.

Other critics charged that Lubitsch's benign depiction of the Nazis whitewashed the real horror. He answered: "I admit that I have not resorted to methods usually employed in pictures, novels and plays to signify Nazi terror. No actual torture chamber is photographed, no flogging is shown, no close-up of excited Nazis using their whips and rolling their eyes in lust. My Nazis are different; they passed that stage long ago. Brutality, flogging and torturing have become their daily routine. Is whipping and flogging the only way of expressing terrorism? No—the American audiences don't laugh at those Nazis because they underestimate their menace, but because they are happy to see this new order and its ideology being ridiculed."[62]

Unlike Chaplin, who in the light of postwar reports, expressed reservations about treating the Nazis with a light touch, Lubitsch continued to defend his work. In a 1943 letter to the *Philadelphia Inquirer*, he wrote: "What I have satirized in this picture are the Nazis and their ridiculous ideology. I have also satirized the attitude of actors who always remain actors regardless of how dangerous the situation might be, which I believe is a true observation."[63] He said at another time: "The many audiences I observed were deeply moved whenever the picture touched the tragedy of Warsaw. Never once have they laughed at the expense of Poland or the Polish people."[64]

Similar reservations about the mockery of Nazi occupation were expressed about Mel Brooks's 1983 remake of *To Be or Not to Be*. Brooks played three roles in the film—Hamlet, Hitler, and the actor-protagonist. Such ham-handed concessions to modern taste as a gay dresser and a Polish-language rendition of "Sweet Georgia Brown" contrasted sharply with Lubitsch's version of the film. One Brooks biographer explained it as a "difference between Lubitsch's essentially European sophistication and Brooks's essentially Jewish bellicose broadness."[65]

Like Lubitsch, Brooks defended his version, claiming that his post-Holocaust audiences had grown accustomed to a heavier dose of farce, but understood the horror behind the façade. Obsessed with the spectacle of Nazism, Brooks manages to weave mocking attacks into nearly everything he films. His irreverent treatment of the Nazis had its most direct antecedent in *The Producers*, a 1967 work that featured a chorus line of high-kicking Nazi-garbed dancers in the stage production of "Springtime for Hitler." Said Brooks: "If I get up on the soapbox and wax eloquently, it'll be blown away in the wind. But if I do 'Springtime for Hitler,' it'll never be forgotten."[66]

Another postwar film that dealt with humor's role in the Holocaust, Jerry Lewis's *The Day the Clown Died*, was never released. The 1971 production, written, directed, and financed by Lewis, was his first serious film. It concerned Helmut Doork, a world-famous clown who starts drinking heavily, gets drunk in the local bistro, and maligns the Führer. Helmut is arrested by the Gestapo, sentenced to a labor farm, and forced to perform to keep the children quiet. The Nazis did force trained clowns, prisoners in some concentration camps, to placate interned children. To research the role, Lewis "went to Belsen, Dachau and Auschwitz. I saw the killing camps, the sprinklers which unleashed Zyklon-B, and I saw the nail scratchings on the walls; the initials, the writings."[67] To prepare for the role, he lost thirty-five pounds in six weeks by eating nothing but grapefruit. Some scenes were filmed in France; camp scenes were filmed at a Swedish military compound. A series of lawsuits between Lewis and the film's producer prevented its release. "It sits in Stockholm, tied up in litigation," he wrote in 1982. "Fortunately, though, the story is timeless. I can release it ten years from now, and it will hold up. One way or another, I'll get it done."[68]

Several dozen plays with Holocaust themes have been written since 1945 in the United States, Israel, and Europe. There are few traces of humor in this "literature of atrocity."[69] Most of these plays, according to one expert, emphasize the Holocaust as "private experience" or "collective catastrophe,"[70] examining such traits as commitment, self-sacrifice, and loyalty. A notable exception, *Auschwitz*, a 1978 comedy by British playwright Peter Barnes, a Jew who was evacuated as a child from wartime London, uses black humor to examine Hannah Arendt's "banality of evil." The one-act play is part of a two-act set. *Auschwitz*, despite the play's title, takes place mostly in a faceless Berlin bureaucracy, and briefly in the death camp itself. The bureaucrats' petty jealousies and attempted trysts, and the sterility of the government forms they shuffle, nearly overwhelm awareness of the victims and the destruction wreaked by the anonymous documents.

Barnes's cynical, self-advancing followers of Hitler fancy themselves as distanced from the duped masses by the critical jokes they pass among themselves. Emboldened by a round of toasts among the characters, the jokes start flying:

CRANACH: Don't laugh. It's an offense to make people laugh. Jokes carry penalties. So don't. Have you tried the new Rippentrop herrings? They're just ordinary herrings with the brain removed and the mouth split wider.

Shrieks from ELSE and STROOP, while GOTTLEB roars and slaps his thigh in delight. Their laughter quickly grows louder and more hysterical.

GOTTLEB: That'll get you five years hard labor, Viktor. Here's one carries ten: My dentist is going out of business. Everyone's afraid to open their mouth.

241

ELSE: The only virgin left in Berlin is the angel on top of the victory column—Goebbels can't climb that high.

GOTTLEB: I sentence you to fifteen years, Fraulein.

ELSE: A German's dream of paradise is to have a suit made of genuine English wool with a genuine grease spot on it.

GOTTLEB: Another fifteen.

STROOP: We can't lose the war, we'd never be that careless.

GOTTLEB: Twenty years hard.

STROOP: The time we'll really be rid of the war is when Franco's widow stands beside Mussolini's grave asking who shot the Führer?

GOTTLEB: Thirty.

CRANACH: Listen, listen, what do you call someone who sticks his finger up the Führer's arse?!

GOTTLEB: Heroic.

CRANACH: No, a brain surgeon!

GOTTLEB: That's DEATH.[71]

Quickly sobered, the bureaucrats return to talk of work—and their duties in connection with the Final Solution. The play's brief epilogue, set in "Block B. Auschwitz II," shows two Jewish comics, Abe Bimko and Hymie Bieberstein, in their "farewell appearance" at a Christmas concert. Their patter is redolent of bad vaudeville:

BIEBERSTEIN: Bernie Litvinoff just died.

BIMKO: Well, if he had a chance to better himself. . . .

They tell a few more bad jokes.

BIEBERSTEIN: I could be wrong but I think this act is dying.

BIMKO: The way to beat hydrocyanide gas is by holding your breath for five minutes. It's just a question of mind over matter. They don't mind and and we don't matter.

Followed by the final stage directions:

THEY *die in darkness.*[72]

Within a generation of World War II's end, novels about the Holocaust experience and its aftermath appeared, some sprinkled with humor or infused with satiric overtones. These novels, some written by survivors, ranged from Tadeusz Borowski's *This Way for the Gas, Ladies and Gentlemen*, a collection of concentration camp stories whose ironic tone highlighted the war's terrors, to several works that weaved in the actual jokes told under Nazi occupation.

Hints of Sholem Aleichem, evoking Jews' naive belief in the triumph of justice, are found in *Jacob the Liar*, by Jurek Becker, a Polish Holocaust survivor. *Soul of Wood*, a collection of stories by Jakov Lind, an Austrian Jew who spent the war in Holland, turns to Kafkaesque depictions of bureaucracy to explain mankind's inhumanity. In Avigdor Dagan's *The Court Jesters*, the protagonists, four concentration camp inmates who are kept alive to entertain their captors, nearly lose their privileged status when one violates their pact "never to say anything in our performance to upset the rulers of our world."[73] Yoram Kaniuk's *Adam Resurrected* is set in an Israeli rehabilitation center and features a Jewish clown who was sentenced to entertain children in a concentration camp. Leslie Epstein's *King of the Jews* lifts several jokes from Warsaw Ghetto journals in his description of cabaret comics in Poland's occupied capital. Jean-François Steiner's *Treblinka*, a story of an actual prisoner uprising in the death camp, makes frequent mention of the inmates' humor:

> A certain brand of humor was a most astonishing aspect of life in Treblinka. An extreme form of the celebrated Jewish humor, a mixture of the tall tale and a gentle self-irony, it played the necessary role of release in this world of death. Today it is difficult to conceive of it, and the survivors sometimes have trouble remembering that it existed. One of the female survivors told us a joke she was in the habit of making. In the last months of the existence of Treblinka a number of young women were sent to Camp

243

Number Two to work in a laundry where the prisoners' linen was washed. One of them had as much passion as lack of talent for singing, and all day long she insisted on humming songs of which she sometimes remembered the words but never the tune. This annoying habit had made her the butt of her companions' jokes. The survivor tells one of those jokes which she made herself.

"Rifka," she told her one day, "I thought I had gotten used to everything here, but there is one thing I can't stand."

"And what's that?"

"Your voice, Rifka, your voice!"[74]

This Way for the Gas, Ladies and Gentlemen, Borowski's collection of stories, first published as individual pieces in 1948, is the most vivid of its genre, and its title was the most reflective of the author's own destiny. A survivor of Auschwitz and Dachau, he took his life in 1951—with gas. The irony in his depictions of concentration camp life comes in contrasting the banel (the prisoners' efforts to carry on a normal life) with the macabre (the Nazis' routine of death that permeated their existence). Tadek, the principal character, and his compatriots speak easily about "the Cremo" and "the Puff." Families are pushed to their deaths while "Tadek and his comrades take pleasure in eating." Two thousand prisoners are put to death in the crematoria during a throw-in at a nearby soccer game. One member of a crematoria detail tells the narrator an effective way to burn people:

"You take four little kids with plenty of hair on their heads, then stick the heads together and light the hair. The rest burns by itself and in no time all the whole business is gemacht."

"Congratulations," I said drily and with very little expression.

He burst out laughing and with a strange expression looked right into my eyes.

"Listen, doctor, here in Auschwitz we must entertain ourselves in every way we can. Otherwise, who could stand it?"[75]

244

Borowski's narrator relates a story about liberation. A group of prisoners seize a hated S.S. guard and are about to kill him, when some American soldiers turn into the camp. An officer, accompanied by a translator, enters the barrack where the guard is being hidden. "Don't seek revenge," the American officer implores.

> "Comrades, our new Kommandant gives you his word of honour that all the criminals of the S.S. as well as among the prisoners will be punished," said the translator. The men in the bunks broke into applause and shouts. In smiles and gestures they tried to convey their friendly approval of the young man from across the ocean.
>
> "And so the Kommandant requests," went on the translator, his voice turning somewhat hoarse: "That you try to be patient and do not commit lawless deeds, which may only lead to trouble, and please pass the sons of bitches over to the camp guards. How about it, men?"
>
> The block answered with a prolonged shout. The American thanked the translator and wished the prisoners a good rest and an early reunion with their dear ones. Accompanied by a friendly hum of voices, he left the block and proceeded to the next.
>
> Not until after he had visited all the blocks and returned with the soldiers to his headquarters did we pull our man off the bunk—where covered with blankets and half-smothered with the weight of our bodies he lay gagged, his face buried in the straw mattress—and drag him onto the cement floor under the stove, where the entire block, grunting and growling with hatred, trampled him to death.[76]

In Romain Gary's *The Dance of Genghis Cohn,* a Yiddish burlesque comic in Warsaw becomes the *dybbuk,* the demon, haunting the S.S. officer who murdered him. The officer is haunted by the scene of Cohn's dying sign of contempt—facing a rifleman, the comic turned his back, lowered his trousers, and shouted, *Kish mir im toches* [kiss my behind]. Hauptjudenfresser Schatz, driven out of his mind by the vengeful Jewish ghost, becomes an alcoholic, muttering phrases in Yiddish, observing the Kosher laws, and shuffling through the dance routines that Cohn once performed on the stage: "In Auschwitz, one day, I told a fellow inmate such a funny joke that he literally died laughing," Cohn brags. "He was undoubtedly the only Jew who ever died laughing in Auschwitz. The German guards were furious."

"For generations," Cohn declares, once in the role of *dybbuk*, "the defenders of a racially pure Germany have called us Jews 'the enemy within,' and now at last they've succeeded in getting us truly inside them."[77]

> "I often catch myself using words in that horrible jargon," mutters Schatz. "In the end, I had to buy myself a Yiddish dictionary, so as to understand myself. A few key words. . . . Rakhmones . . . that means pity. I must have heard it a million times in Poland. Gevalt, help. Hutzpeh, cheek. And the other night . . . can you imagine that? I woke up singing."
>
> Inspector Guth smiles pleasantly. "There's nothing wrong with that," he says.
>
> "It depends," Schatz grumbles angrily. "You know what that ganif made me sing? El molo rakhmin. It's their funeral chant for the dead . . . he woke me up a little after midnight—I later realized that it was the anniversary of the rising of the Warsaw ghetto—and before I knew it he had me singing at the top of my voice the Hebrew chant for the dead . . . he was sitting on my bed, his arms crossed, listening, with a terrifying, mad gleam in his eyes. After that, he made me sing Yiddishe Mamme. The son of a bitch has no tact whatsoever."[78]

Gary also took his own life.

The Last Butterfly has echoes of Kaniuk's *Adam Resurrected*. The fictional account by Michael Jacot of a half-Jewish clown sentenced—for making a joke about Hitler in his theater act—to perform for the Jewish children in Theresienstadt openly questions the propriety of humor in such a setting. Antonin Karas, the clown, is questioned by Vera Lydrakova, his wartime *amour*, after one successful bout of evoking laughter from the children.

> At the end Vera saw Antonin looking seriously at the fort.
> "So serious after such a triumph?" she asked.
> "I'm thinking how funny it is to be happy at a time like this."
> "What better time is there to be happy?"
> He looked at her and he knew the truth.[79]

Notes

1

1. Ber Mark, *The Warsaw Ghetto Uprising,* trans. Gershon Freidlin. New York: Schocken Books, 1975, p. 126.

2. *Ibid.*

3. Robert McAfee Brown, *The Essential Reinhold Niebuhr.* New Haven, CT: Yale University Press, 1986, p. 52.

4. B. D. Shaw, *Is Hitler Dead? and Best Anti-Nazi Humor.* New York: Alcaeus House, 1939, p. 20.

5. *New York Times,* December 3, 1938, p. 7.

6. Joel Dimsdale, ed., *Survivors, Victims and Perpetrators: Essays on the Nazi Holocaust.* Washington, DC: Hemisphere Publishing, 1980, p. 168.

7. *Ibid.*

8. Berel Lang, ed., *Writing and the Holocaust.* New York: Holmes & Meier, 1988, pp. 217–218.

9. Michel Borwicz, *Ecrits des condamnés à mort sous l'occupation nazie (1939–1945).* Paris: Gallimard, 1973, Preface.

10. Ecclesiastes 3:4.

11. Norman N. Holland, *Laughing: A Psychology of Humor.* Ithaca, NY: Cornell University Press, 1982, p. 22.

12. Alan Dundes, *Cracking Jokes: Studies of Sick Humor Cycles & Stereotypes.* Berkeley, CA: Ten Speed Press, 1987, p. 19.

13. Interview with Annette Insdorf, *Art out of Agony: The Holocaust Theme in Literature, Sculpture and Film.* Montreal: CBC Enterprises, 1984, pp. 132–133.

14. Konnelyn Feig, *Hitler's Death Camps: The Sanity of Madness*. New York: Holmes & Meier, 1979, p. 77.

15. Antonin Obrdlik, Gallows humor—a sociological perspective, *American Journal of Sociology*, March 1942, p. 712.

16. Marcel Ophuls, The sorrow and the laughter, *Première*. November 1988, p. 113.

17. *Warsaw Ghetto: A Diary by Mary Berg*. New York: L. B. Fischer, 1945, p. 111.

18. *An Interrupted Life: The Diaries of Etty Hillesum*. New York: Pantheon, 1983, p. 155.

19. Sylvia Rothchild, ed., *Voices from the Holocaust*. New York: New American Library, 1982, p. 409.

20. Richard Grunberger, *A Social History of the Third Reich*. London: Weidenfeld and Nicolson, 1971, p. 331.

21. Norman Cousins, *The Words of Albert Schweitzer*. New York: Newmarket Press, 1984, p. 44.

22. Jacob Boas, *Boulevard des Miseres: The Story of Transit Camp Westerbork*. Hamden, CT: Archon Books, 1985, p. 83.

23. Victor Frankl, *Man's Search for Meaning*. New York: Simon & Schuster, 1959, pp. 54–56.

24. Laughter instead of violence, *USA Today*, April 1982, p. 2.

25. Brown, p. 29.

26. Theodor Reik, *Jewish Wit*. New York: Gamut Press, 1962, p. 27.

27. Raymond Federman, SUNY/Buffalo professor of English, concentration camp survivor and novelist, speculates that writers who have pierced the center of the Holocaust's truth are overpowered by its enormity—and are unable to go on living.

28. Anna Pawelczynska, *Values and Violence in Auschwitz: A Sociological Analysis*, trans. Catherine Leach. Berkeley, CA: University of California Press, 1973, pp. 58–65, 127–129.

29. Dr. Elie Cohen, *Human Behavior in the Concentration Camps*. New York: Norton, 1953, p. 181.

30. Eric Wilhelm, Author finds Holocaust children used games to play out their fear, *Los Angeles Times*. January 12, 1989, p. 10.

31. Alfred Kantor, *The Book of Alfred Kantor: An Artist's Journal of the Holocaust*. New York: Schocken Books, 1987, introduction.

32. George Mikes, *Humour in Memoriam*. London: Routledge & Kegan Paul, 1970, p. 92.

33. Frankl, pp. 54–56.

34. Kantor, introduction.

35. Borwicz, p. 265.

36. Harvey Mindess, *Laughter and Liberation*. Los Angeles, CA: Nash, 1971, p. 48.

37. Henry Shoshkes, *No Traveler Returns*. Garden City, NY: Doubleday-Doran, 1945.

38. Interview with author, 1985.

39. Mikes, p. 92.

40. Egon Larsen, *Wit as a Weapon: The Political Joke in History*. London: Frederick Muller, 1980, p. 43.

41. Rudi Hartmann, *Flüsterwitze aus dem Tausendjährigen Reich*. Munich: Knaur, 1983, p. 8.

42. Lucjan Dobroszycki, *The Chronicle of the Lodz Ghetto 1941–1944*. New Haven, CT: Yale University Press, 1984, p. 327.

43. *Notes from the Warsaw Ghetto: The Journal of Emmanuel Ringelblum*, trans. Jacob Sloan. New York: Schocken Books, 1974, p. 288.

44. Ralph Wiener, *Als das Lachen Tödlich war* [When Laughter Was Fatal]. German Democratic Republic: Greifenverlag zu Rudolstadt, 1988, p. 253.

45. Richard Rashke, *Escape from Sobibor*. Boston: Houghton Mifflin, 1982, p. 59.

46. *Notes from the Warsaw Ghetto*, p. 154.

47. Author's interview with Westerbork survivor Hans Margules, 1988.

48. *Notes from the Warsaw Ghetto*, p. 54.

49. Interview with author, 1984.

50. Boas, p. 117.

51. Norman Cousins, *Anatomy of an Illness*. Toronto: Bantam Books, 1979, p. 27.

52. Interview with author, 1984.

53. Paul McGhee, *Humor: Its Origin and Development*. San Francisco, CA: Freeman, 1979, p. 232.

54. *The Washington Spectator*, Washington, DC, August 15, 1987, p. 4.

55. Leslie Zganjar, The science of laughter: jest for the fun of it, Associated Press, March 27, 1988.

56. Susan Ziemer-Brender, unpublished paper, 1986.

57. Interview with author, 1985.

58. Eliezer Berkowitz, *Faith after the Holocaust*. New York: Ktav, 1973, pp. 33–34.

2

1. Uwe Naumann, *Zwischen Tränen und Gelächter*. Cologne: Pahl-Rugenstein Verlag, 1983, p. 79.

2. *New York Times*, January 19, 1941, p. 7.

3. James and Patience Barnes, Oswald Mosley as entrepreneur, *History Today*, March 1990, p. 16.

4. Peter Beckmann, *Hammer and Tickle: Clandestine Laughter in the Soviet Empire*. Boulder, CO: Golem Press, 1980, introduction.

5. George Mikes, *Humour in Memoriam*. London: Routledge & Kegan Paul, 1970, p. 92.

6. Stephen Robinson, Nepal's PM has last laugh, *The Jerusalem Post*, May 9, 1990, p. 5.

7. Egon Larsen, *Wit as a Weapon: The Political Joke in History*. London: Frederick Muller, 1980, p. 37.

8. Itzhak Galnoor and Steven Lukes, *No Laughing Matter: A Collection of Political Jokes*. London: Routledge & Kegan Paul, 1985, p. vii.

9. *Ibid.*

10. Algis Ruksenas, *Is That You Laughing Comrade: The World's Best Russian Underground Jokes*. Secaucus, NJ: Citadel Press, 1986, pp. 7–8.

11. Mikes, p. 91.

12. *Ibid.*, pp. 16–17.

13. *Ibid.*, p. 98.

14. Eliezer Berkowitz, *Faith after the Holocaust*. New York: KTAV, 1973, p. 11.

15. Galnoor and Lukes, pp. 9–10.

16. *Ibid.*, p. viii.

17. *Ibid.*

18. Zbynek Zeman, *Heckling Hitler: Caricatures of the Third Reich*. Hanover, NH: University Press of New England, 1987, p. 67.

19. *Ibid.*, p. 97.

20. *Ibid.*, p. 14.

21. *Ibid.*

22. Antonin Obrdlik, Gallows humor: a sociological perspective, *The American Journal of Sociology*, March 1942, p. 711.

23. *Ibid.*

24. Associated Press, July 5, 1933.

25. Detlev Peukert, *Inside Nazi Germany: Conformity, Opposition, and Racism in*

Everyday Life, trans. Richard Deveson. New Haven, CT: Yale University Press, 1987, p. 52.

26. Related by Rudi Hartmann, interview with author, 1989.

27. *Schnellbrief, An die Führer der SD-(Leit) Abschnitte, "Gerüchte, politische Witze und Volkshumor,"* Berlin, January 17, 1941.

28. *An die Leiter der Staatspolizei-leit-stellen, Führer der SD-(Leit)Abschnitte, "Gehässige und staatsabträgliche Witze und Gerüchte,"* Berlin, March 13, 1941.

29. Franz Danimann, *Flüsterwitze und Spottgedichte unterm Hakenkreuz.* Vienna: Hermann Bohlaus Nachf., 1983, p. 8.

30. Associated Press, March 10, 1939.

31. Harold Poor, *Kurt Tucholsky and the Ordeal of Germany, 1914–1935.* New York: Charles Scribner's Sons, 1968, p. 198.

32. *Ibid.*

33. *Ibid.*

34. *Ibid.*, p. 3.

35. *Ibid.*, p. 203.

36. *Ibid.*, p. 210.

37. *Ibid.*, p. 203.

38. Peukert, p. 52.

39. Harry Trimborn, Did Hitler's hanging judges act illegally? *Toronto Star*, August 31, 1980.

40. Jahntz/Kahne, *Der Volksgerichtshof: Darstellung der Ermittlungen der Staatsanwaltschaft bei dem Landgericht Berlin gegen ehemaligen Richter und Staatsanwalte am Volksgerichtshof.* Der Senator für Justiz und Bundesangelegenheiten. Berlin, 1986, pp. 87–91.

41. Larsen, p. 47.

42. *Ibid.*

43. Max Vandrey, *Der politische Witz im Dritten Reich.* Munich: Wilhelm Goldmann Verlag, 1967, p. 87.

44. Larsen, p. 46.

45. *Ibid.*, p. 47.

46. Helmut Heiber, *Goebbels*, trans. John Dickinson. London: Robert Hale & Company, 1972, p. 206.

47. B. D. Shaw, ed., *Is Hitler Dead? and Best Anti-Nazi Humor.* New York: Alcaeus House, 1939, pp. 10–11.

48. Larsen, pp. 48–49.

49. Zeman, p. 13.

50. *Ibid.*, pp. 13–14.

51. Obrdlik, p. 713.

52. *Ibid.*, p. 714.

53. Peukert, p. 49.

54. *Notes from the Warsaw Ghetto: The Journal of Emmanuel Ringelblum*, trans. Jacob Sloan. New York: Schocken Books, 1974, p. 151.

55. Walter Langer, *The Mind of Adolf Hitler: The Secret Wartime Report*. New York: Basic Books, 1972, p. 85.

56. Robert Waite, *The Psychopathic God: Adolf Hitler*. New York: Basic Books, 1977, p. 13.

57. Alan Bullock, *Hitler: A Study in Tyranny*. New York: Harper & Row, 1971, p. 224.

58. Albert Speer, *Inside the Third Reich*, trans. Richard and Clara Winston. New York: Macmillan, 1970, p. 123.

59. Waite, p. 13.

60. Robert Payne, *The Life and Death of Adolf Hitler*, New York: Praeger, 1973, p. 34.

61. Waite, p. 13.

62. *Ibid.*, p. 201.

63. *Ibid.*, p. 202.

64. Bullock, p. 427.

65. Larsen, p. 47.

66. *Ibid.*, p. 48.

67. Heiber, p. 205.

68. Marlis Steinert, *Hitler's War and the Germans: Public Mood and Attitude during the Second World War*, trans. Thomas E. J. DeWitt. Athens, OH: Ohio University Press, 1977, p. 195.

69. Krieg den Witz, *The Spectator*, February 17, 1939, p. 262.

70. Heiber, p. 206.

71. *Ibid.*

72. *Ibid.*, p. 207.

73. Associated Press, February 4, 1939.

74. *Ibid.*

75. Associated Press, March 8, 1939.

76. Zeman, p. 67.

77. Heiber, p. 207.

78. Sarah Blacher Cohen, ed., *Jewish Wry: Essays on Jewish Humor*. Bloomington, IN: Indiana University Press, 1987, p. 74.

79. Henry Spalding, *Encyclopedia of Black Folklore and Humor*. Middle Village, NY: Jonathan David Publishers, 1972, p. xiii.

80. Robert Brake, The lion act is over: passive/aggressive patterns of communication in American Negro humor, *Journal of Popular Culture*, Winter 1975, p. 554.

81. Philip Sterling, *Laughing on the Outside: The Intelligent White Reader's Guide to Negro Tales and Humor*. New York: Grosset & Dunlap, 1965, p. 22.

82. Brake, p. 550.

83. Sterling, p. 24.

84. Cohen, p. 59.

85. *Ibid.*, p. 73.

86. Joseph Boskin, Protest humor: fighting criticism with laughter, *Bostonia*, December 1980, pp. 48–56.

87. Cohen, p. 59.

88. Boskin, pp. 48–56.

89. Joseph Boskin, Humor in the civil rights movement, *Boston University Journal*, Spring 1970, p. 6.

90. Soviet-born comic Yakov Smirnoff, who worked in variety shows and on cruise ships in his homeland, says he annually submitted his script to the appropriate official: 1984 interview with author.

91. Arie Zand, *Political Jokes of Leningrad*. Austin, TX: Composing Stick, 1982, introduction.

92. Interview with author, 1990.

93. Interview with author, 1986.

94. Ralph Wiener, *Als das Lachen Tödlich war*. German Democratic Republic: Greifenverlag zu Rudolstadt, 1988, p. 75.

3

1. Antonin Obrdlik, Gallows humor—a sociological phenomenon, *American Journal of Sociology*, March 1942, p. 710.

2. *Ibid.*, p. 715.

3. *Ibid.*

4. *Ibid.*

5. *Ibid.*, p. 712.

6. *Ibid.*, p. 713.

7. Vera Laska, *Women in the Resistance and in the Holocaust: The Voices of Eyewitnesses*. Westport, CT: Greenwood Press, 1983, p. 5.

8. *Ibid.*, pp. 8–9.

9. Ralph Wiener, *Als das Lachen Tödlich war*, German Democratic Republic: Greifenverlag zu Rudolstadt, 1988, p. 101.

10. *Belgian Humor Under the German Heel*. New York: Belgian Information Center, 1942, introduction.

11. Related by Elaine Taibi: interview with author, 1989.

12. Related by Helena Salomon: interview with author, 1990.

13. Heinz Kuehn, *Mixed Blessings: An Almost Ordinary Life in Hitler's Germany*. Athens, GA: University of Georgia Press, 1988, p. 125.

14. Marlis Steinert, *Hitler's War and the Germans: Public Mood and Attitude during the Second World War*, trans. Thomas E. J. DeWitt. Athens, OH: Ohio University Press, 1977, p. 239.

15. Franz Danimann, *Flüsterwitze und Spottgedichte unterm Hakenkreuz*. Vienna: Hermann Bohlaus Nachf., 1983, p. 15.

16. *Ibid.*, p. 16.

17. Kuehn, p. 125.

18. Steinert, p. 203.

19. *Ibid.* p. 234.

20. *Ibid.*

21. *Ibid.*

22. *Proverbs Illustrated by Avas: Polish Political Cartoons*. London: P. S. King and Staples, 1941.

23. *Sein Kampf: 41 Caricatures politiques par Stanislaw Dobrzynski*. Jerusalem: Wydawnictwo "W Drodze," 1944, p. 46.

24. From the archives of the House of Humour and Satire, Gabrovo, Bulgaria.

25. *Ibid.*

26. *Beshkov: Cartoons and Drawings 1923–1945*. Sofia: BZNS Publishing House, 1985, p. 32.

27. Ruth Andreas-Friedrich, *Berlin Underground 1938–1945*. New York: Paragon House, 1989, p. 66.

28. Detlev Peukert, *Inside Nazi Germany: Conformity, Opposition, and Racism in Everyday Life*, trans. Richard Deveson. New Haven, CT: Yale University Press, 1982, p. 51.

29. Andreas-Friedrich, p. 248.

30. Jacob Boas, *Boulevard des Misères: The Story of Transit Camp Westerbork*, Hamden, CT: Archon Books, 1985, p. 119.

31. *Ibid.*, pp. 124–127.

32. Uwe Naumann, *Zwischen Tränen und Gelächter*. Cologne: Pahl-Rugenstein Verlag, 1983, p. 216.

33. *Ibid.*, p. 221.

34. *Ibid.*, pp. 220–221.

35. *Ibid.*, p. 226.

36. *Ibid.*, pp. 226–227.

4

1. Michael Schwartz, Finckenschläge: Zum Tode des Kabarettisten, *Frankfurter Allgemeine Zeitung*, August 1, 1978.

2. Harold Poor, *Kurt Tucholsky and the Ordeal of Germany, 1914–1935*. New York: Charles Scribner's Sons, 1968, p. 50.

3. Lisa Appignanesi, *The Cabaret*. London: Studio Vista, 1975, p. 153.

4. *Ibid.*, p. 157.

5. *Ibid.*

6. *Ibid.*, p. 161.

7. *Ibid.*, p. 157.

8. Helmut Lehmann-Haupt, *Art under a Dictatorship*. New York: Oxford University Press, 1954, p. 68.

9. *Ibid.*

10. Werner Finck, *Zwischendurch: Ernste Versuche mit dem Heiteren*. Munich: F. A. Herbig Verlagsbuchhandlung, 1975, p. 297.

11. Schwartz, Finckenschläge.

12. Appignanesi, p. 156.

13. Uwe Naumann, *Zwischen Tränen und Gelächter*. Cologne: Pahl-Rugenstein Verlag, 1983, p. 25.

14. *Ibid.*, p. 294.

15. *Ibid.*

16. Georg Zivier, Helmut Kotschenreuther, Volker Ludwig, *Kabarett mit K*. Berlin: Berlin Verlag, 1974, p. 36.

17. Schwartz, Finckenschläge.

18. *Ibid.*

19. Werner Finck, *Alter Narr—was nun? Die Geschichte meiner Zeit*. Munich: F. A. Herbig Verlagsbuchhandlung, 1972, p. 8.

20. Interpress Archiv, Internationaler Biographischer Pressdienst, Hamburg, 1977, p. 2.

21. *Das grosse Buch der Humoristen*. Munich: Moewig, 1987, p. 124.

22. Finck, *Alter Narr—was nun?*, p. 53.

23. Werner Finck, *Heiter—auf verlorenem Posten*. Munich: F. A. Herbig Verlagsbuchhandlung, 1977, p. 41.

24. Finck, *Zwischendurch*, p. 180.

25. *Das grosse Buch der Humoristen*, p. 126.

26. Werner Finck, *Der brave Soldat Finck*. Munich: F. A. Herbig Verlagsbuchhandlung, 1975, p. 13.

27. *Das grosse Buch der Humoristen*, p. 127.

28. Oscar Teller, *Davids Witz-Schleuder: Jüdisch-Politisches Cabaret*. Darmstadt: Verlag Darmstadter Blatter, 1985, p. 17.

29. Werner Finck, *Der brave Soldat Finck*, p. 9.

30. Werner Finck, *Das grosse Werner-Finck-Buch*. Frankfurt: Ullstein Verlag, 1985, p. 79.

31. Appignanesi, p. 159.

32. *Ibid.*

33. Finck, *Alter Narr—was nun?*, p. 62.

34. B. D. Shaw, ed., *Is Hitler Dead? and Best Anti-Nazi Humor*. New York: Alcaeus House, 1939, p. 5.

35. Werner Finck, *Der brave Soldat Finck*, p. 10.

36. Naumann, p. 25.

37. Finck, *Das grosse Werner-Finck-Buch*, p. 78.

38. *Ibid.*, p. 8.

39. Finck, *Zwischendurch*, p. 297.

40. *Ibid.*

41. Werner Finck, *Der brave Soldat Finck*, p. 9.

42. Finck, *Alter Narr—was nun?*, p. 61.

43. *New York Times*, June 6, 1935, p. 4.

44. Naumann, p. 294.

45. *Ibid.*, p. 402.

46. Appignanesi, p. 159.

47. Finck, *Alter Narr—was nun?*, p. 69.

48. *Ibid.*

49. Finck, *Das grosse Werner-Finck-Buch*, p. 80.

50. Finck, *Alter Narr—was nun?*, p. 71.

51. *Ibid.*, p. 72.

52. *Ibid.*

53. Finck, *Das grosse Werner-Finck-Buch*, p. 81.

54. Finck, *Alter Narr—was nun?*, p. 73.

55. *Ibid.*

56. *Ibid.*, p. 74.

57. Finck, *Das grosse Werner-Finck-Buch*, p. 26.

58. Helmut Heiber, *Goebbels*, trans. John Dickinson. London: Robert Hale & Company, 1972, p. 206.

59. Heinz Greul, *Bretter, die die Zeit bedeuten: Die Kulturgeschichte des Kabaretts*. Cologne: Kiepenheuer & Witsch, 1967, p. 329.

60. Finck, *Das grosse Werner-Finck-Buch*, p. 7.

5

1. Irving Kristol, Is Jewish humor dead? the rise and fall of the Jewish joke, *Commentary*, November 1951, p. 431.

2. *Ibid.*, p. 433.

3. Natan Sharansky, *Fear No Evil*. New York: Random House, 1988, p. 367.

4. *Ibid.*

5. Interview with author, 1990.

6. Interview with author, 1988.

7. *Shabbat* 30b.

8. *Nida* 23a.

9. *Tanit* 22a.

10. Joseph Dorinson, Jewish humor: mechanism for defense, weapon for cultural affirmation, *Journal of Psychohistory*, Spring 1981, p. 449.

11. Salcia Landmann, The origin of Jewish humor: an analysis of its sources and some examples, *Jewish Journal of Sociology*, December 1962.

12. George Mikes, *Humour in Memoriam*. London: Routledge & Kegan Paul, 1970, p. 85.

13. Landmann, The origin of Jewish humor, p. 44.

14. Israel Knox, The traditional roots of Jewish humor, *Judaism*, Summer 1963, p. 331.

15. *The Warsaw Diary of Adam Czerniakow*, Braircliff Manor, NY: Stein and Day, 1982, p. 296.

16. Richard Grunberger, *A Social History of the Third Reich*. London: Weidenfeld and Nicolson, 1971, p. 340.

17. Milton Meltzer, *Never to Forget: The Jews of the Holocaust*. New York: Harper & Row, 1976, p. 87.

18. Michel Borwicz, *Ecrits des condamnés à mort sous l'occupation nazie (1939–1945)*. Paris: Gallimard, 1973, p. 266.

19. Letter from Dr. E. A. M. Speijer, The Hague, 1990.

20. Related by Leon Lewis, interview with author, 1990.

21. Gabriel Laury, Dark times under blue skies: the allies have landed. Unpublished manuscript, Peekskill, NY.

22. The Prophet Moses is known in traditional Jewish circles as Moshe Rabenu, Hebrew for "Moses our teacher."

23. Laury.

24. Theodor Reik, *Jewish Wit*. New York: Gamut Press, 1962, p. 27.

25. *Ibid.*, p. 49.

26. Emil Dorian, *The Quality of Mercy: A Romanian Diary 1937–1944*, trans. Mara Soceanu Vamos. Philadelphia: The Jewish Publication Society of America, 1982, p. 31.

27. Shimon Huberband, *Kiddush Hashem: Jewish Religious and Cultural Life in Poland during the Holocaust*. Hoboken, NJ: Ktav, 1987, p. 113.

28. *Ibid.*, p. 113.

29. Hans-Jochen Gamm, *Der Flüsterwitz im Dritten Reich*. Munich: Deutscher Taschenbuch Verlag, 1979, p. 24.

30. Jacob Boas, *Boulevard des Misères: The Story of Transit Camp Westerbork*. Hamden, CT: Archon Books, 1985, p. 82.

31. Nachman Blumenthal, *Werter un Wertlech fun der Churbn-Tkufe*. Tel Aviv: I. L. Peretz Publishing House, 1981, p. 19.

32. Archival material, Leo Baeck Institute, New York.

33. Israel Kaplan, *Jewish Folk-Expressions under the Nazi Yoke*. Tel Aviv: Beit Lohamei Hagettaot Ghetto Fighters' House, 1987, p. iv.

34. *Ibid.*

35. David Maisel, trans., *Jewish Jargon under the Nazis: A Glossary of Hebrew and Yiddish Slang and Code Words Used in Ghettos and Concentration Camps*. English translations of Israel Kaplan's work. Boston and Cambridge Centers for Adult Education.

36. *Notes from the Warsaw Ghetto: The Journal of Emmanuel Ringelblum*, trans. Jacob Sloan. New York: Schocken Books, 1974, p. 242.

37. Maisel.

38. Robert Moses Shapiro, Yiddish slang under the Nazis, *The Book Peddler*, Amherst, MA, Summer 1989, p. 30.

39. *Ibid.*, p. 31.

40. *Ibid.*

41. Interview with author, 1988.

42. Interview with author, 1985.

43. Lucy Dawidowicz, *The War Against the Jews 1933–1945*. New York: Bantam Books, 1975, p. 347.

44. *Warsaw Ghetto: A Diary by Mary Berg*. New York: L. B. Fischer, p. 111.

45. *Notes from the Warsaw Ghetto*, p. 225.

46. *Scroll of Agony: The Warsaw Diary of Chaim A. Kaplan*, trans. Abraham Katsh. New York: Collier Books, 1973, p. 97.

47. Israel Bernbaum, Yiddish folksongs of Eastern Europe. Unpublished paper, Queens College, New York, 1972, p. 39.

48. Dawidowicz, p. 273.

49. Lucjan Dobroszycki, ed., *The Chronicle of the Lodz Ghetto 1941–1944*. New Haven, CT: Yale University Press, 1984, p. 92.

50. David Roskies, *Against the Apocalypse: Responses to Catastrophe in Modern Jewish Life*. Cambridge, MA: Harvard University Press, 1984, p. 205.

51. Dobroszycki, p. 92.

52. *Ibid.*, p. 9.

53. *Ibid.*, p. 327.

54. *Notes from the Warsaw Ghetto*, p. 22.

55. Dawidowicz, pp. 323–324.

56. *Ibid.*, p. 294.

57. Related in letter from Manny Mittelman.

58. Genin Slikes, The Last Purim-Present in the Warsaw Ghetto. File in YIVO Institute, New York.

59. *Ibid.*

60. Oscar Teller, *Davids Witz-Schleuder: Jüdisch-Politisches Cabaret*. Darmstadt: Verlag Darmstadter Blatter, 1985, p. 283.

61. Yitskhok Rudashevski, *The Diary of the Vilna Ghetto*. Tel Aviv: Ghetto Fighters House, 1973, p. 137.

62. Teller, p. 283.

63. Dawidowicz, p. 346.

64. *Ibid.*

65. Nahma Sandrow, *Vagabond Stars: A World History of Yiddish Theater*. New York: Limelight Editions, 1986, p. 341.

66. *Ibid.*, pp. 340–341.

67. Leonard Tushnet, *The Uses of Adversity*. New York: Thomas Yoseloff, 1966, p. 29.

68. Ber Mark, *Uprising in the Warsaw Ghetto*, trans. Gershon Freidlin. New York: Schocken Books, 1975, p. 75.

69. Elie Wiesel, *Night*. Northvale, NJ: Jason Aronson, 1985, pp. 86–87.

70. Grunberger, p. 340.

71. Sidra DeKoven Ezrahi, *By Words Alone: The Holocaust in Literature*. Chicago: University of Chicago Press, 1982, p. 31.

72. Related by Judy Baumel, interview with author, 1985.

73. Reeve Robert Brenner, *The Faith and Doubt of Holocaust Survivors*. New York: Free Press, 1980, p. 213.

74. Ulrike Migdal, *Und die Musik spielt dazu: Chansons und Satiren aus dem KZ Theresienstadt*. Munich: Piper, 1986, p. 24.

75. Alfred Kantor, *The Book of Alfred Kantor: An Artist's Journal of the Holocaust*. New York: Schocken Books, 1971, introduction.

76. Ruth Bondy, *Elder of the Jews: Jakob Edelstein of Theresienstadt*, trans. Evelyn Abel. New York: Grove Press, 1981, p. 291.

77. Joza Karas, *Music in Terezin 1941–1945*. New York: Beaufort Books, 1985, pp. 14–15.

78. Migdal, p. 30.

79. *Ibid.*, p. 31.

80. Mary Steinhauser, *Totenbuch Theresienstadt: Damit Sie nicht Vergessen Werden*. Vienna: Junius Verlags-und VertriebsgesellschaftmbH, 1971, introduction.

81. *Ibid.*

82. Migdal, pp. 106–108.

83. *Ibid.*, pp. 85–86.

84. *Ibid.*, pp. 6, 64, 96.

85. Kantor, introduction.

86. Hana Greenfield, Fighting back with satire, *Jerusalem Post Entertainment Magazine*, April 27, 1990, p. 12.

87. Janet Blatter and Sybil Milton, *Art of the Holocaust*. London: Orbis Publishing, 1981, p. 116.

88. Drawn by father of Arnd Lothar Falk; sent to author, 1989.

89. Joel Dimsdale, ed., *Survivors, Victims, and Perpetrators: Essays on the Nazi Holocaust*. Washington, DC: Hemisphere Publishing, 1980, p. 169.

90. Anton Gill, *The Journey back from Hell: An Oral History—Conversations with Concentration Camp Survivors*. New York: William Morrow, 1988, p. 173.

91. Sandrow, p. 349.

92. Konnilyn Feig, *Hitler's Death Camps: The Sanity of Madness*. New York: Holmes & Meier, 1979, p. 349.

93. Joseph Czarnecki, *Last Traces: The Lost Art of Auschwitz*. New York: Atheneum, 1989, introduction.

94. *Ibid.,* p. 28.

95. Gill, p. 363.

96. Jenny Robertson, *Ghetto: Poems of the Warsaw Ghetto 1939–43*. Oxford: Lion Publishing, 1989, p. 77.

97. Interview with author, 1990.

98. Moshe Waldoks and William Novak, *The Big Book of Jewish Humor*. New York: Harper & Row, 1981, p. 61.

99. Salcia Landmann, *Judische Witze Nachlese 1960–1976*. Munich: Deutscher Taschenbuch Verlag, 1972, p. 209.

100. Ralph Wiener, *Als das Lachen Tödlich War*. German Democratic Republic: Greifenverlag zu Rudolstadt, 1988, p. 239.

6

1. *Notes from the Warsaw Ghetto: The Journal of Emmanuel Ringelblum*, trans. Jacob Sloan. New York: Schocken Books, 1974, p. 288.

2. Emil Dorian, *The Quality of Mercy: A Romanian Diary 1937–1944*. Philadelphia: Jewish Publication Society of America, 1982, pp. 289–290.

3. Author is stumped. A review of countless books of jokes from World War II Europe has not turned up a single one about Hitler and a pig.

4. Moshe Waldoks and William Novak, *The Big Book of Jewish Humor*. New York: Harper & Row, 1981, p. 61.

5. Richard Grunberger, *A Social History of the Third Reich*. London: Weidenfeld and Nicolson, 1971, p. 338.

6. *Ibid.,* p. 336.

7. Ruth Andreas-Friedrich, *Berlin Underground 1938–1945*. New York: Paragon House, 1989, p. 75.

8. *Scroll of Agony: The Warsaw Diary of Chaim A. Kaplan*, trans. Abraham Katsh. New York: Collier Books, 1965, p. 83.

9. Exodus 14:11.

10. The Yiddish expression *Landsman*, or "countryman," is a familiar term of greeting among Jews from the same town or country.

263

11. *Encyclopedia of Jewish Humor*, ed. Henry Spalding. New York: Jonathan David, 1969, pp. 184–185.

12. *Notes from the Warsaw Ghetto*, p. 152.

13. *Ibid.*

14. *Ibid.*, p. 49.

15. Shimon Huberband, *Kiddush Hashem: Jewish Religious and Cultural Life in Poland During the Holocaust*. Hoboken, NJ: Ktav, 1987, p. 120.

16. Lucjan Dobroszycki, *The Chronicle of the Lodz Ghetto 1941–1944*, trans. Richard Lourie et al. New Haven, CT: Yale University Press, 1984, p. 328.

17. *Scroll of Agony*, p. 231.

18. *Ibid.*, p. 205.

7

1. Zbynek Zeman, *Heckling Hitler: Caricatures of the Third Reich*. Hanover, NH: University Press of New England, 1987, pp. 10–11.

2. *Ibid.*, p. 10.

3. *Ibid.*, p. 47.

4. Theodor Reik, *Jewish Wit*. New York: Gamut Press, 1962, p. 49.

5. Max Vandrey, *Der politische Witz im Dritten Reich*. Munich: Wilhelm Goldmann Verlag, 1967, p. 89.

6. Hans-Jochen Gamm, *Der Flüsterwitz im Dritten Reich*. Munich: Deutscher Taschenbuch Verlag, 1979, p. 79.

7. Vandrey, p. 74.

8. Zeman, p. 83.

9. *d'Orient*, Indonesia, April 1936, p. 31.

10. *Oyfgang*, Havana, April 1934, cover.

11. Zeman, p. 46.

12. Reinhard Hippen, *Satire gegen Hitler: Kabarett im Exil*. Zurich: Kabarett-geschichten pendo-Verlag, 1986, p. 10.

13. *Ibid.*

14. Lisa Appignanesi, *The Cabaret*. London: Studio Vista, 1975, p. 162.

15. Frederick Brainin, Ballad of Leo Slezak, *International Poetry Review*, Spring 1983, pp. 121–122.

16. Hippen, p. 72.

17. *Ibid.*, p. 18.

18. Appignanesi, p. 163.

19. Interview with author, 1981.

20. Hippen, p. 149.

21. Appignanesi, p. 169.

22. Uwe Naumann, *Zwischen Tränen und Gelächter*. Cologne: Pahl-Rugenstein Verlag, 1983, p. 182.

23. Appignanesi, p. 166.

24. *Ibid.*, pp. 166–167.

25. Naumann, p. 124.

26. *Ibid.*, p. 151.

27. Egon Larsen, *Wit as a Weapon: The Political Joke in History*. London: Frederick Muller, 1980, p. 52.

28. *Ibid.*, p. 53.

29. Naumann, p. 148.

30. *Ibid.*, p. 183.

31. Anthony Rhodes, *Propaganda—The Art of Persuasion: World War II*. Secaucus, NJ: Wellfleet Press. 1987, p. 37.

32. *Ibid.*, p. 38.

33. Nazis, insulted/collect, call on /U.S. for more, *New York Herald Tribune*, February 19, 1941, p. 1.

34. *Ibid.*

35. *Ibid.*

36. Zeman, p. 97.

37. Rhodes, p. 119.

38. *Ibid.*

39. *Ibid.*

40. Zeman, p. 97.

41. *Ibid.*

42. *Ibid.* p. 103.

43. Martin Esslin. *Brecht, A Choice of Evils: A Critical Study of the Man, His Work and His Opinions*. London: Eyre Metheun, 1959, p. 55.

44. *Brecht, Collected Plays*. Volume 6. Ed. Ralph Manheim and John Willett, New York: Vintage Books, 1976, p. 456.

45. *Ibid.*, p. 198.

46. *Ibid.*, p. 284.

47. *Ibid.*, p. 300.

48. R. F. Patterson, *Mein Rant: A Summary in Light Verse of 'Mein Kampf*. London: Blackis & Son, 1940, p. viii.

49. *Ibid.*, p. x.

50. *Ibid.,* pp. 5–6.

51. *Ibid.,* p. 69.

52. Jordan Young, *Spike Jones and His City Slickers.* Beverly Hills, CA: Disharmony Books, 1982, p. 13.

53. David Robinson, *Chaplin: His Life and Art.* New York: McGraw-Hill, 1985, p. 506.

54. Clayton R. Koppes and Gregory D. Black, *Hollywood Goes to War: How Politics, Profits & Propaganda Shaped World War II Movies.* New York: Free Press, 1987, p. 31.

55. Robinson, p. 508.

56. *Ibid.,* p. 485.

57. Joan Howard Maurer, *The Three Stooges Book of Scripts.* Secaucus, NJ: Citadel Press, 1984, pp. 180–221.

58. *Walt Disney's Donald Duck: 50 Years of Happy Frustration.* Tucson, AZ: HP-Books, 1984, p. 32.

59. William Paul, *Ernst Lubitsch's American Comedy.* New York: Columbia University Press, 1983, p. 225.

60. Koppes and Black, p. 297.

61. Leland A. Poague, *The Cinema of Ernst Lubitsch.* Cranbury, NJ: A. S. Barnes, 1978, p. 90.

62. Naumann, p. 292.

63. Herman G. Weinberg, *The Lubitsch Touch: A Critical Study.* New York: Dutton, 1968, p. 227.

64. Naumann, p. 292.

65. Neil Sinyard, *The Films of Mel Brooks.* New York: Exeter Books, 1987, p. 86.

66. *Ibid.,* p. 14.

67. Jerry Lewis and Herb Gluck, *Jerry Lewis, in Person.* New York: Atheneum, 1982, p. 280.

68. *Ibid.,* p. 283.

69. Elinor Fuchs, ed., *Plays of the Holocaust.* New York: Theatre Communications Group, 1987, p. xi.

70. *Ibid.,* p. xii.

71. *Ibid.,* pp. 130–131.

72. *Ibid.,* pp. 14–15.

73. Avigdor Dagan, *The Court Jesters.* Philadelphia: Jewish Publication Society, 1989, p. 19.

74. Jean-François Steiner, *Treblinka.* New York: Mentor, 1979, pp. 191–192.

75. Tadeusz Borowski, *This Way for the Gas, Ladies and Gentlemen*. New York: Penguin Books, 1976, p. 142.

76. *Ibid.*, pp. 162–163.

77. Romain Gary, *The Dance of Genghis Cohn*. New York: Signet Books, 1968, p. 10.

78. *Ibid.*, p. 83.

79. Michael Jacot, *The Last Butterfly*. New York: Ballantine Books, 1974, p. 114.

Index

Abraham, Moses, 185–186
Accomodation jokes, 204–205
Adler, Bruno, 228
Ad Loloyada, 135
Africa, 43, 135
African-Americans, humor of, 42–44
AIZ, 218
Allies, 29, 36, 58, 67, 97, 107, 141, 160, 161, 163, 192, 216, 226, 228, 229
Amalek, xi
America/Americans, 30, 37, 42–44, 114, 134, 138, 143, 162, 216, 220, 225, 226, 228, 231, 233, 235, 237, 238, 241
Amery, Jean, 13
Amsterdam, 9, 71, 219, 221
Andreas-Friedrich, Ruth, 70
Anecdoty, 45
Angeloushev, Boris, 69
Angriff, 41–42, 116
Anschluss, 108, 198
Anti-Nazi humor, 189–212
Anti-Semitism, 29, 33, 40, 41, 42, 148, 152, 185, 192, 236
    examples of jokes concerning, 195
Appignanesi, Lisa, 114–115
Arab world, x

Arbeitsverbot, 115
Arendt, Hannah, 241
Argentina, 237
Artists' Quarter, 223
Arts, *see* Cartoons; Drawings; Paintings
Ashkenazic Jews, 135
Auschwitz, 8, 9–10, 11, 13, 14–15, 20, 141, 152, 158, 159–160, 161, 240, 244, 246
Auschwitz, 241–242
Austausch, 141
Austria/Austrians, 12, 14, 25, 32, 41, 51, 54, 57, 64, 114, 116, 126, 140, 152, 198, 219, 220, 225, 243
Austro-Hungarian Empire, 161
Avas, 68
Axis, 19, 93, 229, 235

Babylonia, 134
Bach, Johann Sebastian, 142
Backe, Herbert, 76
Bacon, Francis, 191
Badchan, 135
"Ballad of Leo Slezak," 220–221
Barnes, Peter, 241–242
Baroque, 142
Baumel, Judith Tydor, 16, 21

Bavaria, 36, 159, 215–216, 217
BBC, 225, 226–228
BDM *Bund Deutscher Madchen* (League of German Girls), 79, 80, 81, 199
Becker, Jurek, 243
Belgium, 222
Belsen, 240
Benny, Jack, 238, 239
Berg, Armin, 223
Berg, Mary, 9, 150
Berk, Hans Schwarz van, 116
Berkowitz, Eliezer, 21
Berlin/Berliners, 18, 19, 31, 33, 34, 36, 37, 39, 40, 42, 66, 68, 70, 73, 86, 113, 117, 118, 123, 124, 125, 141, 153, 221, 229, 233; *see also* West Berlin
Berlin Sports Palace, 70
Bern, 222
Bernell, Agnes, 224
Beshkov, Iliya, 69
Bhattarai, Krishna Prased, 26
Bible, 134
Birkenau, 158
Bismarck, Otto von, 165
Bitter humor, 208–212
Boas, Jacob, 71
Borge, Victor, 222–223
Borowski, Tadeusz, 13, 243, 244–245
Boskin, Joseph, 43–44
Boston University, 43
Brainin, Frederick, 220
Brandt, Willy, 27
Brecht, Bertolt, 33, 113, 223, 231–233
Brezhnev, Leonid, 103
Britain, *see* Great Britain
British Board of Film Censors, 237
British Mandate Authority, 230
British Political Intelligence Department, 226
British Union of Fascists, 26
Brooks, Mel, 8, 239–240

Buber, Martin, 142
Buchenwald, 126, 160–161
Budapest, 14, 29, 160, 163, 219
Bulgarians, 69

Cabarets, 17, 19, 26, 32, 33, 36, 40–41, 42, 63, 67, 71, 111–129, 138, 149, 150, 153–158, 161, 216, 219–220, 221–227, 243
Café Europe, 157
Caracas, 219
Carlsbad, 145
Cartoons/cartoonists, 30, 37, 65, 68–69, 215–216, 217, 229–230, 236, 238
Cassin, René, 8
Catholic Church, 34, 42, 84, 119, 145
CBS, 226
Chamber of Culture (*Reichskulturkammer*), 115, 124
Chaplin, Charles, 96, 215, 236–237, 239
Chasidim, 137, 162, 169
Cheers to Life, 153
Chelm, 135
Chile, 237
Christ, *see* Jesus
Christianity/Christians, 91, 99, 117, 118, 184, 202
Churchill, Winston, 94, 169, 234
Church of England, 223
Club of Wasted Talent, 153
Cologne, 66
Columbus, Christopher, 184, 225
Commentary, 133
Communism/Communists, 30, 32, 40, 44, 45, 50, 91, 105, 164, 171, 199, 217, 218
Conferenciers, 114, 115–116
Cornichon, 222
"Corporal Tom Jones," 226
Corruption, 200
Cossacks, 211
Cousins, Norman, 20

Croatians, 73
Crusades, 135
Czarnecki, Joseph, 161
Czechoslovakia/Czechs, 6, 9, 14, 29, 30, 37, 64, 73, 152, 160, 218, 219, 222
Czerniakow, Adam, 137, 147–148

Dachau, 35, 36, 67, 71–73, 101, 106, 113, 129, 240, 244
Daffy Duck, 238
Dagan, Avigaor, 243
The Dance of Genghis Cohn, 245–246
Das Kabarett der Komiker (Cabaret of Comics), 124
"Das Magdalenennaus," 42
Dawidowicz, Lucy, 149
The Day the Clown Died, 240–241
Denmark, 65, 219, 231
Der Aufhaltsame Aufstieg des Arturo Ui, 231–233
"Der Flüsterwitz," 46
"Der Fuehrer's Face," 235–236, 238
Der Liebe Augustin, 219
Der Pojaz, 159
Der Stürmer, 29, 142, 185, 192, 197
"Der Yiddisher Gelechter," 145–146
Des Pres, Terrence, 7
Die Blutnacht, 71
"Die Bonzen," 198
Die Juden in Deutschland, 33
Die Katakombe, 41, 113, 115, 116, 117–118, 119, 122, 123
Die Stachelbeere, 219
Disney, Walt, 236
Dobrzynski, Stanislaw, 68
Dolfuss, George Herbert, 54
"Donald Duck in Nutziland," 236, 238
Dorian, Emil, 140
d'Orient, 217
Dorinson, Joseph, 135
Drawings, 159–160, 161
Dresden, 162

DuBois, W. E. B., 43
Dutch, *see* Holland/Dutch
Dybbuk, 245

Eastern Europe, 26, 28–29, 45, 133, 135, 211
East Germany, 72, 219
Economy, German, 199–200
Efimov, Boris, 69
Egypt, 138, 149, 205
Ehrenzweig, Robert, 226–227
Ehrlich, Max, 19–20
Einsatzgruppen, 17
Eisen, George, 14
Elijah, Prophet, 135, 202
Emigration, 196
"The Emperor's New Clothes," 223
England/Englishmen, 26, 31, 69–70, 104, 162, 227, 228, 231; *see also* Great Britian/British
Enlightenment, age of, 136
Epstein, Leslie, 7, 243
Esau, 143
Essen, 228
Esterwegen, 123
Etrogim, 141
Europe/Europeans, ix, x, xi, 4, 18, 26, 29, 30, 36, 44, 46, 63, 118, 125, 133, 136, 138, 140, 143, 149, 192, 205, 208, 209, 216, 217, 220, 224, 225, 230, 233, 235, 237, 238, 240, 241; *see also* Eastern Europe
Evangelical Church, 85
Evening Standard, 30, 37, 229
Exodus, 4
The Exodus from Egypt, 161

Fachenheim, Emil, 8
Faith, humor and, and the Holocaust, 1–22
Fantl, Pavel, 160
Farkas, Karl, 223

Feigenbaum, Zofia, 137
Fields, W. C., 20
Ferdl, Weiss, 36, 67, 116, 120, 126, 127–129
Fietje, 66
Films, 235–241
Final Solution, x, 143, 230, 242
Finchenschläge, 117
Finck, Werner, 36, 40–41, 42, 111, 113, 114, 116–126
Finland, 231
Firer, 177–178
Flavor of humor, 189–212
Flüsterwitze, 18, 46
Food Distribution Committee, 80
Four and Twenty Black Sheep, 223
France, 217, 240
Franco, Francisco, 242
Frank, Anne, 4
Frank, Hans, 212
Frankl, Viktor, 11, 14–15
Frederick the Great, 34, 103
Free German League of Culture, 223
Freud, Sigmund, 12, 33, 140, 191, 215
Frick, Wilhelm, 53
Friedlander, Judith, 162–164
Front for German Culture, 119

Galgenhumor (gallows humor), 63
Gallup Poll, 237
Gandhi, Mahatma, 91
Gary, Romain, 245–246
Gemmecker, Albert, 71
German Academy, 95
German Bank, 105
German economy, 199–200
German justice, 196
Germany. *See* East Germany; Nazi Germany; West Germany
Geschonneck, Erwin, 72
Gestapo, 9, 31, 37, 39, 49, 64, 77, 80,

88, 90, 113, 122, 125, 126, 129, 160, 178, 186, 204, 238, 240
Ghetto Uprising, 4
Glasnost, 45
God, example of joke concerning, 194
Goebbels, Joseph, 32, 33, 38, 39, 40–41, 42, 49–59, 67, 69, 70, 75, 76, 90, 96, 100, 101, 103, 106, 107, 115, 116, 118, 119, 120, 122, 124–125, 165–166, 172, 176, 178–179, 186, 203, 220, 228, 230–231, 237, 238, 242
Goering, Emmy, 57
Goering, Hermann, 34, 39–40, 50–59, 74, 76, 90, 96, 103, 116, 119, 120, 129, 186, 199, 200, 203, 204, 228, 238
Goethe, Johann Wolfgang von, 119, 122
Goetz, Frederick, 17
Gogol, Nikolay, 25
Gondor, Bertalan, 160
Goodman, Joel, 20
Gorbachev, Mikhail, 26, 45
Gotfurt, Frederick, 223
Graffitti, 37
Graphic arts, *see* Cartoons; Drawings
Grayer, 177–178
Great Britain/British, 27, 30, 31, 40, 65, 68, 143, 164, 216, 226, 227, 229, 230, 233, 237, 241; *see also* England, Scots
The Great Dictator, 236–237, 239
Groschen, 177–178
Gross, Walter, 123
Grossdungen, 34
Grossenhain, 42
Gross Rosen, 20
Grosz, George, 37
Grunbaum, Fritz, 116, 126
Grunberger, Richard, 10, 137
Grynszpan, Herschel, 51

Guernica, 85
Guilaford, 224

Halifax, Lord, 230
Haman, 135, 139, 141, 148–149
Hamantashen, 148
Hamburg, 42, 66, 125, 142
Hanukah, 141
Hanover, 18
Harris, David, 45
Haum, Hanns ut, 42
Havana, 217
Hays Office, 236
Heartfield, John, 218–219
Hecht, J., 137
Heckling Hitler: Caricatures of the Third Reich, 215–216
Heine, Thomas Theodor, 216
Herr Wendriner steht unter der Diktatur, 32
Herszkowicz, Jankele, 146–147
Herzfelde, Helmut, 218
Hess, Rudolf, 59, 69, 104
Hillesum, Etty, 9
Hindenburg, Paul von, 52, 56, 103, 104–105
Hippen, Reinhard, 219
Hippocrates, 7
Hirnaschal Briefe, 227
Hirohito, 93, 95
Hitler, Adolf, xi, 4, 5, 6, 8, 16, 17, 19, 25, 26, 30, 32, 33, 34, 35, 37, 38–39, 45, 47, 48, 50, 51, 53–59, 64, 66, 67, 68, 69, 71, 72, 74–78, 80–84, 86–108, 116, 118, 119, 120, 126, 136–137, 138, 140, 141, 142, 148, 149, 151, 154, 160, 161, 165, 167–170, 172, 173, 175–179, 183, 185–187, 191–192, 193, 194, 196, 199–200, 201, 202–203, 209, 210, 212, 215–216, 217, 218, 223, 225, 227, 228, 229–230, 231, 233–235,

236, 237, 238, 239, 240, 241, 242, 247
Hitler Youth, 81, 100
"Hogan's Heroes," 8
Holland/Dutch, 9,11, 14, 26, 71, 84–85, 123, 161, 217, 222, 243
Hollywood, 235–241
Holocaust, ix, x, xiii, 4, 7, 8, 10, 11, 13, 16, 18, 21, 43, 135, 144, 145, 148, 152, 192, 193, 194, 217, 240, 241
  humor and faith and, 1–22
Hoshana Rabba, 141
Hoshanas, 141
House of Commons, 219
Huberband, Shimon, 211
Humor; *see also* Laughter
  bitter, 208–212
  faith, and the Holocaust, 1–22
  flavor of, 189–212
  of Hitler, 39
  Jewish, 131–187
  of optimism, 61–110
  postwar, 8, 213, 217, 219, 233, 239–247
Humor rooms, 20
Humor therapy, 19–21
Hungary/Hungarians, 27, 29, 160, 163
Hussein, Saddam, ix, x, xi
Hutcheson, Francis, 63

India, 20
Indonesia, 217
Inquisition, 135
Institute for the Study of the Jewish Question, 33
International Women's League for Peace and Freedom, 222
In Which We Serve, 65
Iraq, x
Iron Curtain, 45

Israel/Israelis/Israelites, ix–x, xi, 7, 20, 134, 135, 136, 144, 205, 241
Italy, 26, 31, 216

Jacob, Biblical, 143
Jacob the Liar, 243
Jacot, Michael, 247
Jerusalem, 141
Jesus, 10, 19, 34, 56, 76–77, 101, 194, 202
Jewish humor, 131–187
Jewish Institute of Religion, xii
Jewish Political Cabaret, 227
Job, 136
Jokes, 17–19
 circulating from 1933 to 1945, 164–187
 under Nazi occupation, 46–59
Jones, Spike, 235–236
Judenrat, 7, 137, 144, 146, 212
Juden unerwunscht, 141
Judische Rundschau, 197
Jüdisches Nachrichtenblatt, 19
Justice, German, 196

Kafka, Franz, 243
Kaiser Wilhelm, 218
Kaiser Wilhelm Memorial Church, 107
Kalmar, Rudolf, 72–73
Kameradschaftabenden, 153
Kanar, Zwi, 145
Kaniuk, Yoram, 243, 246
Kantor, Alfred, 14, 15, 153, 159
Kaplan, Chaim, 202, 212
Kaplan, Israel, 143
King of the Jews, 7, 243
Kisch, Egon Erwin, 42
Knesset, 7
Koestler, Arthur, 133
Kovno Ghetto, 146
Krakow, 66, 138

Kraft durch Freude (Strength through Joy), 80, 82, 199
Kremlin, 45
Kristallnacht, 41, 127, 143, 184, 198
Kristol, Irving, 133, 134
Krokodil, 230–231
Kuwait, x

Landmann, Salcia, 136
The Lantern, 225
Larsen, Egon, 26–27, 223, 227–228
The Last Butterfly, 246–247
The Last of Hitler, 8
Laughter, under oppression, 23–59; *see also* Humor
League of German Girls (BDM), 79, 80, 81, 199
League of Nations, 30, 229
"Lebensraum for the Conquered," 230
Lefortovo Prison, 134
Lehrburger, *see* Larsen
Leicester, 224
Leningrad, 45
L'Espoir, 65
Levant, 135
Levi, Primo, 13
Levy, Josef, 186
Lewis, Jerry, 240–241
Ley, Robert, 58
Lind, Jakoy, 243
Liszt, Franz, 101
Literatur am Naschmarkt, 219–220
Lithuanians, 143
Little Red Riding Hood, 78–80, 201
Little Theatre, 223–224
Lodz Ghetto, 18, 144, 146, 147, 212
Lombard, Carole, 238
London, 26, 37, 125, 218, 219, 223, 225, 227, 229, 230, 237, 241
Long Island University, 135
Lorre, Peter, 103
Los Angeles, 236

Low, David, 30, 229–230
Lubitsch, Ernst, 238–239, 240
Lublin, 21
Lublin Ghetto, 146
Lucas, Robert, 226–227
Lukes, Steven, 27
Lulavim, 141
Luther, Martin, 75
Luxembourg, 222, 226

M, 103
Mach, Sano, 64
Maidanek, 21
Mann, Erika, 222
Mann, Heinrich, 133
Mann, Katja, 222
Mann, Thomas, 222
Mannheim, 218
Man's Search for Meaning, 15
Marcus, Rabbi David, 134
Mark, Ber, 150
Marx, Groucho, 20
Marxism, 231, 234; *see also* Communism
Matzahs, 141
McDougall, William, 25
McGhee, Paul, 20
Mechanicus, Philip, 11
Meekcoms, Rachella Velt, 9–10
Mein Kampf, 95, 202, 233
Mein Krampf, 19
Mein Rant: A Summary in Light Verse, 233–235
Mendelssohn, Felix, 100
Messiah, 144, 202
Methusaleh, 84
Mexico City, 219
Mezuzoths, 208
Mickey Mouse, 40, 230–231
Miese Meschine, 148
Migdal, Ulrike, 154
Mikes, George, 27–29
Milch, Erhard, 51–52

Milton, Sybil, xv
Mindess, Harvey, 16
Moltke, Helmuth von, 210
Mordechai, 135
Moscow, 226
Moses (Moshe Rabenu), 12–13, 83, 139, 205
Mosley, Oswald, 26
Motion Picture Producers and Distributors of America, 236
Muller, Josef, 34–35
Munich, 17, 36, 67, 71, 116, 125, 127, 215–216, 222, 229
"Muselmänner" (Muslims), 12
Music, 142; *see also* Songs
Mussolini, Benito, 5, 19, 26, 33, 57, 82, 93, 94, 95, 102, 107, 161, 223, 229
"The Myth of the Twentieth Century," 100

Napoleon, 69, 83, 103
The National Socialist World, 96–97
Naumann, Kurt, 41–42
Naumann, Uwe, 63
Nazi Germany, x, xi, xiii
    cabaret world of, 111–129
    history of suppression of humor in, 23–59
    humor against, 189–212
    humor and faith in, 1–22
    humor of optimism in, 61–110
    humor outside, 213–247
    Jewish humor and, 131–187
Nazi occupation, jokes and poetry under, examples of, 46–59
Neibuhr, Reinhold, 3, 5, 12
Nepal, 26
Nero, 51
The New Order, 231
Newspapers, 17, 19, 30, 31, 41–42, 45, 78, 116, 122, 125, 140, 142, 147, 185, 192, 197, 216, 218, 231, 239

New York City, 8, 125, 144, 218, 219, 223

New York State, 19, 216

New York Times, 26

New Zealanders, 229

Nichtarische Bach-Cantata-Gesellschaft, 142

Nietzsche, Friedrich Wilhelm, 69

Ninth of Av, 141

No Laughing Matter: A Collection of Political Jokes, 27

North America, 125

Norway, 65–66, 211, 219

Novels, 243–247

Nuremberg trials, 9, 76, 225

Obrdlik, Antonin, 9, 37, 64

OBS—*Odna Baba Skazala*, 45

Office for the Beauty of the Lumbering, 79

Ohne Butter, Ohne Eier, Ohne Fett, 158–159

Olympic Games of 1936, 141

Ophuls, Marcel, 9

Oppenheim, Israel, 144

Oppression, laughter under, 23–59

Optimism, humor of, 61–110

Orwell, George, 17, 25

Ostropoler, Hershel, 46

Oxford University, 27

Oyfgang, 217

Paintings, 160

Palestine, 135, 219, 230

Paraguay, 237

Paris, 125, 218, 219, 231

Passover, 18, 138, 141, 149

Patterson, R. F., 233–235

Paul, Jean, 25

Pawelczynska, Anna, 13

Pearl Harbor, 237

People's Court (Volksgerichtsnof), 34, 204

Peppermill, 222

Persia, 148, 149

Persian Gulf war, ix, x

Pharoah, 149

Philadelphia Inquirer, 239

Philadelphia Symphony Orchestra, 142

Picasso, Pablo, 85

Ping Pong cabaret, 221

Plays, 71–73, 161, 225, 231–233, 241–242; *see also* Cabarets

Poetry/poets, 35, 46, 69–71, 99–100, 121–122, 127–128, 137, 154–159, 220–221, 226, 233–235

Poland/Poles, 3–5, 6, 13, 21, 29, 32, 41, 66, 68, 73, 74, 135, 145, 149, 150, 152, 161, 170, 221, 230, 231, 238, 239, 240, 243

Poor, Harold, 114

Porky Pig, 238

Potemkin Village, 152

Pour le Semite, 137

Prague, 30, 42, 153, 159, 216, 218, 219

Press, 17, 30, 31; *see also* Newspapers

The Producers, 8, 240

Propaganda Ministry, 67; *see also* Goebbels

Pro-victim humor, 189–212

Prussia, 57, 210

Puppet show, 71

Purim, 135, 141, 148–149

Questioning jokes, 204, 205–208

Rabbah, 134

Rabbi of Ger, 169–170

Rabinovic, Abram, 46

Race laws, 201

Radio, 17, 26, 36, 67, 125, 225–229

Radio Luxembourg, 226

Radio Moscow, 226

Raim, Edith, xv

Rashi, 144

Rathenau, Walther, 165

Reagan, Ronald, 26

Redemption, 202–203

Reichskulturkammer, 115, 124

Reichstag, 30, 40, 51, 229, 231
Reik, Theodor, 12, 140
Remarque, Erich Maria, 183
Rembrandt, 84
Rheingold, 225
Rhymes. *See* Poetry
Ringelblum, Emmanuel, 3–4, 18, 144, 193, 211
Roder, Karl, 73
Rohm, Ernst, 104, 187
Romania/Romanians, 140, 161
    anti-Semitism in, 195
Roosevelt, Franklin Delano, 50, 81
Rosen, Willy, 159
Rosenbaum, Borge, 222–223
Rosenberg, Alfred, 100
Rosh Hashanah, 3, 21, 142
Rostov, 144
Roth, Wolfgang, 19
Rothschild, Lord, 169, 220
Royal Air Force, 55, 228
Rozencwajg, Karol, 147
Ruksenas, Algis, 27
"Rumkowski, Chaim," 146–147
Russia, czarist, 26, 68; *see also* Soviet Union

Sachs, Jan, 220–221
Saratoga Springs, 20
"Satire against Hitler: Cabaret in Exile," 219
Saturday Review, 20
Schacht, Hjalmar, 53, 75–76, 168–169
Schiller, Johann von, 169
Schlepper, 145
Schnog, Karl, 35
Schnorrer, 193
Schwarz-Bart, André, 13
Schwarzheide, 14, 159, 160
Schweitzer, Albert, 10–11, 142
Scots, 31; *see also* Great Britain
Self-Aid Societies, 212

Sephardim, 135
Serbs, 73
Shadchan, 193
Shanghai, 219
Sharansky, Natan, 134
Shavuoth, 141
Shaw, George Bernard, 216
Shema, 6
Shlmazel, 140, 150, 193
Shlmiel, 140, 193
Shoah, 8
Sholem Aleichem, 133, 243
Siberia, 221
Simplicissimus, 216
Skalbimircz, 145
Skarzyt Camp, 145
Slavs, 73
Slezak, Leo, 220–221
Slovakia, 64, 159
Sobibor, 18
Social Democrats, 89, 199
Soldatensenger, 226
Solidarity, 29
Songs, 26, 32, 33, 65–66, 78, 100–101, 137, 145–146, 148, 149, 153–154, 224, 235
Soul of Wood, 243
South America, 125
Soviet Information Bureau, 69
Soviet Union/Soviets/Russians, 9, 26, 27, 29, 32, 42, 44–46, 69, 73, 74, 134, 144, 149, 198, 217, 230–231
Spanish Civil War, 85
Speer, Albert, 39
Speijer, E. A. M., xv
Sprachregelungen, 237
"Springtime for Hitler," 8, 240
SSJF (Radio Station Jewish Fantasy), 38
Stalin, Joseph, 102, 103
Stalingrad, 32, 228
"Standing Room Only," 230
Steiner, Jean-François, 243–244

Stockholm, 241
Stokowski, Leopold, 142
Strauss, Leo, 155–158
Streicher, Julius, 29, 142, 192, 197
Strength Through Joy, 80, 82, 199
Stuttgart, 125
Styria, 221
Succahs, 141
Succot, 141
Süddeutschen Zeitung, 17
Sudeten, 153
The Survivor—An Anatomy of Life in the Death Camp, 7
Survivor's syndrome, 20
Svenk, Karel, 153
Sweden/Swedes, 32, 33, 163, 216, 219, 222, 227, 231, 240
Swift, Jonathan, 224
Switzerland, 219, 222, 227
Sydney, 219
Szyk, Arthur, 231

Talmud, 133, 134, 135, 144, 205
Tefillin, 13
Tel Aviv, 135
Teller, Oscar, 149
Terezin. *See* Theresienstadt
"Terezin March," 153–154
Tetje, 66
Thatcher, Margaret, 27
Theater, *see* Plays; Puppet show
Therapy, humor, 19–21
Theresienstadt, 6, 15, 138, 152–160, 247
This Way for the Gas, Ladies and Gentlemen, 243, 244–245
Three Stooges, 237–238
Tingeltangel Club, 41, 124
To Be or Not to Be
   of Brooks, 239–240
   of Lubitsch, 238–239
Tochis, 180
Tomlin, Lily, 20

Tommies, 70
Transnistria, 161
Treblinka, 151, 221
Treblinka, 243–244
Tsvever, 177–178
Tucholsky, Kurt, 32–33, 114
Tunisia, 138
Twain, Mark, 3

Ulbricht, Walter, 27
Umach b'shmo, xi
"Uncle Emil" resistance group, 70
United Artists, 236
United States. *See* America/Americans
U.S. Office of Strategic Services, 226
Untermentschen, 137

Valentin, Karl, 126–127
Vesper, Will, 31
Vicky, 37
Vienna/Viennese, 18, 20, 72, 103, 116, 140, 147, 153, 219, 220–221, 226–227, 231
Vilna, 144
Vilna Ghetto, 145, 148, 209
Volkischer Beobachter, 42, 78, 122, 125
Volkism, 5
Volksgerichtsnof (People's Court), 34, 204

Wagner, Richard, 220, 225
Wallace, Oliver, 235
Wallenberg, Raoul, 163
Wandering Jew, 205
Wannsee Conference, 143
Warsaw, 238, 239
Warsaw Ghetto, 3–5, 7, 9, 18, 21, 38, 74, 137, 144, 145, 147–148, 149, 150, 162–164, 169, 177, 193, 202, 208, 209, 211–212, 243
Weimar Republic, 32, 37, 95, 113, 165, 217, 229
Weiner, Rabbi Erich, 153

Weinert, Erich, 226
Weisz, Viktor, 37
West Berlin, 34, 107
Westerbork, 11, 18, 71, 141
West Germany/West Germans, 34, 154
Wiener, Ralph, 18
Wiener journal, 140
Wiesel, Elie, 151
Winter Relief Work (*Winterhilfswerk*), 41,
    122, 200
Witze machen verboten, 35
Wolff, Kurt Egon, 221
World War I, 39, 77, 98, 114, 218,
    235
World War II, ix, 3, 5, 6, 16, 17, 26, 27,
    29, 41, 44, 58, 68, 113, 116, 117,
    133, 135, 136, 139, 192, 204, 217,
    220, 231, 235, 237, 238, 243

humor after, 8, 213, 217, 219, 233,
    239–247
losses and shortages of, 201–202

Yehilla, 147
Yeke, 205
Yirmiya, 134–135
Yom Kippur, 141, 142
"You Natzi Spy," 237–238

Zeman, Zbynek, 215–216
Zera, 134
Zichrona l'olam, 182–183
Ziemer-Brender, Susan, 20–21
Zionism, 197
Ziv, Avner, 20
Zolkiev, 137
Zurich, 222
Zwischen zwei Kriegen, 32

About the Author

Steve Lipman graduated from the State University of New York in Buffalo and received his master's degree from Ball State University. He was awarded fellowships from both the National Journalism Center and the John McCloy Foundation. Mr. Lipman is a staff reporter for the *New York Jewish Week*. Formerly the editor of the *Buffalo Jewish Review*, he has contributed stories and articles to the Associated Press, as well as to many notable publications, including *The New York Times* and *Newsday*.